Revelation of Self in Language

Narrative Identity as Emergent in Conversation

SURANJANA BARUA

Revelation of Self in Language

Narrative Identity as Emergent in Conversation

SURANJANA BARUA

Tulika Books

Published by

Tulika Books
44 (first floor), Shahpur Jat, New Delhi 110 049, India
www.tulikabooks.in

First edition (hardback) 2023

ISBN: 978-81-950559-6-8

Printed at Chaman Offset, Delhi 110 002

To the first storyteller I knew –
my late sassy grandmother, Surabala Borpujari –
and to my parents, Mallika and Niren Barua,
who excitedly or patiently listen(ed) to all my stories …

Contents

Foreword

Indexicals is a hot topic now, within the so-called 'third wave' of sociolinguistics, but when we started twenty years back – and Suranjana was one of the students freshly out of the MA (Linguistics) batch of the University of Delhi who took the bait gladly and willingly – we were making inroads into the domain by throwing up the challenge of deciphering 'social meanings' from social 'texts' (conversations), and very loudly NOT from social contexts. The hypothesis that I was interested in testing as a supervisor was to show how language need not be predicated upon the predictable social variables (like class, caste, gender, etc.); that is, how language (in the form of social 'texts') need not index social contexts.

To set up such a hypothesis, let alone test it from real-life conversational situations, was a challenge – and was resisted locally, quite aggressively, to say the least. There was pressure from an unexpected gendered coalition against the topic and the theme, and the idea that two male professors are proposing to supervise a thesis (even though it was only an MPhil) on gender. Finally, the unfamiliarity of the committee with Judith Butler's work, especially her first book *Gender Trouble*, on which I was running a reading group at that time with my students, Suranjana being at the forefront of the group, saved the day and we were 'allowed' to proceed with the dissertation.

On the one hand, mine was essentially a Foucauldian project, and on the other, an attempt to rid sociolinguistics of its inherent bias of sentencing forever a social group or individual to their social context, with no hope of ever emerging out of one's class, caste or other minority status. The alternative was to study language not from a given (and somewhat predestined) social identity but to read identity off social texts, like conversations. Can we predict social identity from the 'text'?

The first project (Suranjana's MPhil) asked: Are small children inherently gender-biased? Is bias predicated on their social class, their gender? Well, the dissertation threw up surprising results, which will be eventually shared when we as a community of scholars have travelled a bit more, but there was no doubt that more needed to be done. And, who else but Suranjana! She has a personality that lends itself naturally to a certain flavour of research work that necessarily involves 'interaction'; it is a kind of fieldwork that defines the broader sociological field of the ethnography of communication.

That is how the longer journey of the PhD project began: Is self predicated upon social contexts? And, can we read self off from 'texts'? The results and findings are now in front of you; the results are perhaps not that unexpected, and that is because the self is an even bigger concept, bringing within its ambit the philosophy and psychology of the individual(s). Such results also attest to the fact that texts cannot be clinically emptied of their socio-psychological contexts.

As hinted above, a PhD is not merely a thesis to be written up and defended, and deposited in the library to gather dust. It is a journey of the self, and what better journey of the self than studying self from the perspectives of gender, philosophy, psychology and, above all, language? The work encased within the following pages is therefore significant at multiple levels, apart from being a valuable descriptive resource to theorize on and to validate the findings of various non-mainstream, though by no means insignificant, sociolinguistic theories.

Although the dissertation – and therefore the book – is organized around the need, and later the act, of storytelling, through its enunciation of real stories as texts, it suggests that stories are indeed one aspect of our manifest self – a medium of projection of the self. If the consciousness of the self in a child is awakened in the form of a 'theory of mind', telling stories is a confirmation of the establishment of that self through a recognition of the other. It is therefore reasonable to expect storytelling to provide the 'text' for studying the self, even if narrative as a primitive category of human existence is not a very easy concept to establish or argue for. However, 'narrative' can be a more compelling unit of communication, which, in addition, situates it firmly within an alternative sociolinguistic framework that emerges at the interface of the social and the linguistic, bridging the gap, so to speak, between the two – reminiscent also of the discursive level of interactional order suggested in the sociological theories of Erving Goffman where conversation is organized (in particular, in Goffman 1981).

However, once its need is established, the act of storytelling requires an even more determined and elaborate examination. And here the book (as was the dissertation) succeeds in convincingly demonstrating the most appropriate application of the technology of conversation analysis. This aspect of the work conveys our conviction that it is not through a sort of merely associative literary 'sploshing' that we learn more about the self, but rather through a painstaking, and perhaps more scientific, method of analytically and linguistically analysing real-life texts of our times. It is not through waffling about life but by surfacing linguistic evidence in the form of conversation fragments that an unblemished view of the self is revealed.

A true conversation analysis must aim to capture the effort made by participants to attain a certain level of knowledge that is not bound to vocabulary or grammar. One of the most effective bases for studying interactions has been the ethnography of communication model of Hymes (1961), and built upon by John Gumperz in Gumperz and Hymes (1964, 1972). The effective unit in such interactional studies has been recognized as the speech event or the context of speech. Despite its limitation that it still fails to capture the reality of everyday practices (Brown and Levinson 1979), interactional studies have succeeded in establishing the centrality of discourse as a significant locus for research in language and culture – the overwhelming argument presented in this book is a reaffirmation of this centrality.

The mention of culture along with language is important as the former is an essential component of the type of narrative units that Suranjana's work entails – which I will now term as 'interactional narrative units' (INUs), where the narrative does not merely remain a dormant socio-psychological element but is enlivened by infusing its interactional dimension through culturally significant interpretations. This is dotted throughout the book, but more so in chapter 5, where several conversation extracts highlight such interpretations. This aspect of the book not only firmly keeps it within its interactional domain – as identified above – but also forces a stance that is unique and at the same time different from Goffman's sociologically exact observations.

This aspect brings into focus another aspect of the book (and its underlying thesis), that a 'text' is also a product of human interactions, mirroring their emotions, desires, regrets, etc. That is, a text is not just a complex linguistic element, but also an instrument through which participants understand themselves and make others understand them; the fact that most of the interactions reported here involve couples demand such a framework. This book thus excels in excavating the 'humanness' of the conversational units by bringing forth their psychological interpretations; cultural presuppositions play an important role in affording such interpretations. This feature, evident in the findings of the extracts analysed, brings the work much closer to Garfinkel's (1967) ethnomethodological framework.

It is not surprising, therefore, that chapter 5 ends with the following sentence: 'As such, even our most intimate projections of selfhood within conversation are in relation to and with others, contextually accomplished and culturally conforming.'

After a brief detour through the strategy of 'stories that supress other stories' that narrators often employ – thereby reducing the interactional aspect of INUs, which is as per my assumptions laid out above – and the conclusions in the form of moral residues that remain, the most important question that arises for future is: how does interaction in fact take place? The book does not deal with this, but a possible path of enquiry opens up if we consider Gricean ideas of speaker intentions through implicatures; given that inferences originate in discourse, a possible discursive theory of meaning may result from such an enquiry.

References

Brown, P. and S.C. Levinson (1979), 'Social Structure, Groups and Inter-action', in H. Giles and K. Scherer, eds, *Social Markers in Speech*, Cambridge: Cambridge University Press.

Garfinkel, H. (1967), *Studies in Ethnomethodology*, New York: Prentice-Hall.

Goffman, E. (1981), *Forms of Talk*, Philadelphia: University of Pennsylvania Press.

Gumperz, J.J. and D. Hymes, eds (1964), 'The Ethnography of Communication', special issue, *American Anthropologist*, vol. 66, no. 6.

—— (1972), *Directions in Sociolinguistics*, New York: Holt, Rinehart, and Winston.

Hymes, D. ([1961] 1968), 'The Ethnography of Speaking', in T. Gladwin and W.C. Sturtevant, eds, *Anthropology and Human Behavior*, Washington, DC: Anthropological Society of Washington, DC; reprinted in J.A. Fishman, ed., *Readings in the Sociology of Language*, The Hague: Mouton de Gruyter, 1968, pp. 99–119.

Delhi, March 2023

TANMOY BHATTACHARYA
Professor of Linguistics
University of Delhi

Preface and Acknowledgements

This book hinges on the premise that humans are default storytellers. A story is a human being's first encounter with the universe and with the world at large. It is that fantastic make-believe world we imagine, come to inhabit, and derive pleasure and life lessons from. Stories introduce us to our societies and anchor us in our cultures – they are our escape pods from harsh reality and yet (as some theorists say and as you will find out in later pages of this book!) stories sort of 'prepare' us for life itself and, in that sense, are our life coaches. But *what* does our personal storied universe really look like? And *why* do we tell stories about ourselves? What is it that makes *us* interesting as the heroes of our own worlds?

This book makes the claim that our stories about ourselves (or, our *selves*) are not mere 'historical recreations' of our own pasts. We tell stories *about* ourselves, *for* others, at a particular moment in time and towards a certain end. In this sense, our life stories are startling portrayals and yet contingent projections of our 'selves' as good and worthy individuals for the benefit of 'others' from whom we seek recognition and validation for our very existence through this act of storytelling. Thus, humans are not just perennially geared towards storytelling – it is imprinted in our cultural and cognitive DNA, so to speak – but stories are also a yardstick of human sociality (example, gossip) and 'immortalize' our personal lives by becoming articulated and thus externalized at a moment of interlocution with and for an *other*. *What* exactly our life stories reveal about us and *how* narrating a life story positions us as good selves for others to acknowledge us are, in a nutshell, the primary curiosities that this book indulges in.

The book piques these curiosities by asking two questions initially: who are we, and why do we tell stories? It starts with enquiring into storytelling as a basic trait of humans *as a species* and then launches into an investigation of storytelling *as a socio-cognitive feature*. Why we tell stories that project *a good self* is another question the book addresses with a brief philosophical detour that seeks to help the reader appreciate concepts such as Self and Other. There are nuances of the *gendered self* that the book also addresses: in particular, the notion of how a 'good, ethical human being' takes on different hues when it coagulates into an embodied, biologically sexed and gendered identity of female/male. Assorted associations of *gendered ethics and morality* drawing from feminist studies as well as ethico-moral explorations of human subjectivity are other important dimensions the book encapsulates.

The subtitle of the book – 'Narrative Identity as Emergent in Conversation' – gives hints as to the direction this enquiry takes into the 'relevation of self'. A well-known model of analysing conversation (Conversation Analysis or CA) is tweaked in the service of analysing the narrative as a field of study through elucidation of its main components, namely form, function and plot. The latter chapters of this book exemplify how CA, which looks at the minutest of interactive features of talk, can be used in studying the narrative.

Just as each story is complete in itself and yet incomplete in the sense that there is always *time* which takes it forward into newer possibilities of reinterpretation (thereby breaking the beginning–middle–end sequence), so too, any exploration of narrative identity as emergent in conversation will be complete and incomplete at the same time: it will be complete *at* a particular moment of interlocution, but will be incomplete in the sense that there will always be more possibilities of *re-narration* at some other point of time in the future. Thus, each narrative presented in this work presents a slice of life but is ensconced in, and circumscribed by, time and space. The predicament of a young university student who faces incredible problems and social ostracization at the hands of her peers who gossip about her personal life underlines the importance of implicatures in narratives and the role of rumour in social life. Other narratives analysed in this book showcase how couples perform coupledom through 'duetting' while narrating their life story and yet highlighting individual gendered identities at the same time; how the *cultural imaginary* comes into play and how social roles and expectations *position* us as gendered human beings, not just in lived experience but even in our narratives. The book also proffers the novel theoretical concept of the *ancillary narrative* proposed as a story told, not by way of sharing a life story but as a mechanism for protecting the self. As the narratives of a sister (who had lost her brother in a road accident) and a husband (who was an acid attack and accident survivor) show us, *which* aspects of a story we choose to highlight or *how* we tell multiple stories just to subvert our painful past are as important in storytelling as the storyline itself.

Thus, a life story is not just a slice of one's life with a beginning–middle–end sequence that narratives typically have – rather, life stories are *linguistic selfies* that a self (or selves in the case of duet narratives) takes with an other for the benefit of encapturing certain aspects of her/his identity, and in the process, a unique narrative identity emerges *every time* a story is unfolding in a moment of interlocution.

I am indebted to …

Smt. Mallika Barua, with whom my story begins: educator and headmistress of a school for decades, acclaimed drama artist, talented sitar player and one of the most dignified human beings I have ever encountered …

Late Shri Niren Barua, the centre of my universe: well-known newsreader and drama artist for All India Radio Guwahati, whose deep baritone was heard and recognized throughout Assam for decades, and whose gregarious and effervescent personality made for stories that are legends till today! …

Smt. Sagarika and Shri Pallab Kataki, my aunt and uncle – advocates by profession but spiritual scientists by vocation; Shri Nilanjan and Smt. Juri Barua, my brother and sister-in-law – simple, kind, down-to-earth people who ground me; Rajdeep and Nivedana Kataki and my nephew Praneel (Parikshit Barua) whom I lead on ever-new adventures and to whom I owe my fascination for the storied world …

Dr L. David Lal, assistant professor of political science at IIITG – colleague, friend, academic collaborator, fellow adventurer, soulmate, whose roles in my life defy categorization yet who re-defines me …

All my teachers from Holy Child School and Cotton College (Guwahati, Assam), and University of Delhi (Delhi), who taught me so much – especially Shri Pradip Acharya and Shri Amlandeep Das (at Cotton College), and Professor K.V. Subbarao, Professor R.K. Agnihotri and Professor Tanmoy Bhattacharya (at University of Delhi), names I take till today with happiness and awe! The last two named were my supervisors both for MPhil and PhD. I owe Professor Tanmoy Bhattacharya a special mention here: it was he who nudged me into the world of academics, and I could think of no one else to write the Foreword to this first academic title of mine in Linguistics. I am so grateful for his time and thank him for his precious words.

Late Shri Arun Sarma, acclaimed dramatist and litterateur of Assam, recipient of Sangeet Natak and Sahitya Akademi awards and my lifelong mentor; late Shri Abon Borpujari and late Shri Prakash Goswami, friends of my father who truly were my friends too …

Professor Gautam Barua, Director, IIITG and my guru in institute administration whose work ethics and personal example have left a deep imprint on me; Professor (Retd.) Madan M. Sarma, Tezpur University, Assam, whose relentless pursuit of creativity in the lettered world inspires me; and Professor Gautam K. Borah, Tezpur University, Assam, whose astute understanding of the socio-cognitive dimensions of language astounds me …

Professor Ayesha Kidwai, Jawaharlal Nehru University, New Delhi, whose solid support for my interdisciplinary academic leaning in those early days of research life really boosted my self-confidence – she stood by me when it mattered; Professor Rukmini Bhaya Nair, IIT Delhi, to whom I owe an intellectual debt; Professor Imtiaz Hasnain, Aligarh Muslim University, whose scholarship in the field of sociolinguistics I look up to; Prof. Aadil Amin Kak, University of Kashmir, my friend, philosopher and guide; and Prof. Rajesh Kumar, IIT Madras, a well-wisher who has mentored me over the years …

Smt. Asha Sanwal, University Hostel for Women, University of Delhi, who has nurtured me for decades; and Shri Basanta Deka and Smt. Kiran Deka, Orchid Publication, Guwahati, Assam, who continue to witness my journey …

All the respondents who have contributed to my research life over the past nearly twenty years. They remain unnamed in the spirit of research, but they are always in my head and heart. It is to them that I owe my deep fascination for language as it is spoken at a particular moment of interlocution, and they have enriched my life beyond measure just by letting me into theirs …

All my students at Tezpur University, Assam and Indian Institute of Information Technology Guwahati (IIITG, Assam) whose questions, curiosities, presentations and discussions keep me alive and alert to the possibilities of language …

All my former and current PhD scholars – Dr Dimple Choudhury, Ms Barshapriya Dutta, Ms Ayesha Dkhar and Ms Porixita Kakoty – who fondly call me ‘Guruji’ but from whom I have learnt so much about language and life. We teach each other to expand our horizons; Barsha has been particularly helpful with cross-checking references in this manuscript …

The editorial team of the journal *Language and Language Teaching* with whom I have shared so many tasks, concerns and responsibilities over the past many years; my experience as a team member of this journal has lent credence to my life as a student of language and linguistics …

The Ministry of Civil Aviation (Government of India) and the Aviation English Language Proficiency (AELP) Testing Team at AELTO/TSP-Guwahati; my engagement as an English Language Expert and Aviation English Trainer has opened newer avenues for me to experience language in action and has taught me that human lives, literally, hang in the balance over language …

All my friends – specially Ms Prarthana Das, Mr Prakash Raj C.D. and Mr Abhishek Singh, whose personal stories establish without doubt that they are simply heroic; Mr Rahul Sarkar, Dr Vibha Pandey and Dr Minakshi Bhattacharya, whose friendship has stood the test of time …

Smt. Minnie Pandey, Shri Santosh Kumar Choudhury, Dr Om Prakash, Dr M. Pandey and Mr Punit Mishra, who proffered help and insightful comments for this work …

Haobam Basantarani (Basanta), without whose persistent efforts and extraordinary patience this book would not have seen the light of day; her painstaking work and her deeply insightful queries and concerns as part of the editorial team at Tulika Books made me look at my own research with renewed vigour and from newer perspectives …

Tulika Books, New Delhi and Ms Indira Chandrasekhar (publisher and managing editor), whose willingness to engage with new authors and ideas is revolutionary, to say the least. 'Tulika' translates into the quill and just as one has to take utmost care in writing with a quill – with measured and precise strokes to ensure the ink does not spill – so too they are in spirit; I am thankful to Mr Arun Kerketta and the entire team at Tulika Books.

You, the reader, with whom I engage through this written word … our stories connect right here, at this moment in time …

Transcription Conventions

The transcription system used in this book reflects the standard that has emerged in the Conversation Analysis framework. The system has been developed chiefly by Jefferson (1989: 193–96) and the symbols, explained in the table below, were also adapted in Barua (2005). The last three symbols – { }; H; 1,2 – have been adapted from Dressler and Kreuz (2000).

Symbol	*Designation*
A:	Current speaker (designated by letter/initials)
CAPS	Capitalized letters indicate that a section of speech is louder than the surrounding speech.
Underscoring	Underlined fragments indicate stress or emphasis.
°Soft°	Degree signs enclose speech that is quieter than the surrounding speech.
>fast<	Faster than surrounding speech
< slow>	Slower than surrounding speech
@voice@	Speech enclosed by @ is in an animated voice.
“ ”	Double quotation marks indicate the quotation voice.
a:	A colon indicates prolongation of the immediately prior sound. The number of colons indicates the length of the prolongation.
.	A period indicates a falling intonation.
,	A comma indicates a continuing intonation.

?	A question mark indicates a rising intonation.
↑↓	Pointed arrows indicate a marked rise or fall in pitch in the immediately following utterance.
'no	A marked fall in pitch on a syllable.
da-	The dash marks a stop or cut-off in sound.
.hhh/hhh	Indicate inbreath and outbreath respectively. The length is indicated by the number of hs.
hu, ha, he	Laugh particles. If enclosed in parentheses (he) indicates occurrence while talking.
(0.4)	The number within brackets indicates a time gap in one-tenth of a second.
(.)	A period enclosed in parentheses indicates a pause in the talk of less than two-tenths of a second.
()/():	An untranscribable passage or an unidentifiable speaker.
(guess)/(A)	Transcriber's guess of dubious hearing or speaker identification.
(( ))	Comment by the transcriber.
→	Arrows in the left margin point to specific parts of an extract discussed in the text.
=	Latched utterances having no gap.
[ ]	Overlap onset is marked with a single left square bracket and a single right square bracket marks end of overlap.[1]
[EB:41:031104]	Extract headings indicate transcript source of the researcher.[2]
{ }	Backchannel communication.
H	Audible breathing.
1,2	Unique discourse number and numbered lines within each utterance.[3]

Notes

1 Though the convention is to put the square bracket marking overlap onset between relevant lines in the data, following recent studies, the '[]' symbol for onset overlap is put on the relevant lines in this study to mark, as precisely as possible, the exact point of overlap, and thereby minimize the interference of the gloss and translation.

2 The headings may contain information about the data source, the tape number from which the extract is cited, the date and series number of recording, etc.

[3] Each extract cited has a unique discourse number. Further, as per CA conventions, lines in every cited extract are usually numbered beginning with 1,2, 3, …, etc. However, in a departure from convention, every extract line where different narratives from the same narrator or narrators are cited, the extract will have the original number as in the original transcript. This is to give an idea to the reader as to when within the interview the particular line(s) occur: if, for example, the lines cited in a transcript are 28–48, they occur fairly early in the interview; if the lines cited are numbered as 880–910, they occur towards the end of the interview.

Abbreviations

1,2,3	first/second/third person
acc	accusative
agr	agreement
CA	Conversation Analysis
caus	causative
cl	classifier
comp	complementizer
comp mkr	comparative marker
cop	copula
cpm	conjunctive participial marker
d	distal
dat	dative
det	determiner
dm	discourse marker
DM	deference marker
do	direct object
ec	echo word
emph	emphatic
erg	ergative
fem	feminine
fut	future

gen	genitive
hon	honorific
imp	imperative
impf	imperfect
incl	inclusive
inf	infinitive
io	indirect object
loc	locative
masc	masculine
mkr	marker
neg	negative
nom	nominative
nh	non-honorific
noz	nominalizer
obj	object
p	proxemic
perf	perfect
pl	plural
pres	present
prog	progressive
pron	pronominal
pst	past
q	question
Q into	question intonation
rel pro	relative pronoun
sg	singular
sub	subject
TA	term of address
TCU	Turn Construction Unit
ToR	Term of Reference
TRP	Transition Relevance Place
voc	vocative
y/n	yes/no

1

Who We Are and Why We Tell Stories

Understanding Self, Goodness and Narrative

We, the Storytelling Apes: *Homo Fictus*[1]

Human beings are eternal storytellers. Since time immemorial, humans have had myths, legends, fables, religious parables, folktales, prayers, proverbs, epic poems, chants, rhymes – all of which revolve around some or other story form. Stories have fuelled civilizations; established cultures and rituals; made their mark on material inscriptions of cultures and generally carved inroads into, and been present in, every living society that humans have created. We also invent narratives for individual gain, for maintaining relationships, for reiterating cultural norms, for ensuring social and moral order, and generally, to make sense of the world. What constitutes this human(e) act of storytelling? Why is it essential for us to 'study' it? Can it even *be* studied?

To understand this rather quaint characteristic of human beings as storytellers, one should take a leap of faith first and understand one's own (individual) relation with storytelling. When and how did *you* first encounter stories in *your* life? What is *your* life story? How and why do *you* think humans came up with storytelling? The answer to the first of these questions – When and how did *you* first encounter stories in *your* life? – will possibly be *memory-based*: you might remember your parents or grandparents or some aunt or uncle sitting down with you or trying to get you to sleep and narrating a story. 'Once upon a time, long, long years ago ...', or so the story would have started, and you would have been possibly drawn (if you were fortunate enough to have had good storytellers in your childhood!) into the world of these stories – the characters and the dramatic twists and turns of their lives; the myriad complicated situations that they encountered would have intrigued you no end until the story came to the typical fairy-tale ending of 'And they lived happily ever after.' If something was very appealing or inconsistent within the story, you would have probably asked questions: *Why* did the crow throw pebbles and *How* did the water rise? *What* happened when Cinderella lost one shoe? How did Lord Shiva control the flow of river Ganga? Again, if your and my encounters with these early storytellers of our lives are in any way common, you would surely have heard something of a *moral* of a story – 'That is why, unlike Little Red Riding Hood, it is important *not* to trust strangers'; 'That is why, like Birbal, you *must* have your wits around you', so on and so forth.

The answer to the second of the questions posed above – What is *your* life story? – would also be memory-based, but if you sat down to tell someone your life story, what do you think is going to happen? Would you be able to tell *all* the things that have happened to you and about all the people you have encountered in your life? No, of course not! This sort of hyperrealism is impossible to be rendered even in personal narratives, for several reasons. First, because of constraints of time – you have to begin somewhere and end some time because both you and your listener have other things to do and lives to live! Second, because you would not be able to narrate all that has happened in *real* time – if, for example, you are a forty-year-old man working in a company, you *cannot* take forty years to narrate your life story, for you will have turned eighty by then! Third, because even *you* do not know everything about your life story. For example, how do you think your parents felt when they realized they were about to have you? This part of your life will necessarily be a *reconstruction* since you are not really there as a conscious thinking, feeling human being to understand how your parents felt about having you. *What is remarkable is that every time we tell our own life story, we actually reconstruct ourselves and our lives* (as we shall see in the course of this book). If you still need proof, try telling your life story to the same person but on two different occasions and at different times – if you record your own telling, you will realize that there are both subtle and not-so-subtle differences in the way you rendered the story both times. If you have different listeners for your story, say, a family member or a long-lost friend or a co-passenger, you will realize, again, that you tell your life story differently – you will 'tailor-make' your story so that it appeals to your listener. The emotional angle you invest in your story will be different depending on whether the person is a family member who knows you deeply inside out, a long-lost friend with whom you are back in touch and wish to fill in the blanks of the intervening years, or a stranger you just met on a train journey and started sharing anecdotes with. Further, you may also notice if you pay attention to how *you* tell *your* life story, that while narrating, you will inevitably weave it around events and people but you would also structure it around some theme – maybe how you became the person you are today; how you faced certain challenges; how certain 'villains' in your story created problems for you; of gains or losses; of romantic love and separation; and so on. While there are endless possibilities to how you tell your story (are you a 'sombre' storyteller or a 'fun' one?), there are limited options regarding how the story itself will be structured and around which 'mega themes' of the story world (there are just a few as we shall see!).

Therefore, even a cursory but conscious glance at two of the questions regarding how *you* encountered stories in *your* life and what *your* life story is gave us quite a few insights: we realized that stories establish connections between people; they serve a certain purpose; they have structures and themes; they are finite, and constraints of time, context and audience influence them; they are perspectival as they encode a viewpoint; and finally, stories are linked to identities and have a moral underpinning.

Let us take a step back in human history now to flesh out an answer to how and why human beings came up with storytelling.

How and Why Do Humans Tell Stories?

The Universal Allure of Stories across Time and Cultures: The Evolution of Storytelling

> Human minds yield helplessly to the suction of story. No matter how hard we concentrate, no matter how deep we dig in our heels, we just can't resist the gravity of alternate worlds. (Gottschall 2013: 3)

What accounts for this deep and primeval need in humans to tell stories? How did they begin to tell stories and how do humans tell stories now? Why do humans 'yield helplessly to the suction of story'? Stories are a cultural universal. Every human society that has been studied by anthropologists or historians, or dug up by archaeologists, contains evidence of storytelling. As a *National Geographic* entry on storytelling notes: 'Storytelling is universal to the human experience.'[2] All cultures have told stories down the ages; in fact, some of the earliest evidence of stories comes from cave drawings in Lascaux and Chavaux, France, dating as far back as 30,000 years ago. These cave drawings depict animals, humans and other objects, which appear to represent visual stories – some of the scenes depicted on those cave walls were possibly associated with some kind of oral storytelling (ibid.). The oral tradition of storytelling found expression in myriad forms ranging from epics, myths, legends, fables, to folklore, etc., and found able allies in performative arts like rhymes and songs. As Nair (2003: 13) notes: 'the activity of story-telling has its roots in a pre-literate, primarily oral, certainly pre-modern, even perhaps a "primitive" ethos. At the same time, the irrepressible urge to tell a simple story, or alternatively, simply tell stories, is one which contemporary civilization has hardly managed to rid itself of.'

The advent of writing revolutionalized the art of storytelling by bringing a different sense of permanence: epic poems such as *The Iliad* (Greek) and *The Tale of Gilgamesh* (Sumerian), for instance, which were first recited and then passed down by word of mouth, were later written down. The latter, along with the *Book of Genesis* in the Old Testament, is deemed to be one of the oldest of written stories; both contain allusions to a mythical flood and 'may tap into lingering cultural memories of real, geological events in the Middle East from the end of the last Ice Age', according to a BBC article.[3]

This penchant for fiction might be for a lot of things based on real/ imagined events occurring in the environment and could have been an *evolutionary adaptation*:

> Some thinkers, following Darwin, argue that the evolutionary source of story is sexual selection, not natural selection. Maybe stories, and other art forms, aren't just obsessed with sex; maybe they are ways of getting sex by making gaudy, peacocklike displays of our skill, intelligence, and creativity – the quality of our minds. ... Or maybe stories are a form of cognitive play. (Gottschall 2013: 27)

On the other hand, evolutionary literary scholar Brian Boyd notes that 'a work of art acts like a playground for the mind' (Boyd 2009: 15). Boyd suggests that the free play of art, in all its forms, does the same sort of work for our mental muscles that rough-and-tumble play does for our physical muscles – *stories prepare us for the world.* According to other evolutionary thinkers in addition to Boyd, like Steven Pinker (1997) and Michelle Scalise Sugiyama (2005), story is where people go to *practise the key skills of human social life.* Alternatively, stories could be low-cost sources of information and vicarious experience that delight in order to instruct. 'Through stories we learn about human culture and psychology, without the potentially staggering costs of having to gain this experience first hand' (Gottschall 2013: 28).

Another evolutionary take concerns the origins of storytelling as *social gossip*:

> If being human is all about talking, it's the tittle-tattle of life that makes the world go round, not the pearls of wisdom that fall from the lips of the Aristotles and the Einsteins. We are social beings, and our world – no less than that of the monkeys and apes – is cocooned in the interests and minutiae of everyday social life. They fascinate us beyond measure. (Dunbar 1997: 4)

For Dunbar, primates groom each other not to pick out niggling nits but as a form of gossip, a way of exchanging social information. Grooming also establishes social order in the ape world: 'To be groomed by a monkey is to experience primordial emotion. ... The experience is both physical sensation and social intercourse' (ibid.: 1). As human groups became larger such tactile grooming became impossible, and hence we started to speak as a form of social gossip and grooming. There is, therefore, an inherent evolutionary *sociality*, and conversations grew along cognitive lines of both forming groups and communal participation: 'Socio-biologists now speculate that stories, like gossip, were an ancient means of social grooming, through which individual members of the human species both ratified their own existence in the eyes of the community, and the community's extension in themselves and others' (Nair 2003: 17).

As human social groups grew and communal bonds sealed in, *stories possibly became a recourse for subverting boredom or cultural irrelevance* and thus, conversationalists possibly began to 'display an almost programmed commitment to grading or evaluating the stories they are submitted to along a cognitive axis that registers boredom, implausibility and cultural irrelevance. It is as if the "self" that a teller projects through her narrative is being communally tested, examined for its *social robustness*' (ibid.: 10).

It is therefore a self-serving circularity: we have *become* social thanks to storytelling, and it is possibly equally true that *because* we are social, we tell stories.

Storytelling in the Human Mind and in Children's Play

The ubiquitousness of storytelling in human beings makes one wonder if it was worked into evolution for some reason. It begs the question Gottschall (2013: 24) asks, that since evolution is 'ruthlessly utilitarian, how has the seeming luxury of fiction not been eliminated from human life'? Apart from the overt oral and written stories that humans make up and encounter in social life, there are also our encounters with the fictional world as dictated by modern digital technology. According to Robson's BBC article,[4] the average adult is thought to spend at least 6 per cent of the waking day engrossed in fictional stories on various screens. Add to this the *inner* world of stories that we constantly inhabit – that of daydreaming – and we seem to be swamped with stories!

> ... we spend about half of our waking hours – one-third of our lives on earth – spinning fantasies. We daydream about the past: things we should have said or done, working through our victories and failures. We daydream about mundane stuff, such as imagining different ways of handling a conflict at work. (Gottschall 2013: 11)

Does it indicate that we are neurologically hard-wired for storytelling? Gottschall's position is that the fact that story is a human universal is strong evidence of *biological purpose* (ibid.: 30), and even though the human brain may not have exactly been *designed* for story, it surely has been adapted towards it in the course of evolution.[5] Current studies on split brain neuroscience (Gazzaniga 2000, 2008a, 2008b) seem to suggest the complementary specialization of human cerebral hemispheres – the left brain being more specialized for tasks such as speaking, thinking and generating hypotheses, and the right brain being incapable of speech or serious cognitive work, with its jobs including recognizing faces, focusing attention and controlling visual–motor tasks. Gazzaniga and his collaborators identified specialized circuitry in the left hemisphere that is responsible for making sense of the incredible amount of information that the brain is always receiving from the environment. This set of neural circuits is engaged in detecting order and meaning in that flow of information, and to organize it into a coherent account of a person's experience – in other words, into a story. This brain structure was named as 'the interpreter' (ibid.), which gives credence to the fact of humans being neurologically wired for storytelling.

And because we are *both* evolutionarily and neurologically adapted as well as culturally seeped in storytelling, the human mind is till today a default 'storymaker'. Recall the first question with regard to stories that you were asked at the beginning of this chapter: When and how did *you* first encounter stories in *your* life? Who was your first storyteller? What kind of stories did this person tell you? Your trying to recall this person and the kind of stories she/he told, is perhaps itself being retrieved by you mentally in the form of a story: 'The first storyteller I encountered was my mother. I remember she used to tuck my younger brother and me in bed and read us stories from the Panchatantra.' Our introduction to stories and simultaneous initiation into culture is not by accident: Nair (2003) suggests that stories are a means of combining the causal and logical explanations of 'real' events with emotional recognition which ensure that the lessons taught to us as children, and then throughout our lives via stories, lay the cornerstones of our most crucial beliefs:

> As 'art', stories often present or encourage 'false' beliefs; what needs to be emphasized is that this fact does not in any way adversely affect our ability to reason in and through them. Indeed, by driving a wedge between 'words' and the 'world', between representations and reality, *they may encourage exactly the kind of sophisticated reflexivity that is needed for abstract, structured, linear thought.* (Nair 2003: 16; emphasis added)

Hence, the kind of reflexivity and questioning that stories ingrain in us sort of prepare us for life ahead. In this sense, our childhood introduction to stories becomes our *cultural repositories for knowledge* and prepares us for adult social life that is beset with all kinds of problems. In fact, 'story is so central to the lives of young children that it comes close to defining their existence. What do little kids do? Mostly they do story' (Gottschall 2013: 7) – it is ingrained into their very being. This is the reason why 'experts in child psychology agree that pretend play is *for* something. It has biological functions. Play is widespread in animals, and all but universal in mammals, especially the smart ones. The most common view of play across species is that it helps youngsters rehearse for adult life' (ibid.: 41).

In the last century itself, developmental psychologists Mead (1934) and Piaget (1932) examined sex differences emergent in games that children play. In games, children learn to take on the role of the other and come to see themselves through others' eyes; they also learn respect for rules and the fact that rules can be made and changed. Lever (1976), in examining sex differences in her study of 181 fifth grade, white, middle-class children aged ten and eleven, found that boys play in larger and age-heterogenous groups, play competitive games, and their games lasted longer probably because they required a higher level of skill, were less boring and involved more dispute resolution than girls whose games tended to end with the eruption of dispute. Lever's findings seem to be in line with the Piagetian claim that boys through childhood become increasingly fascinated with the legal elaboration of rules and the elaboration of fair processes of adjudicating conflicts – a fascination that he says does not hold for girls. Girls have a more 'pragmatic' attitude towards rules and are more tolerant towards them, more willing to make exceptions and more easily reconciled to innovation. As a result, the legal sense that Piaget considers essential to moral development 'is far less developed in little girls than in boys' (Piaget 1932: 77). This Piagetian idea is supported by Lever, for whom boys in their games are more concerned about rules while girls are more concerned about relationships often at the cost of the game. In this sense, boys' social orientation is positional and that of girls is personal, and they seem to indicate gendered developmental difference in children. Even recent work in this line of research (Paley 2004; Konner 2010) seems to suggest that for children, pretend play is not just important but also that children's pretend play is relentlessly focused on *trouble*. Lots of studies corroborate the findings that boys and girls spontaneously segregate themselves by sex: boys engage in much more rough sort of play while fantasy play is more frequent in girls, more sophisticated and more focused on pretend parenting.[6] Further, boys are generally considered to be more aggressive and less nurturing than girls, with the differences being present and measurable by the seventeenth month of life. All of these seem to suggest that our childhood games and our storied worlds prepare us for something – do stories then make us who we are and also influence the gendered being we eventually become?

The usages of storytelling have been touted to be many: from *escapism* to *problem-solving* to *forming of groups* that hark back to our inherent human tribalism. But if stories were just pleasurable frippery, then, as Gottschall (2013) argues, evolution would have long ago eliminated them as a waste of energy long ago. For him, it is hard to 'reconcile the escapist theory of fiction with the deep patterns we find in the art of storytelling. If the escapist theory were true, we'd expect stories to be mainly about pleasurable wish fulfilment. In story worlds, everything would go right and good people would never suffer' (ibid.: 48).

While it is indeed true that many of us are drawn to fiction because fiction gives us pleasure, it certainly does not explain why 'most of what is actually in fiction is deeply unpleasant: threat, death, despair, anxiety' (ibid.: 49). This seems to reflect the tendency of children's stories being not always 'fairy tale-*ish*'. If not escapism then as *The National Geographic Encyclopedia* entry cited earlier[7] suggests, the reason human beings are drawn to stories is that *it helps us feel in control.* That is, it helps us to find order in things that have happened to us and make sense of the events of a random world. Stories can also let us see how others think and feel. In other words, they can allow us to *empathize* with the people around us.[8] Stories also allow us to *share information in a memorable way*, which might have helped our ancestors cooperate and survive. By telling a story rather than merely reciting or spelling out dry facts, we remember the details more clearly. Yet another function of storytelling has been its problem-solving characteristic: in fact, psychologist and novelist Keith Oatley calls stories the 'flight simulators of human social life' (Oatley 2008).[9] As humans evolved to live in bigger societies, we needed to learn how to cooperate, without being a 'free rider' who takes too much and gives nothing, or overbearing individuals abusing their dominance to the detriment of the group's welfare. Our capacity for storytelling – and the tales we tell – may have, therefore, also evolved as a way of *communicating the right social norms*.[10] People we share stories with inevitably become part of our social circle – in-groups and out-groups are formed with our stories!

The Good Self in Stories

The Spiritual Storytelling Ape

How did stories, as they emerged in human social groups or as problem-solving excercises, begin to encode the good and the bad elements? When and why did moral teaching become part of storytelling? One of the answers to this lies in the emergence of spirituality and religion as a basic human characteristic:

> *Homo sapiens* must have already been a spiritual ape when our ancestors began streaming out of Africa. And since all religions share some of the same basic features – including belief in supernatural beings, belief in a transcendent soul, belief in the efficacy of magic (in the form of rituals and prayer) – the roots of spirituality must be sunk deep in human nature. (Gottschall 2013: 119–20)

Of all the expressions of storytelling in human societies, religions have been one of the most potent and effective. Each religion tells its own story about the evolution of the world and the emergence of human beings; about right and wrong, and the punishments and rewards for the chosen way of living. 'Based on what the sacred stories say, believers regulate the practices of their lives: how they eat, how they wash, how they dress, when they have sex, when they forgive, and when they wage total war in the name of everything holy. Why? Religion is a human universal' (ibid.: 119). The biologist David Sloan Wilson proposes that religion emerged as a stable part of all human societies for a simple reason: it made them work better and stories are the way for all humans to cooperate. For Wilson (2003), religion provides multiple benefits to groups: first, it defines a group as a group;[11] second, religion coordinates behaviour within the group, setting up rules and norms, punishments and rewards; third, religion provides a powerful incentive system that promotes group cooperation and suppresses selfishness. Religions teach good things and ethical teachings include how people may be bound together into more harmonious collectives. Is this what explains the good versus bad aspects that are portrayed in our mythical tales? Even in the twenty-first century, when digital technology has pervaded our lives, stories are inevitable: we play games that have 'avatars'; we watch movies on avatars in an alternate world which human had colonized; we go online and get hooked to stories on our preferred OTT platform.

> Story . . . continues to fulfill its ancient function of binding society by reinforcing a set of common values and strengthening the ties of common culture. Story enculturates the youth. It defines the people. It tells us what is laudable and what is contemptible. It subtly and constantly encourages us to be decent instead of decadent. Story is the grease and glue of society: by encouraging us to behave well, story reduces social friction while uniting people around common values. Story homogenizes us; it makes us one. (Gottschall 2013: 137–38)

Do our *personal life stories* also reflect such socio-religious and cultural considerations? Are we moral because religious or cultural stories tell us to be so? Let us take an example to see if our life stories too follow this model, and if life stories too have the same sort of appeal that transformed apes into myth-weaving creatures.

Humans and Their Life Stories

> Story-telling seems to me to permit high quality resolutions of experience, either representing it analytically as fiction or reappraising its contingencies as factual narrative. *It is this ability to crystallize experience, re-form it so that it allows us to reform, or at least review, ourselves, that we celebrate when we share our stories.* (Nair 2003: 12; emphasis added)

Let me tell you two stories – please pick which story you liked more immediately after reading both of them.

> Story A
> There was once a little boy who saw ghosts but no one – not even his mother – believed him. A child psychologist came in to help him and initially even he did not believe the child until he heard an audio-tape in which a ghost was indeed speaking. Surprised, the psychologist asked the child to use his gift and help all ghosts who were reaching out to him. Together, they helped a lot of ghosts finish their unfinished business. The child then asked the psychologist to talk to his wife when

she was asleep. The psychologist did so and suddenly realized that he had actually died one night the year before when he had been shot. He told his sleeping wife that he loved her, thereby finishing his unfinished business, and then his spirit departed in a flash of light.

Story B
There was once a brilliant student who wanted to excel in academics. His roommate inspired him to follow his dreams. He published an original theoretical article which earned him a prestigious teaching job. He was enlisted by a mysterious man to work for his country's Department of Defence to study encrypted enemy telecommunications He became increasingly obsessed with his work. He met his old roommate and his niece often. With this friend's encouragement he got married. One day, after delivering a lecture, he tried to flee from enemy agents but was admitted to a psychiatric ward instead where his wife was told that he had schizophrenia. He came to realize that his old roommate, his niece and the man who hired him were all his hallucinations.

Which of these two stories did you like – was it Story A or Story B?[12] What if I told you that only one of these – Story B – is based on a real person and is a true life story.[13] Which story appeals to you more now? Unless you are an absolute horror story fan, my hunch is that it will be Story B simply because it portrays incredible happenings in the life of an *actual* person.

Life stories – even those that are not made into Hollywood movies – have this sort of an appeal. Our personal stories crytallize our experiences and help others draw moral lessons from them. As discursive units, our stories are reiterable and hence enable us as narrators to review ourselves while enabling our listeners to draw out our identities.

Having traced the emergence of human beings as an eternal storytelling species, we have reached a crucial juncture of our exploration of narrativity in which it becomes imperative to define the contours of our own exploration. In other words, let us now define how *we* wish to examine the storytelling human! The title of this book – *Revelation of Self in Language* – gives a hint of this orientation because it makes the assumption that there is such a thing as 'self' that somehow 'reveals itself' in our narratives. This part of the title also gives a hint as to *how* this self reveals itself: it is through the active collusion of language. The subtitle of this book – *Narrative Identity as Emergent in Conversation* – gives an insight into how we wish for this revelation to proceed: through an examination of narratives in conversation. Several questions must necessarily follow: what is a/the self? How is it different from traditional notions of 'person' or 'subject' or 'identity'? What is the actual role of language in this 'revelation'? Is this 'self', and the language in which it reveals itself, gendered? Given that stories are ubiquitous phenomena of human existence, how should we proceed to examine how and why it emerges in conversation? Finally, what really are these conversations we are talking about and who are the participants of these conversations? Since language mediates between society and the individualization process of a subject, a working hypothesis of this book is that it is within the linguistic structure of the personal narrative – around which human life and experience is inevitably structured – that one finds selfhood being expressed. This contention, that it is in the stories we tell about our lives that our selfhood gets expressed, will be the major concern of this book as we try to locate the issue of selfhood within a historical perspective and then will explore the ways in which the self can possibly manifest itself in 'life stories'.

Drawing on Nair's self-proclaimed 'parodically simple version of the hierarchical embedding that relates those mammoth abstractions – communication, conversation and narrative' (Nair 2003: 3) – the narratives that we will be concerned with in this book are those that are conversational, oral, language-based units of communication. Why would such narratives be important? Simply because they showcase the power of narratives to build and rebuild selves in the moment of conversation. To go back again to one of the questions asked to you at the beginning of this chapter – 'What is *your* life story?' – how do you think you would be answering this if *you* and *I* were meeting? What do you think would define the contours of your storytelling? The answers would probably be: where are we meeting (in which city/place), in which setting (in a crowded market place where everyone is masked and worried about the pandemic or in your house seated comfortably on your sofa?), in which language are we speaking? How has the question about life story fit into our conversation? (I would not ask a total stranger what is your life story! There has to be a certain context for that query.) In other words, by the time we are ready to share our story, a whole lot of social meanings and dealings have already gone into placing the life story within context. I would like to know you from a certain vantage point. Nair proffers the below simple hierarchical version for locating 'storytalk' with the larger umbrella term of 'communication' and hence in this book too, we are taking the narratives as they are elicited or emergent in conversation to explore how exactly human selfhood gets established in language.

The nature and question of subjectivity and human selfhood have, over the years, spawned such concepts as 'subject', 'individual', 'agent' and 'self'[14]

FIGURE 1.1 *Hierarchical Embedding Relating Communication, Conversation and Narrative*

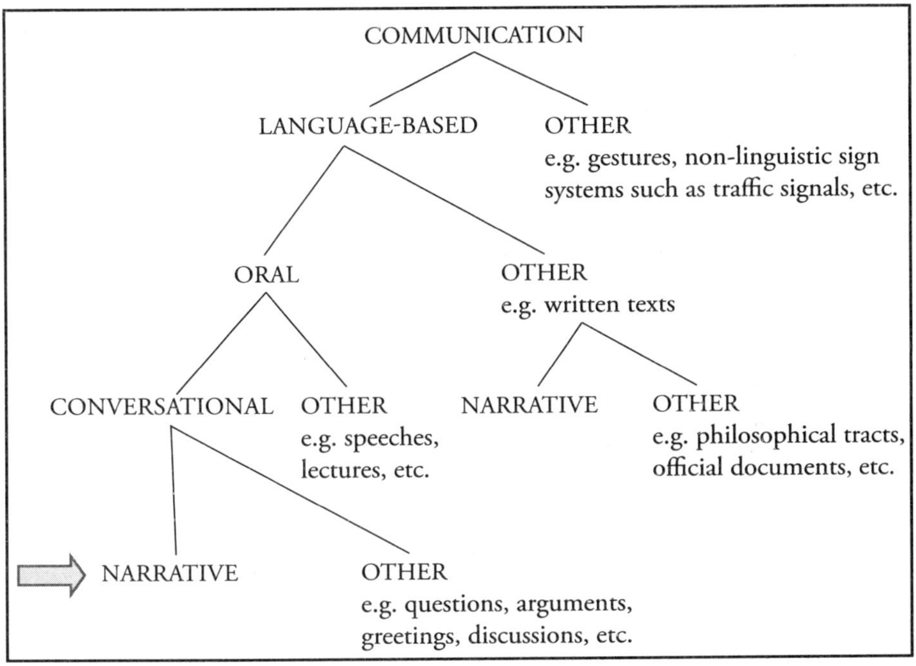

Note: The arrow is inserted on the diagram to highlight the position of the narrative within communication *per se*.
Source: Nair (2003: 3).

in academic deliberations. These terms are often used interchangeably, and each term usually implies different takes on the issue of identity. 'Who am I?' is the cardinal question that one faces regarding identity and an individual usually takes recourse to a complex web of identifications[15] when answering it, none of which alone can define an individual or can help her/him in answering the question. 'Identity' is today acknowledged to be not so much a singular concept as a *network of significations* that hinge on social, political, historical and psychological issues, and as a theoretical construct, it is now a pervasive concept across social and behavioural sciences cutting across disciplines like psychology, psychoanalysis, sociology, linguistics, political science, etc. Since human experience is inevitably structured around stories (as noted in Nair 2003 cited above), it can be surmised that our individual stories about our lives, will reveal aspects of our identity. Moreover, as any social setting presumes conversation between two or more participants, individual narratives as emergent in conversation is a promising area for the revelation of the self in language. Before we embark on this journey however, it becomes necessary to understand the concept of 'self' and for that we take a short detour to better appreciate this concept and all its associated terms such as 'identity', 'persons', 'others', etc.

The Self: A Brief Philosophical Detour

Let us undertake a brief philosophical detour to examine a few theorizations/ issues pertaining to identity and selfhood. For Frankfurt, a 'person' denotes the 'capacity for reflective self-evaluation . . . manifest in second-order desires' (Frankfurt 1971: 7). These latter imply volitions ('to want to be moved by certain desires') or to want certain 'first-order' spontaneous/'unreflective desires' to be the ones to galvanize the person into action. Second-order desires are thus typically identification and *endorsement of one's values and beliefs* which structure one's will. In Frankfurt's view, therefore, a person is someone who can ask, possibly, of herself: Is this the kind of being I ought to be or want to be? Consequently, critical self-reflection and self-determination are inextricable from a morally valuable life. For Taylor (1976) too, it is evaluative responsibility – involving the qualities of reflection, evaluation, will and depth – that is essential to the notion of 'self'. For some other philosophers, a person is *a basic material primitive* to which are ascribed not only mental but also physical predicates. Strawson, for example, considers the concept of person to be logically prior to that of consciousness and deems the former to be a 'basic particular' – an individual material body upon 'which the identification and reidentification of all other things rest' (Strawson 1977: 87). In Giddens 'self-identity' becomes a 'reflexively organized endeavour' (Giddens 1991: 5) and the reflexive self has the following elements. (i) It is something for which the individual is responsible. (ii) It forms a trajectory of development from the past to the anticipated future.[16] (iii) The reflexivity of the self is continuous as well as all-pervasive with self-interrogation and change being inevitable in such reflexivity (iv) Self-identity as a coherent phenomenon is an interpretative self-history and presumes a narrative. (v) Self-actualization achieved through reflexivity implies the control of time and the insistence on 'personal time' is manifest in the *durée* of day-to-day social life. (vi) The reflexivity of the self extends also to the body which is deemed part of an action system rather than a merely passive object. (vii) Self-actualization, as a process of balance between risk and opportunity, involves calculative strategies to be adopted in relation to the future. (viii) It (self-actualization) also depends on authenticity, which means 'being true to oneself'. (ix) For self-actualization to proceed, the individual life course is seen as *a series of passages* that may involve losses which need to be mourned. And finally: (x) The development of the self is internally referential and personal integrity 'as an achievement of an authentic self' comes from integrating the life experiences within the narrative of self-development. In Giddens, we see a glimpse of how the creation of a personal belief system, by means of which the individual acknowledges 'his first loyalty is to himself' (Giddens 1991: 80), can surface through a narrative of self-development. Our assumption that the narrative will be instrumental in the revelation of self in language is given a vote of confidence by Le Page and Tabouret-Keller, who note that 'self-ascription is *always* accompanied by linguistic symbols' (Le Page and Tabouret-Keller 1985: 237; emphasis added).

One of the more influential philosophical theories of 'self' is that of Taylor (1989), for whom self is 'defined by the powers of disengaged reason – with the associated ideals of self-responsible freedom and dignity, of self-exploration, and of personal commitment. These powers – at least the first two – requiring radical reflexivity are the basis for a certain concept of inwardness' (ibid.: 211).

This feature of 'radical reflexivity' can be traced way back to Augustine, while the power of 'disengaged reason' is associated mostly with Descartes. The notion of inwardness in fact was heralded much earlier than Augustine and traces its roots even to Plato.[17] It is as a function of the historical mode of self-interpretation that we have come to think of ourselves in the opposition 'inside–outside', where our thoughts, ideas and feelings are 'within us' and the objects of the world are the domain of the 'without'. With Augustine in the fourth century AD, the Platonian oppositions of spirit–matter, higher–lower, eternal–temporal, immutable–changing were captured in explicit 'inner/outer' terms for the first time. Like Plato, he agreed on the universe as the eternal realization of a rational order, but added to it the emphasis on participation since everything in the world reflects the meaningful order of God's 'Ideas'. Augustine thus contributes to developing the doctrine of the 'will' since it can control the rational intention and has the power to confer or withhold assent. The will in turn determines what we can know and the central crisis of moral experience for Augustine is a weakness of the will (*akrasia*). Radical reflexivity takes on supreme importance as the first-person account of the space in which we encounter God.

For Descartes in the seventeenth century AD, on the other hand, the world (following the Galilean revolution) is mechanical, representative and functional, and a domain of instrumental control. While the moral sources are still within us, the 'Ideas' are no longer ontic (a universe of meaningful order) but ones that we *construct*, and rationality is the capacity to construct order as dictated by knowledge. This signals, for the first time, not a *substantivist* but a *proceduralist* stance of knowledge; in the latter, representation becomes knowledge through being correct, carrying certainty and via the 'objectification of the bodily' that affirms their immaterial status. Aiming to ground natural philosophy within the principles of mechanics, Descartes conceived of a *metaphysical self* which was vested with the philosophical values of 'truth' and 'certainty'. He employed the method of 'doubt' to establish as indubitable the existence of an 'I' that is an immaterial, intelligent, thinking entity subject to consciousness. It is through reason and not learning that the subject comes to conclude *cogito ergo sum* ('I think therefore I am'). By extension, it is no longer the experiential body but a 'disenchanted' stance involving 'neutralizing' the cosmos that helps achieve self-mastery. The new concept of inwardness, self-sufficiency and autonomous powers of ordering by reason also prepared the ground for the modern unbelief.

With the advent of Locke and Hume's empiricism followed by Hegelian 'transcendental idealism' and Nietzschean 'perspectivalism' in the eighteenth and the nineteenth centuries, the idea of self became further enriched. Along with the Cartesian metaphysical self, sense perception and psychological continuity became aspects of self. Identity came to imply the continued existence of the same reflective consciousness. Locke took the subjectivist idea of radical reflexivity further by allowing it to facilitate in the *complete remaking of the self*. In his deterministic account, people are compelled by their strong desires and contingent connections that he calls 'habits'. The Cartesian mind–body dualism receives the fullest expression in Locke's perfectly detachable consciousness from its embodiment. Locke further defines the person as 'a thinking intelligent being that has reason and reflection and can consider itself as itself, the same thinking thing, in different times and places' (Locke 1948: 9). For him, '[*s*]*elf* is that conscious thinking thing – whatever substance made up of (whether spiritual or material, simple or compounded, it matters not) – which is sensible or conscious of pleasure and pain, capable of happiness or misery, and so is concerned for itself, as far as that consciousness extends' (Locke, quoted in Atkins, ed. 2005: 29).

With his emphasis on psychological continuity, Locke brought in the cardinal notions of time and relation to the personal identity. Hume, on the other hand, targeted the 'substrate view'[18] of the human subject by depicting the importance of the *imagination* in receiving sense impressions and arranging them according to association. On the substrate view, the problem of a thing continuing to remain the same thing (despite having different properties at different times) is resolved by making a distinction between properties (*accidens*) and an enduring substrate in which the properties are supposed to inhere (*substantia*). Thus, in relation to the self, *one remains the same thinking thing despite changes in one's perceptions, ideas and emotions* because these are merely properties distinct from the underlying substance that endures: it is the mind that perceives through resemblance, spatio-temporal continuity and cause-effect associations and the imagination that poses a semblance of self.

Also aligned against the substrate view, though not entirely divested of metaphysical overtones, is Hegel's (1977) version of *transcendental idealism*. In his view, the object, as well as our knowledge of it, is constituted by self-consciousness and *the world exists for a mind to perceive it*. In Hegel's account, subjectivity and freedom are 'worldly achievements' mediated through our relations with others and the history of the world is the progress of consciousness of freedom. The full realization of the human spirit that is tied to worldly existence involves individual psychological reflection as well as the communal spirit, and is what Hegel calls the 'Geist'. Freedom consists of the duty to act in accordance with reason – which is not opposed to nature in Hegel – and what facilitates the individual's subjectivity to emerge in the face of 'others' is the *Sittlichkeit* (organic community). It is in the latter that the individual's desires can exist in accord with reason and she can achieve subjectivity since society embodies rational principles in its institutions. For Hegel, *subjectivity is thus always intersubjective* because the individual consciousness is mediated through relations with others that exist for its sake. Consciousness, in order to take itself as an object, expresses itself as desire (for certainty) and as such needs another consciousness to exist as self-consciousness. According to Hegel, the encounter of the two self-consciousnesses in the world is experienced ambiguously by both as a threat to and a promise of self-certainty. Each sees the other as a kind of object (an 'Other') in the external world and the subject is aware of this 'Other' as another subject – something same as oneself.

In Hegel (1977), 'Geist', 'freedom' and 'history' are triple concepts within which human subjectivity emerges in relation with the other. For Nietzsche (1956), on the other hand, much like Freud who was influenced by him, *consciousness is a second-order expression of underlying part-biological and part-evolutionary urges and instincts*. He too targets the substrate view when he notes that concepts like mind, soul and body do not refer to distinct entities, but rather are linguistic strategies employed in different aspects of our lives. As Atkins notes in her commentary on Nietzsche, the substrate view arises from a fundamental 'confusion' where, from the fact that something is done (thinking, willing, feeling, etc.), *a doer is inferred* whose nature is of a thinking/willing/feeling thing (Atkins, ed. 2005: 70). Nietzsche, in claiming that all beings are animated by urges that are both creative and destructive, invests these urges with a transformative energy he deems as the 'will to power' (Nietzsche 1968). What we call the self is in Nietzsche's view just a unity of urges and there is no doer behind a deed. The more integrated the urges, the more effective is the organism's will and this creates the illusion of a single agent of volition.[19] Thus, facts are to be treated with suspicion since a fact is just an expression of the perspective of the dominant complex of urges; rather, it is the composite and conflictual nature of the human organism that gives us the important capacity to see things from different perspectives.

The 'Self' in Relation to an 'Other': Poststructuralist/Postmodern Theorization

Nietzschean ideas influenced much of contemporary thought on self and subjectivity, especially through their influence on Freudian psychoanalysis and the 'genealogical method' in Foucault and Butler. However, for Sartre (early twentieth century), consciousness takes on different existential overtones in terms of the 'self–other' equation. Though consciousness in Hegel was an intersubjective phenomenon, *for Sartre the presence of the other nearly annihilates one's subjectivity*. This is achieved by what Sartre calls the 'look' of the other – something that penetrates the unity of consciousness of the subject. One's relation with the other is not an epistemological issue of *knowing* the other person but becomes an ontological datum – an absolute event of *being*. To be 'looked at' for Sartre means '. . . that I am suddenly affected in my being and that essential modifications appear in my structure – modifications which I can apprehend and fix conceptually by means of the reflective cogito' (Sartre, cited in Atkins, ed. 2005: 98). This relation with the other, and by extension the self, is mediated by what Sartre calls the 'pre-reflective cogito and reflective cogito', respectively:

> Only the reflective consciousness has the self directly for an object. The unreflective consciousness does not apprehend the person directly or as its object; the person is presented to consciousness in so far as the person is an object for the Other. This means that all of a sudden I am conscious of escaping myself, not in that I am the foundation of my own nothingness but in that *I have found my foundation outside myself.* I am for myself only as I am a pure reference to the other. (Ibid.; emphasis added)

In finding one's foundation outside oneself in the Other's presence, not only 'my' relation to objects but 'my' relation to 'myself' gets altered;[20] *my freedom is compromised* and Sartre claims that the only 'alternatives of responding to "the Look" are fear, shame or pride' (Atkins, ed. 2005: 89). The conflict is never resolved, and there can only be assertions and counter-assertions resorted to through strategies such as vanity, seduction, sadism, masochism, indifference, love, etc. These strategies cannot quite escape the Other's annihilating power and as a result, the Other's Ego, in the form of the gaze, is internalized.

The notion of the other is radically transformed in the later decades of the twentieth century with the advent of poststructuralist thought. In Derrida, the other comes to 'inhabit' the self in its language through *differance* – the operation of differing which 'both fissures and retards presence, submitting it simultaneously to primordial division and delay' (Derrida 1973: 87–88). Language is constituted out of a differance since it is based on a system of differentiated signs (traces) that do not bear any immediate or ultimately fixed relation to their signifieds. In assigning primary importance to the context of interaction, Derrida's deconstructive method allows 'the incessant movement of *recontextualization*' (Derrida 1988: 136; emphasis added) and in this sense, 'there is nothing outside of the text' (*il n'y a pas de hors-texte*). The text and context are interwoven with each other and deconstruction strives to show that words are ambiguous and not to be trusted as dependable representatives of something 'out there'. It marks out the system of dependencies between one discourse and the other delineating the trace of the event in each instance that ends up being revealed as an effect. By extension, identity that depends on language will also be relegated to the status of a 'trace'; '. . . an identity is never given, received, or attained; only the interminable and indefinitely phantasmatic process of identification endures' (Derrida 1998: 28). Each identification emerges as a trace of the 'I' that formed itself through language:

> This I would have formed itself, at the site of a situation that cannot be found, a site always referring elsewhere to something other, to another language, to the other in general. It would have located [*situe*] itself in a nonlocatable [*insituable*] experience of language in the broadest sense of the term. (Ibid.: 29)

Language establishes the historical contingency of the subject, its imbrication and articulation through its discursive practices, and reveals the *constituted* nature of human identity. In the context of subjectivity, this Derridean notion of *differance* – the neologism signifying both difference and deferral – assumes importance along with the Freudian notion of the 'unconscious', because *it invoked a self that was a multiple, non-essential and shifting entity whose identity is constantly changing and which no longer had a unitary, rational core.*

Around the third quarter of the twentieth century, the concept of self underwent another radical transformation with the postmodernist stance on social theory. The self was now based on constructed as opposed to found reality, and postmodernist thought which was accompanied by 'incredulity towards the metanarrative' (Lyotard 1984) led to a breakdown of the Enlightenment Project as well as the subsequent twentieth-century rationalism (Harvey 1989). The rational way of thinking presumed a single correct mode of representation, believed in linear progress, absolute truths, and the rational planning of ideal social worlds had a corresponding *unitary sense of the self.* With the advent of postmodernism, the notion of a contingent selfhood came to the fore: the view that ideas cannot be understood apart from the linguistic systems that produce them gained ground and decimated the substrate view of selfhood further – one which envisaged 'inherent' characteristics of the subject as ensuring stability. It transpired that '. . . most of reality is indifferent to our descriptions of it and that *the human self is created by the use of vocabulary*[21] rather than being adequately or inadequately expressed in a vocabulary . . . languages are made rather than found, and truth is a property of linguistic entities of sentences' (ibid.: 7; emphasis added).

'The traditional view . . . that there is a core self which can look at, decide among use and express itself by means of . . . beliefs and desires' (Rorty 1989: 10) was thus sidelined in favour of a recognition that language which is deeply rooted in the social construction of reality established 'truth' as a material, discursive, political and subjective phenomenon, and entailed '. . . letting go of the idea of a True Self that is same in all contexts' (O'Hara and Anderson 1996: 168). With the shift in perspective,

> Subjectivity can be glimpsed as a process of finding yourself becoming a subject over the course of an infinite series of encounters involving reflexivity and creativity in the imaginative transformation of desire and anxiety. The effort and desire involved in communication provoke a self that is new to oneself, specific to that encounter. (Henriques *et al.* 1998: xvii)

Apart from the poststructuralist interrogations of the foundations of a unified self and the postmodern questioning of this notion, there developed, as reported in Henriques *et al.* (1998), other critiques that changed the idea of the self as it was understood and ushered in new ways of looking at subjectivity. One such critique – the postcolonial questioning of the logocentric notion of the subject with the ideologies of racism and imperialism – pointed towards the complexity of relation between culture and psyche in the production of subjectivity and identity. The work of Althusser, Fanon and many feminist thinkers developed to counter the neglect of gender and race as distinct categories irreducible to class and the role of the personal in explaining agency, whereas the approaches in Foucault helped shape a different agenda underscoring discourses and practices which functioned to constitute subjectivity as historically specific. For Foucault, 'continuous history is the indispensable correlative of the founding function of the subject' (Foucault 1972: 12). Drawing on Heidegger (1962), he saw the human subject as a self-questioning being in whose ability to raise questions was a latent power also to perceive the presuppositions that direct the questioning. This power provides one with internal coherence and social meaning, and one's understanding of all social phenomena including subjectivity rests always already upon *interpretive historical presuppositions*. A 'genealogy' of the subject will also involve interpretive historical presuppositions that facilitate 'its conditions of possibility': the constituted nature of the human subject is highlighted by Foucault when he notes:

> I do believe that there is no sovereign, founding subject, a universal form of subject to be found everywhere . . . the subject is constituted through practices of subjection, or, in a more autonomous way, through practices of liberation, of liberty . . . on the basis, of course, of a number of rules, styles, inventions to be found in the cultural environment. (Foucault interview, in Kritzman, ed. 1988: 50)[22]

This emphasis on the 'cultural environment' in the forging of subjectivity is also an indication of the involvement of others in such an interpretive history of the subject. As Hollway says, these are 'others' who facilitate the meaning making processes for the individual: 'Throughout an individual's history, meaning has been achieved, consciously and unconsciously in relation to others. Since infancy, we have used significant others as vehicles for containing some of the ambivalent feelings which it is difficult to acknowledge in ourselves' (Hollway 1995: 94).

A question now arises as to what/who exactly is the 'other' that influences selfhood: is it an external other or an internal one in relation to which a self can express itself? In Kitzinger and Wilkinson's words: '. . . who is the other, and who are "we"? Along what shifting lines of power and powerlessness is

Otherness constructed?' (Kitzinger and Wilkinson 1996: 3). Is it only as another consciousness that we experience otherness? Or are there other ways of being an 'other'? Is an 'other' really indispensable for the construction of the self? Cixous and Clement say, in the context of this seeming imperative to know oneself through the construction of the Other, '. . . if there were no other, one would invent it' (Cixous and Clement [1975] 1986: 71).

An important theorization in the context of otherness, and one that is of cardinal interest to us, comes from existential feminism. Feminist challenges to the phallogocentric and masculinist model of subjectivity as privileged in western theory have noted that the concept of the other has been developed predominantly in relation to woman as the other.

> Humanity is male and man defines woman not in herself but as relative to him: she is not regarded as an autonomous being. . . . She is simply what man decrees. . . . She is defined and differentiated with reference to man and not he with reference to her, she is the incidental, the inessential as opposed to the essential. He is the Subject, he is the Absolute – she is the Other. (de Beauvoir 1997: 18)

Many feminists such as Irigaray (1981), Cixous (1983/92) and Kristeva (1980), and feminist psychoanalysts such as Burman (1994) and Hollway (1995), draw on de Beauvoir's ideas on self and subjectivity. However, recent critiques of this feminist perspective have alleged that sometimes such theorizations unfairly homogenize the experience of women, and representations of women which imply a unitary category of otherness render invisible the different experiences of women of varied ethnic, sexual and class locations; in other words, there are other 'others' that need to be taken into account.[23] This issue of various forms of 'othering' has implications for the notions of power that determine an individual's relation with others. Sampson anticipates this play of power when he says:

> We know that *the self needs the other in order to be a self at all.* We know that when those selves are dominant in a given society, they can construct the other so as to affirm a particular kind of self for themselves. . . . If I find myself in and through you, but no longer control the you that grants me my self, then I am forced to deal with a self that is beyond my control, and I may not enjoy this self with which I must now contend. (Sampson 1993: 153; emphasis added)

Therefore, allied in this discussion of construction of othering are the issues of power that are immanent in a set of discourses through which a dominant individual or group defines itself. This power may be in the form of political calculations which determine *the subject's un/willing subjection within a linguistic framework as well as locate her/his relation with significant others*. Following Foucauldian theorization, it has come to be agreed upon that power does not really exist in the conventional monolithic sense of interrogating origins, principles and legitimate limits. If, however, it does work in microphysical ways through capillary forces on various devices and techniques employed on/by the individual, it is legitimate to ask how power functions in the fashioning of a self in relation to the other. Given the knowledge–power axis, how does knowledge of the other affect selfhood as expressed in self-stories? Other studies have added new dimensions to the power issues within various formulations of the self–other axis. Crenshaw (1992) and Smith (1995), for example, have shown that an important form of controlling the other is when confronted by others' representations of themselves or us; such representations are routinely *deauthorized* and dismissed as incoherent. A second corollary of this defining-through-representation is that representations of otherness can be read as inverted representations of those doing the othering. And thus, instead of reading accounts of others as transparent texts which reveal information about others, such discourses can read as being about the authors themselves, and may reveal how those with power of representation or language may construct themselves. Vidich and Lyman, for instance, point out that the 'early ethnographies reveal as much about the West as about their objects of study' – that is, ethnographic studies sometimes may tell more about the authors than the objects of their enquiry (Vidich and Lyman 1994: 26).

An obvious parallel to be sought is: what goes on in a context of interlocution (where one narrator is delineating the other's character and, in the process, constructing her/his own self)? One may also ask how a narrating self is likely to project itself in relation to the external/other world. A further question can be: what are the likely ways in which a narrating self, for instance, positions herself/himself in relation to others who, as participants in a conversation, may bring their own twist to the tale, so to speak. Are there other reasons for the self to be narrating a story for an other? Nair (2003) proffers an argument for both altruism and psychological gains when one narrates. Regarding the first of these, she notes that storytelling is different from other things we do as humans, like eating, sleeping, going shopping and making love, which are primarily for our own benefit and pleasure. 'Story-telling on the other hand seems to manifest a contrary impulse; *our altruistic pleasure in telling a story comes not from pleasing ourselves but others*, creating silent effects in their minds that we cannot often physically observe' (Nair 2003: 15; emphasis added).

Again, there may be latent power struggles in the psychological gains that good storytellers collect.

> Strong social approval and community bonding are the major psychological *gains* that might accrue for 'good' story-tellers. It is my contention that the main battles over the kind of 'object' narrative is have to be fought mainly in mental terrain. Victories and losses in the realm of story-telling, which seems so overt an activity, have to be understood in terms of covert and hidden mental evaluations and community judgements. (Ibid.)

Within a discourse of a narrating self and a 'narrated-to' other, how does power function to proffer psychological advantages to men's narratives as opposed to women's, or how does one's standpoint other another gendered standpoint? In a discourse involving male and female viewpoints, it would be worthwhile to see what strategies of language, if any, cater to the capillary forces of power in deauthorizing the other. What also transpires in such an undertaking is the shifting nature of this otherness: any exploration of narrative identity must necessarily be a study of the self and the other because *a self emerges at the intersections of language and otherness*, and a major question that emerges now is, what is the role of the agent herself in the constitution of her selfhood? In other words, is the self merely constituted in relation to the other or is her agency (intention/volition) also involved in such an enterprise? In the following section, we locate this question within a historical perspective of constituted versus constituting identity while trying to answer it in terms of symbolic interaction perspective in identity theory to understand the cultural stake in narration.

Constituted/Constituting Self and Identity Theory

The issue of constituting versus constituted subjectivity is an important aspect in the conceptualization of identity. Within social theory, this is sometimes also referred to as the *humanist–anti-humanist* or *individualism–society* dichotomy (see Ritzer and Smart, eds 2001; Ritzer 2011; and Kivisto, ed. 2021). The question at its heart is whether subjectivity is constituted by the history of a subject in relation to the external world, or is its emergence dependent on the subject's individualistic experiences and idiosyncrasies – thereby implying a constituting subjectivity. We have already seen that Foucault allies himself with the constituted nature of human subjectivity which envisages an individual being subject or being conditioned to certain discourses and practices (as opposed to being a subject).[24] Such discourses and practices position as well as produce the subject, though Foucault here allows for human creativity by acknowledging the role of 'inventions to be found in the cultural environment'. Henriques *et al.* also take a more or less anti-humanist stance while also allowing for human agency when they use subjectivity 'to refer to individuality and self-awareness – the condition of being a subject but understand in this usage that subjects are dynamic, multiple, always positioned in relation to particular discourses and practices and produced by them – the condition of being subject' (Henriques *et al.* 1998: 3).

The anti-humanist stance targets the 'individual as agent' view and privileges structures of social formation in determining human behaviour. This is also a prominent theme in some developmental psychology studies like Erikson (1960), Elms (1975), Richards (1974), Shotter (1974), Weinreich (1978) and Trevarthen (1975, 1979).[25] By contrast, the humanist standpoint on the subject (going back to the Cartesian subject based on the 'cogito': the mind guaranteeing its own rationality) envisages a unitary, non-contradictory and rational individual who is an agent of all social phenomena and production including knowledge. In considering the 'individual-as-agent' stance that is at the heart of the humanist side of the argument, one must also take into account the *roles* the agent appropriates out of her own choice. According to Banton, a role is a set of 'norms and expectations applied to the incumbent of a particular position' (Banton 1965: 29), and 'to a certain extent, an individual personality is fixed and he chooses roles in the light of his predilections. But it is also true that the roles an individual takes up may influence his attitude and his whole personality (ibid.: 146).

Burke (2003), following Stryker (1980), calls these roles and positionings *internalized meanings in the constitution of identity.* He states that most disciplines conceptualize identity in one of many ways: identity in the sense of a social category (H.C. White 1992; Calhoun, ed. 1994; Snow and Oliver 1995) is viewed as an organized, coherent force with its own goals and oppositions and denotes a group with self-interested motivation. Social categories to which one belongs help to define who one is by providing meanings in the sense of social identities in terms of group memberships (Abrams and Hogg 1990; Stets and Burke 2000). In Burke's account, a second view of the term identity denotes *an individual's subjective sense of personal sameness and continuity paired with some belief in the sameness and continuity of some shared world image* – a sense of being and becoming (Erikson 1968). When that sense is threatened, then there is an *identity crisis* – often associated with changes in life stages (in adolescence when individuals may lose their sense of self in role confusion). Unlike the former view of identity as a social category, this view is ultra-individualistic with each person being or becoming her/his own unique self (Cote 1986; Streitmatter 1993). The sense of identity that this view invokes is based on personal idiosyncrasies and characteristics that are not necessarily shared by others: for example, being assertive, honourable, trustworthy, etc. Stets (1995) deems these more individualized identities personal identities.

For Burke (2003), a third view of identity, and one that is of interest to us in the context of the constituted versus constituting identity debate, is the *symbolic interactionism perspective* that draws on Stryker's (1968, 1980) theory of identity. It takes identity bases to be found in group, role and person notions, but also takes into account variation in levels of commitment in a relationship as well as the importance of identities within the individual (what is called their 'salience'). This perspective, also focusing on the question *Who am I?* (Stryker and Serpe 1982), hinges between the notions of identity as social category and individualism and is contained in the meaning of the self as an aspect of identification – what it means to be who one is. Many of the answers are linked to roles one plays (for example, 'I am a teacher') and are referred to as role identities. A self in this formulation consists of a collection of identities, each of which is based on occupying a particular role (Stryker 1968). To say 'I am a student' is to identify oneself in a particular manner, though that alone does not tell what it means to be a student – the student role is the 'other' in relation to the teacher role and vice versa. These internalized meanings vary from person to person, but such variations centre on a commonly agreed upon set of core meanings and expectations that are part of the general culture. These meanings are always a part of the self (who I am), and tell one what to expect of and how to respond to oneself. Importantly, given that these internalized meanings are shared, they also tell others how to respond to one.

The symbolic interactionism perspective, as drawn out in Stryker (1980), sets forth a number of premises that Burke (2003) lists as follows:

(i) Behaviour is premised on a named or classified world which carries meaning in the form of shared behavioural expectations that grow out of social interaction. 'From interaction with others, one learns how to classify objects one comes into contact with, and in that process also learns how one is expected to behave with reference to those objects' (Stryker 1980: 53–54).

(ii) Burke notes that roles are not just created out of the interactions and negotiations of people, but exist out there 'enough to be seen, reacted to and labelled within society' (Burke 2003: 2).[26]

(iii) People in society are named and labelled in terms of the positions they occupy which in turn define the roles expected of them.
(iv) The names and expectations that become attached with regard to positional designations become internalized and, in turn, part of our self. Thus we become part of the social structure that is named in (ii). This is called the collective and distributive aspects of the same thing, and we are thus identified and defined by self-labels in terms of positions in society which are themselves tied structurally and serve to tie individuals together (for example, father–child ties as defined by the family's structure).
(v) Social behaviour emerges through the role-making process that involves negotiating, modifying, developing and shaping expectations through interaction. Thus, a person's identities are uniquely shaped by the person's expectations and interactions with others.

Given that the meanings of such role identities are derived from cultural knowledge as well as our own personal experiences in the roles, *we thus negotiate our meanings through our interactions with our role partners.* Stryker (1968) further introduces the two other concepts related to personal identity: 'salience hierarchy' and 'commitment'. Of these, salience hierarchy refers to the way that multiple identities that individuals hold are organized within the self, thereby reflecting the likelihood of the hierarchical way each identity would be activated. Salience provides insights to why and how individual identities differ; for some their occupational identities may hold more salience while for others spousal/family identity may hold more importance. 'The hierarchy of salience of the identities held by an individual represents a unique characteristic of that individual, making him/her different from others' (Burke 2003: 3). On the other hand, commitment is a very strong structural component which represents the connections that one has to others by way of having a particular identity, and it '. . . marks the degree to which one is embedded in the social structure as a function of the identity that one holds and it represents society in the individual-society relationship' (ibid.: 4).

Again, two noteworthy aspects of commitment are: (i) the number of others to whom one is related, i.e. the *extensiveness* of the commitment; and (ii) the strength or depth of the connection to those others, i.e. the *intensiveness* of the commitment. The notion of the self which emerges through this identity theory is role-based with multiple foci where identities are devised in conjunction with one's social structure, location and emotion.

In this sense, identity is as much a creative process as an appropriation of certain roles within the social structure.

This idea within symbolic interactionism of a highly contextual self who gets constituted in relation to others lends itself to a postmodern reading of identity as *partial, contradictory and strategic*. Haraway (1991) too, for instance, says in this context that the postmodern subject negotiates a range of roles and positions without being wholly focused on any particular positioning. She also notes that some of these positionings may be in conflict, and that at any given time a subject positions herself/himself in relation to the context she/he finds herelf/himself in. Symbolic interaction, in lending itself to postmodern readings, therefore provides an important way of looking at the constitution of individual identities in collusion with others in multiple situations. While within this view the problematic issues of selfhood are attributable to the *location of the individual within the social structure*, it also allows for *individual choice* by virtue of the salience and commitment to a particular identity that a person might have. Added to the foregoing discussion on the reflexive self (see discussion on Giddens 1991 and Taylor 1989 earlier, on page 15), the symbolic interactionism perspective has important bearings for the way the self is understood in the narrative context. When behavioural expectations are internalized as identity roles, it is expected that the self will conform to certain moral standards that the particular identity will carry in cultural terms; in other words, it can be seen as *positioning the self as culture-conforming* in many ways. For example, if for a person X, her identity as a 'doctor' is her more salient identity, it follows that she will try to be a 'good doctor' as defined within her culture/social matrix. In this sense, not only is the self identified as a being with the distinct and traditional human attribute of reflexivity and rational thinking, she is also an agent of moral deliberation with regard to her salient identity/identities.

What this symbolic occupation of roles ultimately hints at is a notion of *goodness as definitive of selfhood in a hierarchical manner*: 'I am X who is first of all a good mother, a good lawyer and a good neighbour and when I tell you a story, I position myself as a good individual because I want *you* to acknowledge me as a good person and *you* are helping create this good person in the situation of interlocution.' There were three questions posed at the beginning of chapter which are presented below in light of the above discussion:

(i) When and how did *you* first encounter stories in *your* life?
(ii) What is *your* life story?

(iii) How and why do *you* think humans came up with storytelling?

We dove into the third question and first question in earlier sections, titled 'How and Why Do Humans Tell Stories' and 'The Good Self in Stories', by exploring the emergence of storytelling in humans; trying to understand the ubiquitousness of storytelling in human societies; how the human mind and brain is structured for story; the role of children's play in sustaining stories and their cultural moorings. In order to understand our own life stories as we narrate it to others, it necessitated a brief philosophical detour in order to appreciate the self–other relation in philosophy.

In this last section of this chapter, we shall look at some theorizations which can relate the moral issue of goodness to that of selfhood, and we shall also examine some of the implications of this moral self in the postmodern context of a multi-contextual and cultural setting. The two subsections examine the dynamics of how our goodness, our morality as well as our selfhood can be established through our narratives as contextual, (un)conscious and culture-conforming accomplishments of our language.

A 'Good' Self in the Narrative: Notions of Self, Ordinary Life and Goodness

We now turn our attention to certain theoretical positions that would be tenable with the 'revelation of self' in language and the emergence of narrative identity in conversation. It can be surmised here that what we narrate in our stories is as much about *how* we want to portray ourselves (the 'good' self) as what we do *not* want others to know about us. That is, our stories not only identify us as moral individuals, but also shelter our hearers and even us from unpleasant aspects of our lives – they provide the assurance that 'I' and 'my life' are 'good'. In the following sections, we shall explore a few theories that ground these aspects of the good self and good life within the narrative. Visions of good tie up with understandings of the self in Taylor's postulation that '[w]e have a sense of who we are through our sense of where we stand to the good' (Taylor 1989: 5). He in fact argues that the 'orientation to the good is not some optional extra, something we can engage in or abstain from at will, but a condition of our being selves with an identity' (ibid.: 68).

Our selves are defined by what he calls a 'moral topography' (ibid.) and Taylor allows for a historically local interpretation of goodness by acknowledging that the background of a particular value term involves

(i) an understanding of the kind of interchange, common purposes or mutual needs between people of the society in which the term is current; and (ii) a grasp of qualitative discriminations or their individualistic perceptions of the good (with terms that make sense across a whole range of both explanatory and life uses). He gives the name 'constitutive good' to the good, 'the love of which empowers us to do and be good' (ibid.: 93), and *it is the changing nature of this constitutive good that accounts for changing self-concepts across cultures and time*, in his formulation. Further, ideas of the good not only involve qualitative distinctions but also *hierarchical* ones, in the sense of highly ranked and lower goods: it is (what one considers) the 'highest good' that comes closest to defining one's identity, and the fact that one is turned towards or away from this good can have corresponding positive or negative effects. These latter goods are called *hypergoods,* and these are 'goods which not only are incomparably more important than others but provide the standpoint from which these must be weighed, judged, decided about' (ibid.: 63). It is recognition of such goods that define the *moral of a culture* and articulating the good may help define what is basic while at the same time defining one's identity. Qualitative discriminations

> . . . function as an orienting sense of what is important, valuable, or commanding, which emerges in our particular intuitions about how we should act, feel, respond on different occasions, and on which we draw when we deliberate about ethical matters. Articulating these distinctions is setting out the moral point of the actions and feelings our intuitions enjoin on us, or invite us to, or present as admirable. (Ibid.: 77–78)

It is this articulation that brings us closer to the good as a moral and substantivist source, and by virtue of being connected in a 'complex way with our being moved by them' (ibid.: 73), hypergoods prove the substantivist notion of our morality. Taylor also notes, however, that hypergoods may be a source of conflict in that they rise through historical suppression of earlier less adequate views. For him, the 'moral' is generally defined as 'a set of ends or demands which not only have unique importance but also override and allow us to judge others' (ibid.: 63), and the conventional notions that it throws up are those of *justice*, *respect of others* and *self-dignity* to which Taylor adds the important dimension of *what makes life worthwhile.* All of these require strong evaluation involving moral intuitions that not only include uncommonly deep, powerful and universalistic instincts, but also claims that make assent to, or justify, such intuitions. The 'moral ontology' provides the background assumptions that make sense of our moral reactions and explicates the meaning of (moral) life in its three-dimensional aspect:

(i) the modern sense of respect for the individual;
(ii) the realization of a full life worth living; and
(iii) the dignity of human life in all its ordinariness.

Taylor deems this orientation to the good and the moral as essential to being a human interlocutor capable of answering for herself, as a defining feature of human identity grounded in the lived world. Further, as noted earlier, our orientation to the good (or 'seeing' good) empowers, and it functions in the end as what Taylor calls a moral source for our sense of selfhood. This seeing good is not independent of conscious effort – 'the world's being good may . . . be seen as not entirely independent of our seeing it and showing it as good' (ibid.: 448) – and it changes with historical accession of different notions of goodness. Different senses of what the good is will imply different conceptions of what a human agent is: we strongly demand universal justice, equality and beneficence, justify the demands of freedom and self-rule, and put a high priority on the avoidance of death and suffering in keeping with the constitutive goods of our present-day cultures. Based on these, the triple facets of modern identity that Taylor (1989) draws are:

(i) *modern inwardness*: the sense that humans are beings with inner depth and have the power of reflexivity;
(ii) the *affirmation of ordinary life*: which designates those aspects of human life concerned with production and reproduction, i.e. ordinary life revolving around labour in the sense of making of things necessary for life and our life as within the family and marriage; and
(iii) the *expressivist notion of nature as a moral source*: which puts a premium of self-expression and on eliminating suffering.

Corresponding to these, the new kind of constitutive good that emerged was that of *self-interpretation* and in the new culture, it forged prized autonomy, gave emphasis to self-exploration and had visions of the good life in terms of personal commitment. The modern self was a free and self-determining subject for whom the ordinary life of humans is important, and who has the powers of reflexivity, disengaged reason and creative imagination. Within such theorization, identity emerges as an inter-relationship that hinges on our notions of the good, our understandings of the self, the kinds of narratives that make sense of our lives, and lastly, our conceptions of the society: what it is to be a human agent among other human agents. In later chapters of this book, we hope to see how the notions of the 'good life' (in the Indian context), understandings of self and concepts of society emerge in narratives in various conversation contexts, and how speakers narrate about their lived realities in everyday life while being aware of the other in whose presence the narrative is being presented in the first case.

Ordinary Life as Sequestration of Experience

A different interpretation of what Taylor calls the 'affirmation of ordinary life' is to be found in Giddens (1991) (for his definition of selfhood discussed earlier, see page 15). For Giddens, *the ordinariness and the uneventful character of everyday life is actually a tactic of the reflexive self to counter the risks and anxieties of an unpredictable world.* This character acts a protective cocoon that serves as an 'emotional inoculation against existential anxieties' (ibid.: 40). That is, the 'ordinary life' is a screening-off device (in the form of everyday habits and routines of the self) against risks and dangers in the surroundings of action and interaction, and provides 'ontological security' to the anxiety-prone individual. 'To be ontologically secure is to possess on the level of the unconscious and practical consciousness, "answers" to fundamental existential questions which all human life in some way addresses' (ibid.: 47).

For Giddens (ibid., chapter 2) there are four such existential questions that the individual faces. The first of these is with regard to *existence* itself. To be in the existential self is not the same as to have a self-identity and in 'doing' everyday life, 'all humans answer the question of being: they do it by the nature of the activities they carry out' (ibid.: 48). The second existential question concerns a fundamental temporal aspect: that of human *finitude.* This leads to an existential contradiction whereby, set off against an inanimate world, humans are aware of the finiteness and mortality of their own natures. It also allows humans to 'discern moral meaning in otherwise transient events' (ibid.). The third existential question concerns '*others*'. Discovering the other in an emotional-cognitive way is part of the development of self-awareness itself. In that sense, trust in others 'is at the origin of experience of a stable external world and a coherent sense of self-identity' (ibid.: 51). Lastly, the human being also has to deal with the issue of self-identity, which 'is not something that is just given, as a result of the continuities of the individual action system, but something that has to be routinely created and sustained in the reflexive activities of the individual' (ibid.: 52).

For Giddens, a person's identity lies in '*the capacity to keep a particular narrative going*' (ibid.; italics in original), and what keeps the narrative going for an individual is his day-to-day lifestyle, a fundamental component of which is choice. A lifestyle involves clusters of habits and orientations that connect options in a more or less ordered pattern, which in turn gives human life a semblance of unity – the latter being important to a continuing sense of ontological security. They are, therefore, routinized practices that are adopted rather than handed down, and the selection/creation of lifestyles is influenced by group pressures, the visibility of role models as well as by socio-economic circumstances. These routinized practices are 'incorporated into habits of dressing, eating, modes of acting and favoured milieux for encountering others; but the routines followed are reflexively open to change on the light of the mobile nature of self-identity' (ibid.: 81).

Further, the availability of lifestyles, called 'life chances' by Giddens, also functions as a structuring principle of stratification. Though adoption of a particular lifestyle may be easy enough, some lifestyles are proffered only by life chances and, in this way, work very strongly conditions life chances. Giddens' main contention is that routinized lifestyles/habits have a tendency to keep at bay any contemplation/experience of existential questions of the form noted above that may cause a person anxiety. In order to preserve the ontological security of the individual, there is a 'sequestration of experience' (ibid.: 156) accomplished by the uneventful nature of day-to-day life. Drawing on Goffman's (1971: 252) notion of 'Umwelt' – defined as the core of accomplished normalcy with which individuals and groups surround themselves with – Giddens claims that the 'moving world of normalcy' is achieved by a sequestration of experience. The unpleasant phenomena that are sequestered through these processes of concealment are madness, criminality, sickness, death, sexuality and nature. In order that the individual who is so sequestered from contemplation on fundamental existential questions should not experience personal meaninglessness, Giddens' concern is to remoralize social institutions and individual lives through what he calls *emancipatory politics* and *life politics* (Giddens 1991, chapter 7). He defines the former as a generic outlook that makes primary the imperatives of 'justice', 'equality' and 'participation', and is concerned 'above all with liberating individuals and groups from constraints which adversely affect their life chances' (ibid.: 210). It aims at reducing exploitation, inequality and oppression which operates on a 'hierarchical' notion of power – understood as the capability of an individual or group to exert its will over others. Life politics, on the other hand, is a politics of *self-actualization concerned with lifestyles*; it is a politics of choice and aligns itself with a 'reflexively mobilized order . . . which on an individual and collective level, has radically altered the existential parameters of social activity' (ibid.: 214). In other words, it is a politics of life decisions where power is a capillary force that is 'generative' rather than hierarchical.

Such life decisions help in the process of self-actualization understood in terms of a 'balance between opportunity and risk' (ibid.: 78), and makes fulfilment 'in some part a *moral* phenomenon, because it means fostering a sense that one is "good", a "worthy person"' (ibid.: 79; emphasis added).

What remains to be seen is how the linguistic structure of the narrative actually fits on to this scheme of goodness and life politics in the Taylor–Giddens framework. In the following section, we draw on Ricoeurian ideas of the *narrative identity* to emerge with a concept of self that hinges in a triadic relation to the contingency of language as well as a contingency of conscience. Ricoeur (1992) grafts on to his theory of language, action, identity and narration, a formulation of ethics, morality and practical wisdom to spell out his 'philosophical anthropology', and his theory is that human action can be described, told as a function of narration and prescribed or determined by the predicates of good and obligatory (the ethical and moral dimensions, respectively). In the process, it establishes a self that is animated by an ethical intention to live a good life.

Narrative Identity and the 'Good Life'

Unlike both the Cartesian self (where the cogito is independent of the body and its spatio-temporal setting) and the anti-Cartesian self (where it is merely a product or function of an impersonal system), for Ricouer, the self is essentially embodied, constituted by its material and cultural situation, and has the 'unique ability to initiate something new and imputable to himself or herself' (Ricouer 1992: 35). The self's identity is thus constituted by an inextricable tie between a selfsameness (its *idem* identity) and its selfhood (its *ipse* identity), and these come together as a person's narrative identity. *Character – as an expression of the 'I am' – is an answer to the 'what' of identity*; it 'assures at once numerical identity, qualitative identity, uninterrupted continuity across change and finally permanence in time' (ibid.: 122) and designates the set of permanent dispositions that have sedimented over time to identify the person as 'same'. On the other hand, *ipse* identity – that answers to the 'I can' of identity – is manifested in the *promise of keeping one's word*; it is fidelity to self in the presence of the other and not reducible to the form of *idem* identity. By virtue of both these identities, the self inhabits two orders of causality: the physical and the intentional, and corresponding to these two orders are the twin capabilities of action and imputation. In elaborating on his theory of action and imputation, Ricouer notes that every action, be it speaking, acting (doing or making), narrating or imputing actions to someone, involves initiative which acts as an '. . . intervention of the agent of action into the course of the world . . . that effectively causes change in the world' (ibid.: 109). Action is thus both purposive and related to other actions, and, as an articulation of both strings of action and events and their human contexts, it is the narrative discourse which gives expression to this moment of initiative. The twin poles of selfhood – *ipse* and *idem* identities – expressed as keeping one's word and sameness as character, respectively, are thereby subject to the imaginative variations of the narrative text to reveal identity: 'The narrative constructs the identity of the character, what can be called his or her narrative identity, in constructing that of the story told. It is the identity of the story that makes the identity of the character' (ibid.: 147–48).

In the sense that life is actually lived and not told, one may find this idea of selfhood to be revealed in narrative language untenable, but Ricoeur (1991) gives two arguments to prove otherwise. Firstly, each of us possesses a type of pre-narrative structure of experience; in the doing and undoing of action that makes up the texture of life, there is a *narrative intelligibility* at work that initiates this mixture in a creative manner. Second, life becomes much more than a biological phenomenon since it is *interpretable* in the form of the narrative. Given the narrative excesses of order, coherence and unity, 'there is always more order in what we narrate than in what we have actually already lived' (ibid.: 468), and these characteristics of the narrative serve to give a certain perspective to an individual's life. 'We try to gain by means of imaginative variation of our ego a narrative understanding of ourselves, the only kind of understanding that escapes the pseudo-alternatives of pure change and absolute identity' (ibid.: 437).

In trying to understand my own life story and give it a coherence through a plot, my narrative is a 'redefining of what is already defined, a reinterpretation of what is already interpreted' (ibid.: 469). In this way, *narrative identity continues to make and unmake itself over the course of a lifetime*, and in the refiguring of human action into human narration, it gives expression to the time of initiative or what Ricoeur calls the *historical present* (implied by the verb 'to begin') (Ricoeur 1984: 75). The open-endedness of time as embedded in the textuality of human existence implies the relation between time and narrative as explored in Ricoeur (1981b, 1984, 1985, 1988). He notes: '. . . time becomes human to the extent that it is articulated through a narrative mode, and narrative attains its full meaning when it becomes a condition of temporal experience' (Ricoeur 1984: 52).

In being interpretive mediations that borrow both from our history as well as our imagination, narratives help us to figure our personal identities in much the same way that we do of the identities of characters in stories; in other words, what underpins narrative identity is the narrative function – *what can I know of myself*? I make sense of myself by telling you (and myself) a story of my own life which inevitably intersects with other personages. In the process my narrative reveals something of the distinctive heritage I belong to, and also positions me as a person who can initiate actions or impute action to others. It projects a responsive self who can evaluate actions as praiseworthy or otherwise and lives in the hope that its responsiveness to others will bring a better life for all. The narrative, in providing the component of self-understanding, not only expresses the character of the person but also encodes an ethical dimension.

The foundation for what has come to be known as Ricouer's 'three-cornered ethics' (Muldoon 2002: 84) is set as it establishes a self who is guided by the 'wish for the good life', the fundamental basis for which lies in praxis (human action). Appropriating the Aristotelian notion of 'good life' in his theory of praxis, Ricoeur defines the ethical intention as '*aiming at the "good life" with and for others in just institutions*' (Ricoeur 1992: 172; italics in original). It invests an aspirational quality to the 'good life' which he defines as 'the nebulous of ideals and dreams of achievements with regard to which a life is held to be more or less fulfilled or unfulfilled' (ibid.: 179).

Moreover, in defining the good life, it is ethics (the '*aim* of an accomplished life') that has primacy over morality (defined as the 'articulation of this aim in *norms*' – ibid.: 170; italics in original). As the interpretive key between the aim of the good life and our particular choice in terms of norms that are appropriated in pursuit of such an aim, the 'good life' manifests itself on four levels of praxis: (i) *in the standards of excellence* which act not only as self-appraisal but also a potential norm in all jobs, skills, arts and games; (ii) *in 'life plans'* that include vocational life, family life, life of leisure, etc.; (iii) *in the self-interpretation* of the human agent who judges herself/himself with regard to standards of excellence; and finally, (iv) *in the evaluation of good life itself* from where the intermediary series of rules, standards, goods, plans and self-interpretation are evaluated. In establishing an 'I' who 'speaks', 'acts', 'narrates' and is therefore responsible for her actions, praxis along with the narrative functions as the two modes of self-interpretation (of the 'I-can' form: I can speak/act/narrate/impute action) and forges an ethico-moral self characterized primarily by the power-to-do. In this process of actualization of the good life through the power-to-do, ethics emerges as a movement between naked and blind belief in a primordial 'I can' and the real history where I can attest to this 'I can' (Ricoeur 2000: 13–14). Being-able-to-do (as in 'I can') translates into being-able-to-judge on the ethical plane of self-interpretation where it becomes *self-esteem* – the reflexive moment of the wish for the good life. On the other hand, on the moral plane it emerges as *self-respect* pertaining to the lived reality of everyday life in conjunction with others. It is the reflexive moment of self-esteem that, through solicitude, leads one to the recognition of 'oneself as another': 'I can acknowledge you as the author of your actions and also need you in the aiming at and fulfilling of the good life.' The solicitude for the other which is in the form of 'you' at the interpersonal relation transforms into the idea of justice at the institutional level: it is integral for the latter to prevail in society if the individual desire to live well is to be accomplished. Finally, being-able-to-judge itself comes to have multiple dimensions: at the interpersonal level it establishes the just as the 'good' relative to the other with whom we wish to live well; on the level of obligation it manifests itself as 'legal'; and on the level of practical wisdom it is both the 'power-to-do' and 'self-attestation'. In the end, what surfaces in the aim of the good life is also a recognition of convictions which help us to determine our praxis: 'In drawing upon our deepest wishes for a good life, well-considered convictions become our recourse to the primal resources of ethics which have not yet passed through the norm' (Ricoeur 1992: 352).

It is expected that the ethico-cultural grounding of the self will reproduce goodness as defined by social structures and, correspondingly, there will be an underlying moral formation of the individual for whom the process of subjectivation will be ontological, linguistic, social as well as ethical. It is contended that the narrative, as a faithful articulation of human experience, will also encode this ethical dimension of the self and will be instrumental in the revelation of selfhood.

The above contention, that narrative will be a contingent expression of the constitution of a 'good' self in relation to the symbolic world it inhabits with others, can be seen as a postmodern variation on the theme of selfhood. Herein 'the individual self becomes a medium for the culture and its language' (Kvale 1996: 22), and 'in the very act of telling a story the position of the storyteller and the listener, and their place in the social world is constituted' (ibid.: 21). The techniques of the self are inextricably linked not only to social structures, but also the ability of the person to appropriate notions perpetuated by these same social structures. As noted by Soloman and Sherman (2003): 'Insofar as a person tends to reproduce the world in his or her own self-image, there arises the accompanying effect of the person's recreating, reduplicating and perpetuating the very social structures that significantly created that person's identity to begin with' (Solomon and Sherman 2003: 259).

In this triadic relation, the idea of a contextual and constructed self hinges on a contingency of language, which in turn leads to recognition of the contingency of conscience itself as dictated by moorings of culture. The relation between self and language then ceases to be one of expression or representation and starts to become causal. Rorty further notes that 'confrontation' of one's contingency enables a person to see one's life, or the life of one's community as a 'dramatic narrative' over which one had control though it may not have been so (Rorty 1989: 29).

> The paradigm of such a narrative is the life of the genius who can say of the relevant portion of the past 'thus I willed it', because she has found a way to redescribe the past which the past never knew, and thereby found a self to be which her precursors never knew was possible. (Ibid.)

In other words, narrative invests the individual self with the power of improved self-descriptions rather than a set of foundations; her language can help her reconstruct her past and refashion a self that conforms to her 'relatively valid beliefs' (ibid.: 47). This attribute of 'improved self-descriptions' brings us back to the basic question of identity that personal narratives encode: Who am I? We now begin to see the semblance of an answer to this pertinent question: 'I' am the entity who not only has the power of self-ascription and self-description, 'I' am someone who recognizes the contingency of my desires, beliefs and conscience. As a conscious and reflexive self, 'I' stand identified and defined – even if temporarily – in a situation of interlocution with others through my physical attributes as well as the salience of my mental bearings including thoughts, beliefs, intentions and emotions. What perhaps most defines me is where I stand in relation to my own contingent vocabulary of goodness.

Also important in this connection is the process of self-creation ('the sort of person one wants to be'), which, according to Rorty, is a contingent and 'aspirational' morality on which my selfhood hinges. Rorty's adoption of Oakeshott–Sellars' view on morality is pertinent here. For Oakeshott (1975),

> A morality is neither a system of general principles nor a code of rules, but a vernacular language. General principles and even rules may be elicited from it, but (like other languages) it is not the creation of grammarians; it is made by speakers. What has to be learned in a moral education is not a theorem such as that good conduct is acting fairly or being charitable, nor is it a rule such as always 'telling the truth', but how to speak the language intelligently. . . . It is not a device for formulating judgments about conduct or for solving so-called

moral problems but a practice in terms of which to think, to choose, to act and to utter. (Cited in Rorty 1989: 58)

These hints are the manner in which the individual's ethical orientation may surface in narrative: 'my' contingent conscience is something that enables 'me' to speak intelligently and position 'myself' as a 'good' individual. Not only this, a contingent morality may also employ a system of inclusion and exclusion because, in positioning me/us as the good individual(s), it is expected to function as a contrastive feature of personality which may 'other' another person/group as non-moral. In other words, it may both include as well as exclude, and morality becomes a matter of what Sellars calls 'we intentions' – the core meaning of 'immoral action' is 'the sort of thing we don't do' (Sellars 1968, cited in Rorty 1989: 59). That is, an immoral action is the sort of thing that is done by people of other families, tribes, cultures or historical epoch. The Oakeshott–Sellars' view of morality establishes it as a set of practices via which we think, choose, act and utter, and it can underline our self-understanding as well.

To sum up, the self (as well as 'an other') is a 'tissue of contingencies' with a moral consciousness that (though historically conditioned and a product of time, chance, political and/or aesthetic sensibilities) manifests itself at a 'time of initiative' within a narrative that projects one's 'goodness'. This self will show linguistic manifestations both at the structural symbolic–interactionist level as well as the reflective–narrative level. What needs to be sorted out now is whether this self is a gendered one or not; in other words, how does male/female subjectivity figure in this scheme of things, and does it imply a gendered language in which the self emerges. In the next chapter, we will turn to some of these issues of gendered subjectivity and morality (drawing on Gilligan's [1982] theorization of justice as the male ethic and care as the female ethic), and try to understand the ramifications of such a stance for a theory on 'contingent narrative of good selfhood' which this book is premised on.

Notes

1 Fiction man, 'the great ape with the storytelling mind' (Gottschall 2013: xiv).

2 https://www.nationalgeographic.org/encyclopedia/storytelling/, accessed 15 September 2021.

3 David Robson, 'Our Fiction Addiction: Why Humans Need Stories', available at https://www.bbc.com/culture/article/20180503-our-fiction-addiction-why-humans-need-stories, accessed 15 September 2021.

[4] Ibid.

[5] 'Evolution has given us an "inner Holmes" because the world really is full of stories (intrigues, plots, alliances, relationships of cause and effect), and it pays to detect them. The storytelling mind is a crucial evolutionary adaptation. It allows us to experience our lives as coherent, orderly, and meaningful. It is what makes life more than a blooming, buzzing confusion' (Gottschall 2013: 102).

[6] See also discussion in the subsections '"Essentially" Female/Male Talk' and 'Psychosocial Perspectives on Gendered Disposition'.

[7] See note 2 above.

[8] There are insights from neurological studies that suggest that empathy evolved through the course of human evolution (see Ramachandran's take on mirror neurons in the chapter 'The Neurons that Shaped Civilization', in Ramachandran 2011: 163–87).

[9] The simulator model depends on implicit memory – what our brains know but 'we' don't. Implicit memory is inaccessible to the conscious mind. The simulator theory is based on research showing that 'realistic rehearsal of any skill . . . leads to enhanced performance regardless of whether the training episodes are explicitly remembered'. When we experience fiction, our minds are firing and wiring, honing the neural pathways that regulate our responses to real-life experiences (Gottschall 2013: 65).

[10] See note 3 above.

[11] Sociologist Émile Durkheim wrote, 'Religion is a unified system of beliefs and practices . . . which unite into one single moral community called a Church all those who adhere to them' (cited in Gottschall 2013: 122).

[12] If you watch Hollywood movies, you have realized by now that these two stories are simplified plots of two blockbusters: *The Sixth Sense* (Story A) directed by M. Night Shyamalan and *A Beautiful Mind* (Story B) by Ron Howard.

[13] *A Beautiful Mind* is a biographical drama film based on a professor of mathematics Nobel Laureate in economics and Abel Prize winner John Nash.

[14] As a generic term that invokes identity issues, 'subject' is used in the social sciences for what in common parlance is the 'person', 'individual' or 'human being'. Being 'human' has traditionally meant having the aptitude for rational and moral contemplation, whereas to the 'agent' is attributed the capacity for making deliberate choice and power of self-designation.

[15] There can be quite a few ways of identifying a person – physical attributes (5 feet 4 inches tall/brown eyes . . .), sexual and/or gender categories (girl/boy, male/female, lesbian/gay . . .), character traits (honest/short-tempered/cheerful . . .), socio-economic class (high/mid/low income, working class/capitalist class . . .), racial/linguistic/ethnic features (black/white, Indo-Aryan/Dravidian . . .), nationalities (Indian/American/Indian-American . . .), place of living (city/village) and a lot more.

[16] This trajectory has the coherence of a self-identity given the cognitive awareness of the various phases of the lifespan.

[17] Though Plato does not specifically use the terms himself, his delineation of the 'soul' as eternal and the 'body' as changing acts as the precursor to this mode of

thinking. His ethic of reason with the 'Ideas of Good' arranged in rational order in the cosmos (ontic logos) and reflected in beings achieves a centering on ourselves that also ushers in a unitary concept of mind. For Plato, humans gain self-mastery through reason and the three fruits that it bestows are (i) unity with oneself, (ii) calm and (iii) collected self-possession.

[18] Hume's representational account challenges the substrate view by claiming that we do not really have a perception of substance; all our perceptions are of properties, for example, sound, colour, texture, etc. He raises the objection as to how the soul can exist as a thinking thing when there is no thinking going on, for example, during sleep (this was also a Cartesian problem: if the 'I' exists thinking, what happens to the 'I' when it is sleeping and thus, not thinking). The thinking thing in such a scenario would cease to exist. If it does not cease to exist, then it would exist as something which has no properties – a nonsensical proposition, and Hume therefore concludes that the *self is a fiction* that we construct from the illusory of identity in consciousness generated by the imagination.

[19] 'For Nietzsche, the real nature of human subjectivity is aesthetic and consists in the power to create oneself. The way in which such transformation occurs is through "revaluation of all values"' (Atkins, ed. 2005: 71).

[20] We will see a lot of these philosophical parallels evident in the narratives that we shall analyse in later chapters.

[21] It is such premises that justify our exploration into the examination of narrative identity as emergent in conversation. 'Who am I when I speak and how do I create myself through my language in the presence of an other – forever aware of the other's presence as I narrate and how does my self get threatened, positioned, created and recreated as I tell and retell my life stories in the presence of other/s?' In the chasm between the self and the other, between reflexivity and creativity, narratives invest us with identities that may be fragile but in doing so create snapshots of our identity – almost like a 'linguistic selfie' (Barua 2016a: 309).

[22] The Foucault interview comprises a chapter titled 'An Aesthetics of Experience' in Kritzman (1988: 47–53). It was originaly given on 25 April 1984 to Alessandro Fontana, a collaborator of Foucault, for the Italian weekly *Panorama,* and the translation is by Alan Sheridan as noted in Kritzman, ed. (1988: 43).

[23] Mohanty (1988), for instance, points out that the speaking subject of feminist theory is almost invariably a western woman – 'Third World women . . . never rise above the debilitating generality of the "object" status' (Mohanty 1988: 80). Many other studies (Amos and Parmar 1984; Liddle and Rai 1993; Carr 1988) have also shown how the white western academic feminists, in speaking 'about' or 'for' third world women sometimes collude in 'othering' other women.

[24] Foucault interview in Kritzman, ed. (1988: 50); see note 22 above.

[25] Elms (1975) discusses how a child's development happens through and in relation to the signification of the social world; for Richards (1974), the child is essentially a biological organism who becomes social through encounters with the social world; Shotter (1974) seeks to transcend these theorizations (of the individual – society as antithetical, exclusive, inseparable and oppositional) and presents a structural model of subjectivity by envisaging the child's development into a human to be

partly intentional and partly a product. Weinreich also deals with socialization, which is 'the means by which culture, including notions of appropriate sex roles, is transmitted' (Weinreich 1978: 20). Trevarthen's (1975, 1979) 'generative account' deals with infant predispositions and takes into account 'motives' of the child in development. The centrality of the child as an object of scientific inquiry is highlighted in his studies while also underscoring a number of normalizing practices that are part of the production of the individual as a 'normal' person. Erikson's (1960) position sees the child-rearing practices as producing a personality that is in accordance with the requirements of the society. For him, contradictions, conflicts, non-confirmation to norms are not the cost of entering culture (Freud 1930) but 'socialization failures' that require intervention.

[26] Stryker notes that among the class terms learned in interaction are the symbols that are used to designate 'positions'. These positions are relatively stable, morphological components of social structure which carry the shared behavioural expectations conventionally labelled as 'roles' (Stryker 1980: 54).

2

The Good Selves We Live By

Gendered Self, Ethics and Narrative

Gendered Selves

One of the overarching questions of selfhood remains the following: Is a self always 'gendered'?[1] If so, are language, sense of morality, ways of thinking and being inevitably also gendered? What attributes/language traits of women and men define, and justify (if they do), 'gendered' ethics? Gilligan (1982) has for instance proposed *justice* as the male ethic and *care* as the female ethic which itself reifies stereotypical images of the woman as a 'caregiver' driven by obligation and responsibility, and the man as driven by issues of 'right and justice'. In turn, these invoke *essentialist* notions of femininity and masculinity whereby womanliness and manliness are seen to be made up of, and demarcated by, essential differences between the two. Correspondingly, gender comes to be seen as differentiated manifestations of essentially different 'manly' and 'womanly' attributes, and language is deemed to reflect this sociocultural 'reality'. This chapter examines how male and female selfhood come to be defined in relation to masculine and feminine ethics (in the sense of Gilligan 1982). A basic question that follows from this position is whether justice and care ethics *create* 'male' and 'female' selves, respectively, or does a 'self' come to *appropriate* male/female ethics? Following Ricoeur's postulation that we examined in chapter 1, that the ethical intention is aiming at the 'good life' with and for others in just institutions (Ricoeur 1992: 172), a valid question to ask will also be *if the 'good life' itself can be defined in gendered terms.* In other words, do essential differences between men and women have a bearing on their ethical selves, and do they define their 'internalized meanings' of *who* they are? Further, given our assumption that the personal narrative as a faithful articulation of human experience will reveal selfhood in terms of 'goodness' (as theorized in chapter 1), an allied question would be *whether women and men have different kinds of narratives*, and do women and men have different *orientations* to their narratives?

We begin such an enquiry into the gendered dimensions of selfhood in the first subsection, 'Gendered Subjectivity: Male/Female Self and Other', and gendered language in the second subsection, '"Essentially" Female/Male Talk', by looking at essentialism in terms of language. The second section of the chapter, titled 'Compromised Autonomy: Feminist Perspectives', examines the idea of autonomy in relation to the constructed and discursive subject, while in the third section, titled 'Female/Male Ethics', we examine the issue of gendered ethics.

Gendered Subjectivity: Male/Female Self and Other

In discussing the self–other axis in relation to subjectivity, we had come across de Beauvoir's formulation that '[h]umanity is male and man defines woman not in herself but as relative to him; she is not regarded as an autonomous being. . . . He is the Subject, he is the Absolute – she is the Other' (de Beauvoir ([1949] 1997): 18). On de Beauvoir's view, 'Woman' is constructed only as man's 'Other' and this denies any positive value to a woman's life. She goes on to explain this oppressive relation by two features of women's lives: (i) the mediating role of political structures and social institutions in the formation of subjectivity; and (ii) the lived experience of female embodiment. For her, sexual (and social) inequality that pervades society can be redressed only by a total reorganization of society's political structures whose necessity comes about because subjectivity (and by extension freedom) is not a radically uncaused power of the individual but *an effect of one's situation*. 'Woman' describes a situation that is imposed upon females to systematically limit their capacity to regard themselves as agents of their own lives. The female body is 'one of the essential elements in her situation in the world' (ibid.: 69), because it necessitates that she spend large amounts of time and energy in natural functions associated with her reproductive capacity: menstruation, pregnancy, lactation, etc. With regard to women, freedom is a temporal idea since it supposes future and successive generations, and thus acts as an ontological demand on the female body for the perpetuation of the species. This not only implies that one's freedom is vulnerable to interpersonal relations, social institutions and the body that form part of one's situation, but, de Beauvoir believes, women themselves give forth a range of responses to their oppression ranging from 'conscious complicity' through varying degrees of 'bad faith' to genuine belief in the particular situation of women (de Beauvoir 1997: 665 *et seq.*). Ignorant of the possibility of freedom, *women live as inferiors* because they deem it given in their situation. This insight into the psychological nature of oppression through the 'naturalization' of woman's situation is the key to her understanding of the origins of sexual inequality.

For de Beauvoir, therefore, not only does society give rise to and is premised on sexual inequality, the latter is also ontological by virtue of the ambiguities of the female body. What is woven into the aforesaid ontological demand on women is an issue of *morality*: given the necessity of the species to reproduce itself, woman becomes its essential condition by virtue of the female body being the vehicle of the perpetuation of the species. Female embodiment in this way makes the achievement of subjectivity more difficult, because the strength of woman's involvement in the natural world makes her liable to succumb to her 'physiological destiny' (ibid.: 587). And all of this gives to man an exploitative advantage: with woman being vulnerable to domestic incarceration, men are left free to pursue authentic, self-affirming activities. This historic supersession of women by men not only establishes the former as the Other corresponding to the (male) Self, *it also proffers the woman with an unlikely advantage: that of being a non-entity*. The woman's own involvement in the denial of subjectivity sometimes reinforces the myth of Woman, the self-sacrificing Other, since 'refusal to pose oneself as the Subject unique and absolute requires great self-denial' (ibid.: 250). It is given their self-effacing nature that women can never be understood on the model of a 'subject'. As Irigaray (1997) further notes, a Sartrian frame of the signifying subject and the signified other proves inadequate in that both marker and marked are maintained within a masculinist mode of signification with the female being 'marked off' as it were. In a different vein, Wittig (1983) contends that it is the masculine aspect which is the general aspect: for her, gender is the linguistic index of the 'political opposition' between the sexes. As such, there is only one gender, the feminine, the masculine not being a gender but the general.

Two other theorizations on women and subjectivity are pertinent here: Riviere's ([1929] 2000) postulation of womanliness as a *masquerade*, and Butler's (1990) notion of *performativity*. Riviere, in discussing case studies of women who, because of the contradictory demands made of them in the social environment, experience anxieties and instabilities of identity, claims that 'women who wish for masculinity may put on a mask of womanliness to avert anxiety and retribution feared from men' (Riviere 2000: 130). These women, she argues, put on a show or 'masquerade' of disarming girlishness in order to defuse the perceived disapproval of those around them.

> . . . *womanliness therefore could be assumed and worn as a mask*, both to hide the possession of masculinity and to avert the reprisals expected if she was found to possess it – much as a thief will turn out his pockets and ask to be searched to prove that he has not the stolen goods. (Ibid.: 133; emphasis added)

An example Riviere gives is of an intellectual woman who, in spite of her success and ability in work of a propagandist nature (which consisted principally in speaking and writing), would seek attention/complimentary notice from a man/men at the close of proceedings where she was the key figure.[2] The two types of reassurance the woman would seek from them were: '. . . first, direct reassurance of the nature of compliments about her performance; secondly, and more importantly, indirect assurance of the nature of sexual attentions from these men' (ibid.: 131). Riviere contends that the aim of compulsion was not merely to secure reassurance, but chiefly to make sure of safety by masquerading as guiltless and innocent.

Riviere's hypothesis of 'womanliness' as a masquerade provides a model of feminine identity that is an *ongoing charade or anxious performance* which, though real in effects, is never firmly grounded and never anything other than precarious. This line of enquiry was taken up much later in Butler (1990, 1993), where she replaces Riviere's notion of masquerade with that of gender as a performative. For Butler, 'men' and 'women' do *not* function as stable categories of analysis pre-existing the cultural imposition of gender, and as such 'there is no prediscursive "sex" that acts as a stable point of reference . . . in relation to which the cultural construction of gender proceeds . . . *sex is already gender, already constructed* . . . the "materiality" of sex is forcibly produced' (Butler 1993: xi; emphasis added).

Gender is thus neither the expression of sex, nor does it produce sex; instead it *regulates* sex as a natural condition of the body, establishing it in a pre-discursive domain that refers to it as a duality – a binary norm. In theorizing the notions of discourse, gender and perfomativity, Butler (1990, 1993) elaborates on the discursive mechanism of gender constitution (wherein performative agency is both constrained and enabled through repetition), and the appearance of an abiding substance/gendered self (or a gender core) is produced by the regulation of attributes along culturally established lines of coherence. Within this line of thought, gender is neither a noun nor a set of attributes, but 'within the inherited discourse of the metaphysics of substance' it is a performative – 'constituting the identity it is purported to be' (Butler 1990: 25). This performative aspect of gender draws on the Derridian ([1967a] 1976) notion of 'iterability' of signs by virtue of having a repetitive and citational quality:

> If a performative provisionally succeeds (and I . . . suggest that 'success' is always and only provisional), then it is not because an intention successfully governs the action of speech, but only because that action echoes prior actions, and *accumulates the force of authority through the repetition or citation of a prior, authoritative set of practices*. What this means, then, is that a performative 'works' to the extent that it *draws on and covers over* the constitutive conventions by which it is mobilized. In this sense, no term or statement can function performatively without the accumulating and simulating historicity of force. (Butler 2000; italics in original)

That is, it is not by virtue of intentional individual speaking subjects that 'gender' gets defined – there are 'constitutive conventions' behind each such utterance that actually redefines it. The midwife's statement 'It's a girl', for example, is an initiatory transitive performative that works through such citational power hinging on constitutive conventions; it not only names the 'girl' but invokes the normative process by which 'girl' becomes a viable subject. More importantly, Butler claims that there are political reasons for such a substantializing view of gender; the latter, along with heterosexuality (as a discursive phenomenon drawing on performativity), maintains and reproduces what is called 'heterosexual matrix' (Butler 1990).

This substantializing effect of a gendered psychic disposition or cultural identity is considered an achievement in Butler, for it requires a differentiation from the opposite gender. Yet, on the other hand, there is also the recognition in Butler of the potential inherent in the constructed nature of gendered identity to *subvert* gendered identity. Recognition of the contingency of gendered identity can also allow a human subject the power to be able to recite the same discourse to another purpose, to 'resignify' it and invest it with new meaning. Though Butler does follow Foucault in arguing that the subject is constituted 'in and by discourse', she stresses (in Bell 1999: 164) that this is not a 'unilateral' or 'unnuanced' process but is tenuous, vulnerable and *subject to failure*. The signification process labours within itself an 'agency'. It is only within the practices of repetitive signifying that a subversion of identity becomes possible through resignification. To explicate the processes of resignification and resistance, Butler returns to psychoanalysis, and, by combining the notion of iterability 'with a theory of the "psyche", works to produce an account of gendered subject formation that captures a sense of both structure and agency, constraint and creativity' (Speer and Potter 2002:154). It is then worthwhile to explore not only how, in the Butlerian sense, the 'heterosexual matrix' functions along culturally established lines of coherence to establish identities of 'woman' and 'man', but also how subjects themselves negotiate gendered identities within the culturally inscribed domains of identity and how these may be subject to failure. Further, if, following feminist theorizations, one is identified as woman 'to the extent that one functions as one within the dominant heterosexual frame' (Butler [1990] 1999: xi), what ethical considerations define woman is also a relevant question to explore. In this context, the issue of 'masculine' and 'feminine' ethics will be dealt with in the last section of this chapter. Before that, let us examine how language features in the scheme of gendered subjectivity below.

'Essentially' Female/Male Talk

Essentialism underlined two predominant approaches to gender and spoken interaction in the 1990s, namely, the *difference* paradigm and the *dominance* paradigm. In the former, interaction between sexes is tantamount to two sub-cultures as proposed in the *dual cultures* model of Tannen (1990)[3]: Cameron deemed the dominance and difference paradigms as moments of feminist 'outrage' and feminist 'celebration', respectively (Cameron 1995: 39). In such studies, gender was a variable attribute or *essence* of speaker, with talk being reflective of the essentially independent, internal properties of man/woman. The idea of the essentialist differences between males and females was earlier consolidated by the Separate Worlds Hypothesis (SWH) of Maltz and Borker (1982).[4] For them, as a result of separated peer play[5] in childhood, *the genders evolve different goals for social interactions and communicative styles*. Such differences may later render adult male–female communication as 'cross-cultural communication' (Tannen 1990: 18). Adapting Gumperz's (1982) model of *interethnic communication*, Maltz and Borker (1982) argued that distinct 'subcultures' do indeed evolve in girls' and boys' friendship groups consequent to separated peer play. Girls learn that talk is for

(i) creating and maintaining relationships of closeness and equality;
(ii) criticizing others in acceptable ways; and
(iii) interpreting accurately the speech of other girls.

Boys, on the other hand, learn that talk is for

(i) asserting a position of dominance;
(ii) attracting and maintaining an audience; and
(iii) asserting themselves when another speaker has the floor.

In other words, girls' talk is *collaboration-oriented* while boys' talk is *competition-oriented*. It was shown in Barua (2005) that sometimes the contrary holds true: girls' intra-sex talk *can* be competition-oriented with conversational dominance being manifest in girls' talk, while boys' intra-sex conversation *can* be cooperation-oriented. It was in the context of inter-sex conversation in the above study that the SWH held ground with boys, despite being lesser in number, trying to dominate girls in terms of talk content and conversation length. The study proved the importance of context in the examination of talk-in-interaction and underscores the point that there cannot be sweeping generalizations across speakers to the exclusion of context. Other studies like Nakamura (2001)[6] have also emphasized the importance of contexts even while upholding the SWH. Cook-Gumperz and Szymanski (2001) have also contributed to the SWH by showing how Latino children interactionally orient to their peer group as a gendered context. However, they show that the cultural frame of the Latino family superimposes itself on the gender dynamic of separate worlds and children gain access to other ways of arranging their communicative priorities.

In the case of adult speakers, several influential sociolinguistic studies of the twentieth century looked into 'markers', or isolated linguistic or phonological items, that were assumed to characterize women's or men's speech and their correlation with speaker sex (for example, Labov 1966; Milroy 1980; Trudgill 1974). One of the earliest forays into women's speech was Jesperson (1922) which concluded that women had less extensive vocabulary, used simpler sentence structures and had a greater tendency to speak before they thought, resulting in sentences that were often incomplete. Women were also reported to use 'correct'/prestigious forms more frequently than men in order to make up for their lower social status (Trudgill 1983). Lakoff's (1973, 1975, 1990) influential studies added to the debate on essential language differences when she distinguished between male and female language according to six linguistic features: *lexical distinctions* such as colour terms; strong versus weak *expletives* (for example, Oh dear! or Fudge! instead of stronger expletives such as Damn! and Shit!); 'women's' versus 'neutral' *adjectives*; use of *tag questions*; use of *question intonation* with statements; and strength of *direct speech*. Women's more frequent use of tag questions was subscribed to their lack of confidence in what they say. Coates (1996) has questioned Lakoff's interpretation of tag questions and instead suggested that women's tag questions can be expressions of powerful speech.

Such studies had a certain common concern, which is to emphasize *social and economic insecurity* as the most important reason for variation in language use found across genders. Increasingly, however, the importance of *context of conversation* has been underlined and the *situatedness* of the speaker regarding the use of language has been emphasized. Smith (1979), for example, questions the association of gender with linguistic features of speech, and suggests that (i) the differences may be few and may not be found where expected; (ii) when differences are found, they may be 'sex-preferential' rather than 'sex-exclusive'; (iii) male–female markers do not really reflect differences of sex but may be caused by other social divisions (for example, occupation); (iv) the differences may be 'unsaturated', that is, they are seen only in some members of the society. Apart from the 'difference paradigm', essentialist positions were also taken in the 'dominance paradigm' that looked at male and female talk from the power perspective. Studies in this tradition (for example, Fishman 1978; Zimmerman and West 1975) propose that power inequalities and relations are reproduced in conversation between men and women and examination of linguistic features usually throw up aspects of male conversational dominance. Fishman (1978), for example, used topic change as one of the features while investigating male dominance in interaction, and analysed data in terms of frequency of number of questions asked, statements produced, minimum responses used, and topics introduced and accepted or not as mutual topics. According to her findings, women used many more questions (263) than men (107), half as many statements as men, used minimal responses as backchannel expressions as against for resistance of topics by men, and could not introduce many mutual topics (17 out of 43 instances as against all 28 in men being taken up as mutual topics). West and Garcia (1988) also investigated male dominance vis-à-vis topic changed. Their analysis of five male and female first- and second-year university student dyads (unacquainted before the experiment) showed that while both male and female speakers equally initiated collaborative topic change, only male speakers initiated the unilateral ones. Length of talk-turn as indicator of dominance was studied by Eakins and Eakins (1978), while Aries (1982) also analysed data in terms of distribution of turns taken among participants and the content of interactional behaviour, such as giving opinions, suggestions and agreements, and non-verbal behaviour such as postures. She concluded that while female speakers dominated male speakers in terms of number of turns, male speakers dominated female speakers vis-à-vis non-verbal behaviour.

There have been other studies that have sought to bring out nuances of men's and women's speech by shifting the focus from *micro*-processes of interpersonal interactions to *macro*-processes of engendering power. Acker (1991), for instance, has shown that sometimes institutions themselves engage in gendered practices that proffer advantage to males as opposed to females; in this sense, institutions or organizations are themselves 'gendered':

> To say that an organization, or any other analytical unit, is gendered means that advantage and disadvantage, exploitation and control, action and emotion, meaning and identity, are patterned through and in terms of a distinction between male and female, masculine and feminine. Gender is not an addition to ongoing process conceived as gender neutral. Rather, it is an integral part of those processes which cannot be properly understood without an analysis of gender. (Ibid.: 167)

For Acker (ibid.: 167–68), gendering occurs in at least five interactive processes:

(i) Construction of *divisions* along lines of gender, namely, divisions of labour, allowed behaviours, of locations in physical space and of power including the institutionalized means of maintaining the divisions in the structures of labour markets. Within such practices, men are almost always in the highest positions of organizational power and the definition of skilled work is men's work whereas unskilled work comes under the purview of women's work.

(ii) Construction of *symbols and images* that explain, express, reinforce and sometimes oppose gendered divisions with men inevitably being shown favourably.

(iii) Production of gendered *social structures* in interactions between men and women, women and women, and men and men including all patterns that enact dominance and submission. Here, men are 'actors' while women are 'emotional support'.

(iv) Production of *gendered components of individual identity* which may include consciousness of the existence of the aspects of gender such as in organizations, choice of appropriate work, language use, clothing and the presentation of self as a gendered member of an organization.

(v) *Implication of gender* in the fundamental, ongoing processes of creating and conceptualizing social structures whereby gender is not only a basic constitutive element in family and kinship, but also frames the underlying relations of other structures including complex organizations. It is a constitutive element in organizational logic that has material forms in written rules, labour contracts, managerial directives and other documentary tools for running large organizations including systems of job evaluation. Acker contends: 'Individual men and groups of men do not always win in these processes, but masculinity always seems to symbolize self-respect for men at the bottom and power for men at the top while confirming for both their gender's superiority' (Acker 1991: 166).

This view of gender relationships being defined within institutionalized categories in favour of males is another approach to the study of language and gender. As pointed out in Itakura (2001), some of the above perspectives to the study of language and gender can be summarized under various heads:

(i) The study of *conversational styles* wherein differences between male and female speech have been related to cultural differences/conversational style rather than inequalities in social status (for example, Maltz and Borker 1982; Tannen 1990).
(ii) The study of *conversational competence* which suggests that men and women may possess different types of interactional competence rather than one dominating the other. For example West (1995), who lists different types of competence including co-ordinate entry into conversation (Schegloff 1968) and conversational closing (Schegloff and Sacks 1973), etc.
(iii) The study of *construction of gender in context* that emphasizes the participants' active roles in establishing gender relationships with institutionalized categories being relevant to interactional patterns (for example, Acker 1991; West 1995). The symbolic interactionism perspective (Stryker 1968, 1980) that we discussed in chapter 1 can also afford important dimensions to the issue of gendered identity and gendered talk.
(iv) The study of *gender and dominance in interaction* that seeks to examine whether the distribution of different interactional features between men and women during recordings actually indicate male dominance (for example, Aries 1982; Eakins and Eakins1978; Fishman 1978; Leet-Pellegrini 1980; West and Zimmerman 1983).

This last perspective that establishes male dominance in conversation can sometimes be seen to reflect sociocultural realities; correspondingly, the purported 'superiority' of the male gender will have wide-ranging implications for the issue of selfhood.

Compromised Autonomy: Feminist Perspectives

We have delved into the constructed nature of the gendered self and its language, and following postmodern understanding of the subject as a fractured and malleable entity whose reality is, so to say, always in a particular given moment, we now reconsider the nature of the self and autonomy in the light of the self's actual conditions of existence. What should be of interest here are *relational models of autonomy* (see, for example, Benhabib 1986; Friedman 1997). Such models of autonomy 'emphasize the social situatedness of the individual and the role of personal relations in the acquisition of skills and competencies necessary for the exercise of autonomy' (Atkins, ed. 2005: 280).

According to Mackenzie ([2000] 2005), personal autonomy – as differentiated from political autonomy characterized by the rights to freedom of expression, assembly and religion, rights to participate in the political process, and privacy – requires the exercise of certain basic 'autonomy competencies'. By such autonomy competencies are meant *skills in deliberation, decision-making and action*, and these depend on a 'unified' and 'valued' self-conception. She further argues that it is the affective and cognitive effects of *imaginative thinking* – mediated through the culturally available images and self-representations – that can function to either liberate or constrain one's self-conception. Imaginative thinking on its part can facilitate or limit one's autonomy depending on the images available to it, and, by bringing about the connection between autonomy and imagination, she provides an integration account of the process of self-definition.

A person's point of view and her self-conception, which Mackenzie deems the 'internal audience' and the 'internal observer' respectively, are also integral to a person's self-definition. The *internal audience*, for Mackenzie, is 'caught up within the imaginative project and emotionally identifies with it', while the *internal observer* 'stands outside the imaginative project; may react to it emotionally in a range of different ways; and reflects on and evaluates the desires, emotions and beliefs represented or manifested in the imagining' (Mackenzie 2005: 285). It is the internal audience that simulates different emotions in a person and the internal observer who responds to these emotions with reactive emotions. The twin processes of externalizing and appropriation will have a bearing on both the internal audience and internal observer, thereby eliciting affective responses (for example, pride, shame or embarrassment) as well as evaluative responses (for example, whether the different aspects fall in line with what matters to 'me') in the person. Apart from their ability to mobilize the affective and cognitive forces within an individual, a second feature of the imaginative activities that facilitate autonomy is that they are *socially mediated.* A healthy self-conception and the acquisition of autonomy competencies require social recognition since self-knowledge (presupposed in autonomy) can only be acquired through relations with others, and self-worth (necessary for achieving reflective equilibrium) is bound up with social recognition. Imagination, much like the *cultural imaginary* (our personal repertoire of cultural images and representations that shape our core values, desires, emotions, beliefs and self-concepts), is seen to be ambivalent; it can open up possibilities for imagining oneself or close them down depending on the intention behind the imaginative activity.

The implications of both these features of the imaginative activities – their ability to mobilize the affective and cognitive forces and their socially mediated nature – are immense: since self-integration is deemed 'to be an ongoing and dynamic process . . . because of inevitable tensions and inconsistencies within the self and because the different elements of the self are undergoing transformation' (ibid.: 287), the self's autonomy comes across as *both* compromised and uncompromised. We now move to a bold assertion that we can showcase the imaginative thinking of the gendered subject in his/her narratives which can each be postulated as linguistic evidence of self-definition and hence contingent expressions of selfhood – fragile in being subject to failure – and yet strong in its assertions of identity contextually. A final couple of tasks remain – of examining whether the morality of this contextually constructed gendered self is also contingent on circumstances or a by-product of conscious choice, and are there actually gendered ethics that people live by. In the next subsection, we accomplish the first of these tasks, while in the last section of this chapter, we look into the issue of gendered ethics.

Moral Autonomy and Gendered Morality

Recall from our discussion in chapter 1, Taylor's postulation that 'We have a sense of who we are through our sense of where we stand to the good' (Taylor 1989: 105), and Giddens' idea that 'Fulfilment is in some part a *moral* phenomenon, because it means fostering a sense that one is "good", a "worthy person"' (Giddens 1991: 79; emphasis added). If so, it can be assumed that moral autonomy is contained in the process of self-actualization despite being constrained by the symbolic–cultural order. This would imply the freedom to forge a 'good', 'worthy' and fulfilled individual defined vis-à-vis particularized notions of goodness. In the words of Friedman: 'The core of moral autonomy is simply the notion of *behaving according to norms or ideals that, given one's social nature, one has determined for oneself to be justified as moral guidelines* (Friedman 2000: 213; italics in original).

Such a relational conception of moral autonomy (i) acknowledges the nature of human interconnections and its relevance to autonomy; (ii) takes into account the emotional understanding underlying a moral agent's choice of moral guidelines; (iii) does not require impartiality in the form of reasoning since it considers empirical contingencies of a particular person's identity or life; (iv) belongs not to the public realm but to the private realm of close personal relationships. Moral autonomy is therefore defined as 'self-determination in moral understanding and choice, personal or individual while autonomy may be defined as self-determination in the quite general sense of choosing how to act and live one's own life' (Friedman 2000: 216).

This social and relational account of autonomy, Friedman contends, is a feminist perspective on the issue of moral autonomy which radically differs from the traditional view of autonomy. Feminists have rejected traditional formulations of moral autonomy not only because such ethical theories do not recognize the moral importance of emotions and interpersonal relations, but also because they endorse the non-impartial nature of any actual ethical standpoint (see relevant chapters in Card, ed. 1991; Alcoff and Kittay, eds 2007). Feminists argue that 'one's reasoning habits and capacities are shaped by one's experiences' (Friedman 2000: 213), and that in neglecting the situatedness on the moral standpoint as well as the interpersonal nature of moral reasoning, it is the *feminine* aspect of moral understanding that has gone unrepresented. If anything, it points to a deep-rooted exclusion of femininity from theorizations on subjecthood and moral reasoning. Lovibond traces the roots of 'the consciousness of this metaphysical misogyny' (Lovibond 2000: 17) back to the masculinism of Greek rationalist thought, while drawing its links to modern theorizations of the *ethic of justice as male and the ethics of care as essentially female modes of thought.* The 'full and perfect form' of moral goodness as necessitated and evidenced in the male, combined with the assumption of male superiority in the hierarchy of things, spearheads the tradition whereby 'man' comes to denote both humanity in general and the male sex as its natural representative. For Lovibond, it is this gendered conceptual structure (having this underlying metaphorical misogyny) that goes on to demarcate the ethic of justice and the ethic of care as masculine and feminine ethics, respectively.

This genealogy traces the origin of the modern masculine 'ethics of justice' that represents the thinking of a morally competent person as centred on the search of universal rules demarcated by reason, while the feminine 'ethics of care' in the modern world sees moral intelligence as consisting of primarily, if not exclusively, 'sensitivity' to others. Sensitivity here includes

> . . . emotional responsiveness, capacity for vicarious distress etc., as opposed to the theoretical awareness of life's evils which exist more or less inertly in all of us. For the former approach the characteristically ethical question is: 'Has everyone got what is due to them in this situation', while for the latter it is: 'Has everyone got what they need here?' (Or, '. . . is everyone happy?'). (Ibid.: 21)

Lovibond contends that the care-centred component of rationality has been systematically underemphasized at the level of theory, and therefore 'feminism needs to grasp historically and resist politically, the imaginary link between femininity and the indeterminate or infinite' (ibid.: 23). She introduces another gendered contrast in this issue of morality: women can recognize themselves as the de facto custodians of the *domestic or indefinite part of ethics*, while men are the *custodians of the juridical or definite part.* This is also a contrast that introduces, in Benhabib's words, a 'split between the public realm of justice in which history is made and the atemporal realm of the household, in which life is produced' (Benhabib 1986: 410). Benhabib contends: 'The dehistoricization of the private realm signifies that, as the male ego satisfies his passage from nature to culture, from conflict to consensus, women remain in a timeless universe condemned to repeat the cycles of life' (ibid.).

Man's 'passage from nature to culture' alludes to the transformation of the moral standpoint from the male perspective, and with it there came about the distinction between justice and the good life. As formulated in early contract theories, it aimed at defending privacy and autonomy of the self – first in the religious sphere, and then in the scientific and philosophical spheres of free thought. 'Justice' becomes the centre of the moral universe and 'what-ought-to-be' came to be defined by what everyone would rationally agree to in order to ensure civil peace and prosperity were derived from the rational form of the moral law. On the one hand, bourgeois man underwent a transition from *socially accepted rules of justice* to their generation in the light of the principles *of social contract*;[7] on the other hand, the privatization of the self, the domestic/familial sphere, came to encompass personal decision-making and issues pertaining to friendship, love, sex, etc., and these were deemed beyond the pale of justice. The autonomous (male) self is a narcissist who sees the world in his own image, and 'through the sobering experience of war, fear, domination, anxiety and death' (ibid.: 409), arrives at the social contract: establishment of the law to govern all. Competition becomes domesticized and channelled towards acquisition and the law curbs anxiety by defining the boundaries between self and other. Within this discourse of narcissistic, competitive men bound by the social contract, the experience of the female finds no expression.

> Woman is simply what men are not; namely, they are not autonomous, independent, but by the same token, non-aggressive but nurturant, not competitive but giving, not public but private. *The world of the female is constituted by a series of negations. She is simply what he happens not to be.* Her identity becomes defined by a lack – the lack of autonomy, the lack of independence, the lack of the phallus. The narcissistic male takes her to be just like himself, only his opposite. (Ibid.: 410; emphasis added)

In Benhabib's assertion thus, 'the definition of the moral domain, as well as the ideal of moral autonomy . . . lead to a privatization of women's experience and to the exclusion of its consideration from a moral point of view' (ibid.: 405).

A few questions are in order here: What does this historical subjugation of woman's experience in moral and political thought do to her notions of selfhood and morality (the 'exclusion' of which does *not* imply non-existence)? Further, does the 'limitless' ethic of care and responsibility' as opposed to 'limited' ethics of justice and right really define women's morality? How does being subject to a cultural imaginary that is itself subject to symbolic misogyny affect moral autonomy and the carving of an integrated self with worth? In such a scenario, does goodness itself become a performative on the lines of gender? In the last section of this chapter, we try to answer some of these questions by looking at the theorizations of the two gendered ethics of justice and care, mainly in the studies of Kohlberg and Gilligan, and by examining their implications for a theory of subjectivity in greater detail.

Female/Male Ethics

Gilligan (1982) lays the groundwork for a women's voice in morality – the care perspective – that centres around relationships, connection, context and responsibility or care. While similar notions were also presented at about the same time by Noddings (1984), it was Gilligan's work that had the widest impact in feminist studies.

> The difficulty women experience in finding or speaking publicly in their own voices emerges repeatedly in the form of qualification and self-doubt, but also in intimations of a divided judgment, a public assessment and private assessment which are fundamentally at odds. . . . *Women's deference is rooted not only in their social subordination but also in the substance of their moral concern.* Sensitivity to the needs of others and the assumption of responsibility for taking care leads women to attend to voices other than their own and to include in their judgment other points of view. Women's moral weakness, manifest in an apparent diffusion and confusion of judgment, is thus inseparable from women's moral strength, an overriding concern with relationships and responsibilities. The reluctance to judge may itself be indicative of the care and concern for others that infuse the psychology of women's development and are responsible for what is generally seen as problematic in its nature. (Gilligan 1982: 6–17)

Women are seen to not only define themselves in the context of human relationship, but also judge themselves in terms of their ability to care while refraining to judge others in view of their caring. Women's place in man's life cycle has been seen as that of nurturer, caretaker and helpmate; for Gilligan too, the developmental strand invested with the intimacy of relationships is a critical line of psychological theory which has been blind to their experiences. Paradoxically, the very traits that traditionally have defined goodness of women (their care for and sensitivity to the needs of others) are those that mark them as deficient in moral development. For women, the moral problem arises from conflicting responsibilities rather than competing rights, and requires for its resolution a mode of thinking that is contextual and narrative rather than formal and abstract. *Morality as care in women centres on the moral development of responsibility and relationships, just as morality as fairness in men ties moral development to the understanding of rights and rules.* Thus, for women, a morality of rights and non-interference may appear indifferent and unconcerned, just as for men, a morality of responsibility and obligation may appear diffuse and inconclusive.

Gilligan contends that these psychosocial realities of women's moral development are not adequately represented within the discipline of psychology. She traces the masculinist thread in psychology back to Freud (1905) who built his theory of psychosexual development around the experiences of the male child that culminate in the Oedipus Complex.

Freud said that women's superego – which, in men, was tied to castration anxiety and was heir to the Oedipus Complex – was compromised. Since the superego in women was never so 'inexorable, so impersonal, so independent of its emotional origins' as in men, he concludes that women 'show less sense of justice than men, that they are less ready to submit to the exigencies of life, that they are more influenced in their judgements by feelings of affection or hostility' (Freud 1925: 257–58). In Freud (1908: 199), he tied the 'undoubted intellectual inferiority of so many women' to 'the inhibition of thought necessitated by sexual suppression'. The strategies of withholding and denial that women have employed in the politics of sexual relations – the puberty that heralds accession of libido in boys marks a renewed repression in girls (Freud 1905: 220–21) – appear similar to their evasion or withholding of judgement in the moral realm. Gilligan's own take on the above issue is famously gendered:

> From the different dynamics of separation and attachment in their gender identity formation through the divergence of identity and intimacy that marks their experience in adolescent years, male and female voices typically speak of the importance of different truths, the former of the role of separation as it defines and empowers the self, the latter of the ongoing process of attachment that creates and sustains the human community. (Gilligan 1982: 156)

Elsewhere,

> . . . in the transition from adolescence to adulthood, the dilemma itself is the same for both the sexes, a conflict between integrity and care. But approached from different perspectives, this dilemma generates the recognition of opposite truths. These different perspectives are reflected in two different moral ideologies, since separation is justified by an ethic of rights while attachment is supported by an ethic of care. (Ibid.: 164)

Much like some linguistic features that are deemed to differentiate men's and women's speech (discussed earlier in this chapter), women and men are hence seen to differ with respect to psychosocial standpoints and moral standpoints. Women, with their care perspective, define the self as embedded in relationships which tend to be web-like networks. Moreover, they seek to resolve conflicts of responsibilities by including everyone, and seek safety in connection and fear isolation. Men, on the other hand, abide by the ethic of justice, conceive the self as autonomous, tend to form hierarchies, resolve conflicts of rights by competing, and find safety in independence and fear intimacy.

Psychosocial Perspectives on Gendered Dispositions

Several psychological studies have added to this debate on the developmental difference between women and men, and its consequence for the issue of morality. Chodorow has shown, for instance, that Freud cast a problem in theory as a problem in women's development. She shows that the reproduction within each generation of certain general and nearly universal differences that characterize masculine and feminine personality and roles can be attributed not to anatomy but to the fact that women universally are largely responsible for child care (Chodorow 1974, 1978).[8] For boys and men, separation and individuation are critically tied to their (male) gendered identity which gets *threatened by intimacy*, while for girls and women, their identity hinges on experiencing others' needs and feelings as one's own and it gets *threatened by separation*. McClelland (1975) also establishes sex role to be one of the most important determinants of human behaviour. On the basis of his studies on men, McClelland divided the concept of achievement motivation into what appeared to be two logical components: a motive to approach success ('hope success') and a motive to avoid failure ('fear failure'). Horner (1972) identified another category as the unlikely motivation to avoid success ('fear success'). According to the latter, women appeared to find competitive achievement problematic as a conflict area between femininity and success; anticipation of success produces anticipation of certain negative consequences – for example, threat of social rejection and loss of femininity (Horner 1968: 125). Sassen (1980) however points out that Horner found success anxiety to be present in women only when achievement was directly competitive, i.e. when one person's success was at the cost of another's failure. In a related study, May (1980) identified the male pattern of fantasy in his studies of sex differences in projective imagination as 'pride' that leads from enhancement to deprivation, whereas the female fantasy pattern is 'caring': a narrative of deprivation followed by enhancement in which connection, though leading through separation, is in the end maintained or restored. Illuminating life as a web rather than succession of relationships, women portray autonomy rather than attachment as the illusory and dangerous quest, thus pointing towards a different history of attachment, stressing continuity and change in configuration (rather than replacement and separation), elucidating a different response to loss and changing the metaphor of growth.

Gilligan notes, of this difference in the psyche of men and women:

> The imagery of hierarchy and web, drawn from the texts of men's and women's fantasies and thoughts, convey different ways of structuring relationships and

> are associated with different views of morality and self . . . images of hierarchy and web inform different modes of assertion and response: the wish to be alone at the top and the consequent fear that others will get too close: the wish to be at the centre of connection and the consequent fear of being too far out on the edge. These disparate fears of being stranded and being caught give rise to different portrayals of achievement and affiliation, leading to different modes of action and different ways of assessing the consequences of choice. (Gilligan 1982: 62)

Taking a similar stance prior to Gilligan, Miller (1976) also had deemed it problematic if all affiliations are cast in the mould of dominance and subordination, and suggested that the parameters of female development are different from that of males, while Haan (1975) and Holstein (1976) show that moral judgements of women differ from that of men; the former are tied to feelings of empathy and compassion, and are concerned with the resolution of real as opposed to hypothetical dilemmas. But since the categories by which development is assessed are derived from research on men, divergence from the masculine standard is thought of as failure of development. Consequently, the thinking of women is often classified with that of children. Such sex difference in favour of males was also reported in Kohlberg's studies and Gilligan, both in Murphy and Gilligan (1980) and in Gilligan (1982), sought to establish Kohlberg's findings as valid for only one aspect of moral orientation, that which focuses on justice and rights. Kohlberg (1958, 1976, 1981) attributes six stages of development of moral judgement from childhood to adulthood. In Kohlberg (1976), he extends Piaget's description of children's moral development to adults, and distinguishes three perspectives of moral conflict and choice. Tying moral development in adolescents to the growth of reflective thought at that time, Kohlberg terms the pre-conventional, conventional and post-conventional views on morality to reflect the expansion in moral understanding from an individual through a societal to a universal point of view. Among these comprehensive, differentiated and reflective modes of thought which encompass a trajectory from personal through social to universal principles, (i) pre-conventional judgement is egocentric and derives moral constructs from individual needs; (ii) conventional judgement is based on the shared norms and values that sustain relations, groups, communities and societies; and (iii) post-conventional judgement adopts a reflective stance on societal values and constructs universal principles.

In their study, Murphy and Gilligan (1980) attributed the earlier low scores of women in Kohlberg's moral judgement studies to the failure of taking into consideration women's particular concerns.[9] Distinguishing between an ethic of justice and rights and an ethic of care and responsibility, Murphy and Gilligan came to the conclusion that women's moral judgement is more contextual, more immersed in details of relationships and narratives. Citing various findings from three studies – 'the college student study', 'the abortion decision study' and 'the rights and responsibilities study' – Gilligan went on to establish the different and feminine voice in moral judgement while admitting that '[w]hen the experience of self and the understanding of morality change with the growth of reflective thought in adolescence, questions about identity and morality converge on the issue of interpretation' (Gilligan 1982: 51).

This feminine voice in moral judgement, Gilligan contends, charts a three-stage sequence in the development of the ethics of care in women. In the first transition from *selfishness to responsibility*, women consider needs other than their own. But in the second transition, *from responsibility to goodness*, the needs of the self have to be deliberately uncovered. The new goodness turns inwards in acknowledging the self and accepting responsibility for choice. That is, in the ethics of care, an initial focus on caring for the self in order to survive is followed by a transitional phase where this is deemed selfish and a new understanding of the connection between the self and the other ushers in responsibility. At this point the good is equated with caring for others. However, the realization of exclusion of herself as a recipient of that care creates a disequilibrium that initiates the second transition. The transition from the first to the second perspective – the shift from selfishness to responsibility – is a move toward social participation. 'Whereas from the first perspective, morality is a matter of sanctions imposed by a society of which one is more subject than citizen, from the second perspective, moral judgment relies on shared norms and expectations' (ibid.: 79). The third perspective focuses on the dynamics of relationships and dissipates the tension between the selfishness and responsibility. This transition is *from goodness to truth* where the woman scrutinizes the logic of self-sacrifice in the service of a morality of care. Thereafter, through a new understanding of the interconnection of self with the other, care becomes the self-chosen principle of a judgement that remains psychological in its concern with relationships and response but becomes universal in its condemnation of exploitation and hurt. This moral judgement however has negative undertones with regard to identity:

> The essence of moral decision is the exercise of choice and the willingness to accept responsibility for that choice. To the extent that women perceive themselves as having no choice, they correspondingly excuse themselves from the responsibility that decision entails. Childlike in the vulnerability of their dependence and consequent fear of abandonment, they claim to wish only to please, but in return for their goodness they expect to be loved and cared for. (Gilligan 1982: 67)

In order that the care ethic should not result in the lopsided development of the moral perspective in individuals, Gilligan regards both the care and the justice ethic as complementary but necessary and integrated in morally mature persons:

> Women's insistence on care is at first self-critical rather than self-protective, while men initially conceive obligation to others negatively in terms of noninterference. Development for both sexes would therefore seem to entail an integration of rights and responsibilities through the discovery of the complementarity of these disparate views. For women, the integration of rights and responsibilities takes place through an understanding of the psychological logic of relationships. This understanding tempers the self-destructive potential of a self-critical morality by asserting the needs of all persons for care. For men, recognition through experience of the need for more active responsibility in taking care corrects the potential indifference of a morality of noninterference and turns attention from the logic to the consequences of choice. . . . In the development of a postconventional ethical understanding, women come to see violence inherent in inequality, while men come to see the limitations of a conception of justice blinded to the differences in human life. (Ibid.: 100)

Psychosocial ethics of care and rights as theorized above reveal gendered identity and this is a major concern in the examination of self-stories in the later chapters of this book. For a better perspective of the kind of issues that may emerge in such postulation of the care ethic in women and justice ethic in men, we now look into the relative merits and demerits of the Gilliganian position before examining a few other perspectives in this context.

Gendered Ethics: Multiple Dimensions

One of the objections raised against the ethic of care as hinted in the beginning of this chapter is that women's orientation towards care and personal relationships reflects the stereotypical social role of the traditional, full-time heterosexual wife and mother. Friedman says that in a major sense it limits women's lives since it 'requires female heterosexuality, promotes women's dependence on men and consequent economic and social vulnerability, and submerges women's own desires and aspirations in the moral project of caring endlessly for others' (Friedman 2000: 210). Amongst other objections to Gilligan's work, Friedman also contends that the empirical correlation between gender and the moral perspective is not uniform and the data are open to various interpretations (ibid.: 209–11). A third objection is that the empirical research underlying Gilligan's ethics of care is based only on white, middle-class heterosexual women and her writings do not reflect the differences among women. Articulating differences among women due to factors such as sexual orientation, race, class, religion, ethnicity, nationality, age and ableness have since become major feminist concerns.

The positive implications of Gilligan's ethic of care cannot however be denied, and Friedman (2000: 207–09) lists some of these:[10]

(i) it has stimulated philosophical debates to consider whether moral concepts and metholodologies are in some substantive sense, gender-based or gender-biased;
(ii) her justice–care dichotomy has provided an alternative to utilitarianism and Kantian frameworks, both of which regard the moral viewpoint as impartial, impersonal, universal and principle-based, and give great importance to matters of justice;
(iii) her conception of a moral perspective centred specifically on caring and personal relationships move these concerns to moral centre stage and establish the personal point of view as an appropriate, and perhaps the only possible, standpoint for justified moral reasoning;[11]
(iv) Gilligan's work added a feminist perspective to another trend in philosophy with its defence of the role of emotion in moral life. The denigration of emotion was part and parcel of the cultural devaluation of women; and
(v) her work in part establishes women as more relationally oriented than men, deeming the latter to be more individualistic than the former while also positioning men as ignoring the importance of relationships.

One of the fallouts of Gilligan's emphasis on inter-relationships, her defence of emotions and the personal point of view is also a renewed interest in the socially mediated nature of the subject and its constitution through social relationships, and the resultant communicative ethic of need interpretations. In the light of a history of non-representation of women's concerns and voices, Benhabib (1992), for instance, objects to a narrow domain of the moral circumscribed to only matters of justice when she claims that the constraints of 'universalism' and 'equal participation' are to the exclusion of matters of care and personal relationships that are relegated to questions of the 'good life'. She argues that universalism covers all moral matters including care associated with women, and not simply those of justice associated with men (ibid.: 185–87). 'Universality is not the ideal consensus of fictitiously defined selves, but the concrete process in politics and morals of the struggle of concrete, embodied selves, striving for autonomy' (Benhabib 1986: 406). In formulating her idea of interactive universalism, Benhabib takes a stance against the Kohlbergian conception of the moral domain as based upon a strong differentiation between justice and good life.[12] Though Kohlberg agrees with Gilligan that an orientation of care and response 'usefully enlarges the moral domain' (Kohlberg 1984: 340), he nevertheless maintains 'that reasoning about the just would lend itself to a formal structuralist analysis . . . while questions about the "good life" have not been amenable to this type of statement' (Kohlberg 1982: 316). In his view, justice and rights, and responsibility, are not two tracks of moral development, but rather two moral orientations. He views the choice of orientation to be 'primarily a function of setting and dilemma, not sex' (ibid.: 349). This differentiation between justice and the good life is a cornerstone in Kohlberg's critique of Gilligan, and he goes on to define 'the spheres of kinship, love, friendship and sex that elicit considerations of care . . . [which] are understood to be spheres of *personal* decision-making, as are for instance, the problems of marriage and divorce' (ibid: 229–30; emphasis added). Questions of the good life, though included in the moral domain as extended by Gilligan's theory, are named in the 'personal' as opposed to 'oral' issues. In contrast to Kohlberg's position above, Benhabib (1992: 173; note 11) pertinently remarks that though frequently invoked by Habermas and Kohlberg and others, it is unclear how this distinction between justice and the good life is drawn and how it is justified. She asks if the distinction corresponds to sociological definitions of the public versus private: 'If so, what is meant by the private? Is women-battering a "private" or a "public" matter?', and goes on to claim that another way of drawing the same distinction is to separate what is universalizable from what is culturally contingent (ibid.). Benhabib contends that unlike Habermas who relegates questions of the good life to the aesthetic–expressive sphere (ibid.: 421), for her it is constitutive of selfhood itself:

> Identity does not refer to my potential for choice alone, but to the actuality of

> my choices, namely to how I as a finite, concrete, embodied individual shape and fashion the circumstance of my birth and family, linguistic, cultural and gender identity into a coherent whole that stands as my life story . . . how does this finite, embodied creature constitute into a coherent narrative those episodes of choice and limit, agency and suffering, initiative and dependence? *The self is not a thing, a substrate, but the protagonist of a life's tale.* The conception of selves, who can be individuated prior to their moral selves, is incoherent. (Ibid.: 161–62; emphasis added)

Benhabib (1986, 1992) lays out the communicative ethic of need interpretation through formulating the concepts of 'generalized other' and 'concrete other': the former requiring that each individual be viewed as a rational being entitled to the same rights and duties, whereas the latter views individuals as having a concrete history, identity and affective-emotional constitution. For Benhabib, in the former, we 'abstract from the individuality and identity of the other', while in the latter, we 'abstract from what constitutes our commonality and focus on individuality' (Benhabib 1992: 159). Since the 'generalized other' cannot individuate, we need the concrete other and Benhabib's 'communicative ethic of needs interpretation' provides the suitable framework enabling moral and political agents to define their own concrete identities on the basis of recognizing each other's dignity as 'generalized others'. This ethic, therefore, will include not only rights but also needs, and not only justice but possible modes of the good life – and, what is of interest to us, it will enable the delineation of a finite, individualized and embodied being through coherent life narratives which in turn may list the episodes of choice and limit, agency and suffering, initiative and dependence that ultimately position and reveal a moral subject who is fired by an ethical intention in the sense of Ricoeur (1992) to live a good life with and for others.[13]

Even a preliminary attempt to graft the feminist theories of this chapter on to the philosophical notions of subjectivity in the previous chapter is bound to throw up a plethora of questions. However, let us not be bothered to come up with a singular theory that would suffice to explain all the linguistic phenomena at hand; such an attempt would be at odds with various underlying postmodernist assumptions of a speaking narrating subject who constructs selfhood in a moment of interlocution. Rather, the attempt is to be aware of the theoretical concerns regarding the self and the other that may actually surface in one's life stories and many such ways in which one's selfhood may find expression in language. The question to ponder over is not only how I perform my gendered identity, but also how the material inscriptions of my cultural imaginary demarcate the limits of my lived experience, and hence selfhood, and how I forge my identity in language despite such delimitation. Moreover, how does language itself encode and express the lived and embodied reality of identity in both the Ricouerian senses of *idem* and *ipse* identity? The semblance of one type of answer to this line of questioning perhaps lies in the coming together of the Ricouerian themes of narrative identity, Giddens' postulation of the sequestration of experience, and the postmodern-feminist concern of the self as an embodied, discontinuous, malleable and socially constructed reality. Tied with the ethical aim of the good life as in Taylor and Ricoeur, we anticipate an 'I' who expresses itself and gets expressed in one's language through one's moral positioning with regard to matters of good living. One may say in a rather Cartesian vein – 'I care therefore I am.' To say so means, 'I am what I care about and the goodness that matters to me, defines me.' This 'I', it is claimed here, reveals itself linguistically within the contextual narrative of its own life as worth living and preserving. Towards this end – of examining the revelation of self in language – in the next chapter we look into the structure of the narrative in some detail along with the framework with which we shall examine narratives from various contexts of talk-in-interaction,[14] with the help of Conversation Analysis framework whose basic tenets we shall examine.

Notes

[1] The sex–gender distinction is well established: of course, there will be the sexes differentiated in terms of 'male/female', but are masculine/feminine (hence gendered) ways of thinking, being, conscientiousness also biologically attested? Or are we all human(e) by that yardstick? Is it even possible in a general sense to think about a self that is *not* gendered (notwithstanding the discussion on self–other in the previous chapter)? See the discussion that follows the subsection 'Gendered Subjectivity: Male/Female Self and Other'.

[2] Yet another example Riviere (2000) gives is of a capable housewife who puts on the semblance of a rather uneducated, foolish, bewildered woman when dealing with builders in her own home so as to come across as helpless and hence 'womanly'.

[3] Tannen (1990) proposes that power inequalities and relations are reproduced in conversation between men and women as in Fishman (1978) and Zimmerman and West (1975).

[4] The SWH draws on Whiting and Edward's (1988) systematic observation of early and middle childhood in six cultures which was based on carefully constructed naturalistic time samples and found that children tend to segregate in same-sex

groups with differentiated activities. While boys' games were more competitive, active and aggressive, requiring larger groups with complex social structure, girls' games were portrayed as more cooperative, passive and verbal as well as lacking in complex social structure. See foregoing discussion in chapter 1, subsection 'Storytelling in the Human Mind and in Children's Play', on how children's role-playing and storytelling reify gendered roles that prepare one for life.

5 See discussion earlier on gendered play in chapter 1, subsection 'Storytelling in the Human Mind and in Children's Play'.

6 Nakamura (2001), for instance, shows in her study of twenty-four monolingual Japanese children (ages three to six years) that while some styles are more variable and context-dependent (for example, sentence final particles used during play), others are more rigid and context-independent (for example, use of first person pronouns).

7 Benhabib (1986) contends that social contract theorists not only translated the division between justice and the good life into a split between the public and the domestic, but by portraying men to be the ultimate picture of autonomy, they left out the women altogether.

8 Parented by a person of the same gender, '. . . girls come to experience themselves as less differentiated than boys, as more continuous with and related to the external object-world, and as differently oriented to their inner object-world as well' (Chodorow 1978: 167).

9 Consideration of women's persistently low scores when compared with their male peers led Murphy and Gilligan to propose a distinction between 'post-conventional formalism' and 'post-conventional contextualism': the former derives a solution to all moral problems from concepts like social contract or natural rights, whereas the second approach acknowledges that 'while no answer may be objectively right in the sense of being context-free, some answers and some ways of thinking are better than others' (Murphy and Gilligan 1980: 83).

10 Friedman and Bolte also give a number of similar reasons as to why care ethics is significant in addition to summarizing important feminist ethical developments regarding the areas of (i) care ethics, (ii) applied ethics, (iii) the ideal of autonomy and (iv) discourse ethics; see Friedman and Bolte (2007) for further discussion on these lines.

11 'The personal point of view reflects someone's distinctive history, embodiment and network of social relationships, not to mention her desires and emotions. It seems to be irreducibly partial and particular' (Friedman 2000: 208–09).

12 For Kohlberg, '. . . moral judgments or principles have the central function of resolving interpersonal or social conflicts, that is conflicts of claims or rights. . . . Thus moral judgments and principles imply a notion of equilibrium, or reversibility of claims. In this sense, they ultimately involve some reference to justice, at least in so far as they define "hard" structural stages' (Kohlberg 1984: 216).

13 For more perspectives on the ethics of care, see Card (1988), Harding (1987) and Held (2006). Card (1988) draws attention to the moral damages that the issue of women's voice in ethics should address and asks the pertinent question as to what extent both justice and caring are higher order (Card 1988: 131). Harding (1987)

offers perspectives in intersectional areas of gender with other social categories like race, class, etc. For instance, he points out the affiliation between the ethics of African men with Euro-American women, and reports that ethics of African and American blacks differ from the ethics of European men; the former are more concerned with relationships and less with autonomy. Held (2006) extends the ethics of care from person to political and global dimensions examining care ethics in terms of both moral theory and society.

[14] The narratives presented in this work have various sources all documenting my own life story as a researcher of narrative theory and identity. A majority of these narratives were part of my PhD research (Barua 2012a), while the first one reported in the next chapter was collected during later phases of research.

3

Micro to Macro

A CA Model for Analysing Narratives

Narrating as Rewriting of the Self

Adding to the universally accepted adage that human beings are storytellers, we now add as our motto, 'People narrate stories to make sense of the world, their lives and their own selves.' Given the conceptualization of narrative intelligibility (that we discussed in chapter 1, under 'Narrative Identity and the "Good Life"'), life appears to us as the field of a constructive activity deriving from the narrative intelligence through which we attempt to recover '*the narrative identity which constitutes us*' (Ricoeur 1991: 436; italics in original).

This process of recovering narrative identity – what Freeman (1991, 1993b, 2004) calls 'rewriting the self' – ensures that we create our lives even as we narrate (about) them.

> What I call *rewriting the self* . . . may often be regarded as a developmental process and project. . . . It is a process of refiguring the past in turn re*con*figuring the self in a way that moves beyond what had existed before. The backward movement of narrative therefore turns out to be dialectically intertwined with the forward movement of development. (Freeman 2004: 77; italics in original)

As against the view that life is formless and that the narrative is an external imposition on it, this Ricouerian/Freeman stance contends that human life may be profitably understood as a kind of literature. Ricoeur (1981a) cites four reasons why human experience is narratively structured and therefore is a kind of literature: (i) semantics of human action;[1] (ii) its 'autonomization';[2]

by which is meant that our deeds escape us and have effects that we did not intend; (iii) the relevance and importance of a deed;[3] and (iv) the view that human action is an open work.[4] By virtue of this last characteristic, *human action consists of events which in time will become episodes within the narrative*. That is, events will become episodes retroactively by virtue of their inter-relationships with other events, both antecedent and subsequent. Further, one does not know what is happening until the moment is past and, in this sense, only endings serve to transfigure events into narratives. Ricouer (1981a) calls it a paradox of the hermeneutical circle that not only do beginnings and middles of stories determine their endings but also vice versa: only when a story has ended is it possible to discern the meaning and significance of what has gone before.

This view of the 'beginnings and middles of stories being defined by the end' in terms of a plot lends to the narrative composition a three-part mimetic process of *pre-configuration*, *configuration* and *re-configuration*, which Ricoeur (1984) explains while discussing Aristotle's analysis of tragedy. In tragic poetry, *mythos* or emplotment refers to the ability to plot events together into a system while the aim of the poem is *mimesis* – the imitation/representation of human action (praxis). Of the three-part mimetic process, the first, mimesis1 (pre-configuration), is pre-understanding of the world of practical actions and events – how incidents/circumstances unfurl without repeated instructions as to what is the beginning/middle/end of the story. Mimesis2, on the other hand mediates between mimesis1 and mimesis3 (this last is the reception of the plot by a reader) by taking up the heterogenous set of incidents, events and characters, and transforming disparate entities into a story taken as a whole. Together, this three-part mimetic process invests in the narrative two distinct dimensions: the *episodic* (chronological) dimension, which refers to the events of which the story is comprised, and a *configurational* (non-chronological) dimension, which refers to the second mimetic process of seeing or grasping 'eliciting a pattern from a succession' (Ricoeur 1981b: 174). In other words, the episodic dimension lends a *linear representing of time*[5] in the structure of 'then' and 'and then' to answer the question 'What next?' and the configurational dimension transforms the succession of events into a *meaningful whole*. Mimesis is therefore not simply reduplication but a creative reconstruction or semantic innovation (Ricoeur 1984) representing human experiences and reality whereby emplotment refashions the ordinary experience of time, borne by daily acting and suffering within the narrative grid.

Despite the above elucidation of the 'mimetic process' that establishes beyond doubt that 'human life is . . . narratively structured' (Freeman 2004: 63), the question remains as to how and why do humans really narrate about their lives – in chapter 1 we asked this question more or less from the point of view of storytelling as a *human* characteristic, i.e. how and why Homo sapiens as a species tell stories. Now we need to ask the question of individual narrative from a *humane* standpoint, i.e. how and why do each of us tell stories in order to establish our humane identities – specifically, what do we accomplish when we tell stories about ourselves to others? After all, narrating about one's life is not an easy accomplishment; Ricouer (1992: 161) notes in this context that a person narrates in spite of the obvious problems in recounting her/his life story, which he sums up as:

(i) the equivocalness of the author/narrator;
(ii) the entanglement of one's life in and with the lives of others;
(iii) the 'narrative incompleteness' of one's life; and
(iv) the dialectics of remembrance of the past and anticipations of the future.

That is, one tends to narrate the story of one's life in spite of the fact that one did not create that life and does not really know the beginning (birth) and end (death) of one's life – it is 'open ended' in that sense.[6] In such a scenario, the question that emerges is whether one is *both* author and narrator of the life which one did not create in the first place, or *neither* since each life is so dependent on other lives and stories? One's life is always entangled with *other* lives and one's present is always reconstructed by both remembrances (or rather, reconstructions) of the past and anticipations for the future. One way of looking at this issue is to acknowledge that people narrate about their experiences and their lives despite apparent problems imminent in such narration because narratives give them the freedom to recreate themselves. Daiute and Lightfoot note in this regard, narration is an important discursive phenomenon in that it shows:

(i) how people make sense of life by telling 'what happened', 'what happens' and 'what will happen'; and
(ii) how imagining, exaggerating, hiding, performing, joking and other symbolic activities of narrating support or limit life and its development. (Daiute and Lightfoot 2004: xii)

Narration is an imaginative engagement whereby processes of self-fashioning make sense of our past, present and future, and it merits our attention in terms of its understanding of what constitutes narrative structure. In the sections below, we examine how narrative can be identified (what is its form), why it is narrated (its function) and what can be its possible dimensions (its plots and usages). Additionally, in the final section of this chapter, under 'Conversation Analysis to Examine Narratives of Interlocution', we examine the framework by which details of mundane everyday talk-in-interaction employing narrative techniques will be shown to throw up larger realities of how the self is identified in language and how others orient to that self by examining an actual life story from a university student. The framework that will be employed for the analysis of the narrative form as a discursive phenomenon is that of Conversation Analysis (CA), and we shall also examine the implications of using CA that traditionally looks at *micro* features of interaction for analysis of the narrative structure – traditionally understood to be the largest *macro* discursive feature.

The Narrative: Form, Function and Plots

Quite a number of disciplines that take the narrative as a cardinal unit of analysis, such as narrative psychology, begin from the ontological perspective that *we live in a story-shaped world*; that is, our lives are guided by a 'narratory principle' – the readiness to organize our experience, to interpret our social actions and even to enact our roles according to the requirements of narrative plots. What warrants the ubiquitousness of narratives is that even experiences that are common to all, namely day/night dreams, are experienced and reported as narratives often with mythic undertones.[7] It is not too far-fetched then to assume that our lives are also summed up in terms of narratives. The prototype of narrative that emerges in everyday lives is *interpersonal storytelling* and it has been reiterated enough throughout this book how the contingencies of context, self, other and language itself may impinge on the establishment of the identity that surfaces through interpersonal storytelling; in other words, narrative identity both in the sense of *idem* and *ipse* will be evident in a life story as narrated at a particular moment in time and particular location.

The *sine qua non* of this narrated-story world is a sequence of utterances representing the past wherein the sequence of events is recapitulated 'in the same order as the original events' (Labov and Waletzky 1967: 21). Since this epochal work by Labov and Waletzky, the analysis of oral narratives has become part of sociolinguistics, and how stories are told, how they are designed, how they are received, their content, function and organization, are of interest to sociolinguistic inquiry. Although narratives can be of many types, namely, the 'literary narrative' (works of authors), the 'fictional narrative' (fairy/folk tales), the 'historical narrative' (about the history of the world/a country or of a tribe), the 'medical narrative' (giving people's medical histories), etc., we are looking at *the personal narrative* – elicited/emergent in the course of interviews with various individuals in various contexts as we shall see – that we hope to show is instrumental in the 'revelation of self in language'.

Narrative Form

As already noted above, a prototypical narrative is a basic sequence of utterances representing the past; the sequence of events is recapitulated 'in the same order as the original events' (Labov and Waletzky 1967: 21). Sacks' classic example of a child's story involving temporal sequencing is: 'The baby cried. The mommy picked it up' (Sacks 1995, vol 1: 236) – in this, if the sequence of utterances is altered, it will be a 'different story'. Labov (1972) notes that there can be other means of recapitulating past experiences which do not follow temporal sequencing. For example, syntactic embedding (as in 1 below) or the past perfect (as in 2 example) can be used to recreate past experiences:

(1) a A friend of mine came in just
in time to stop
this person who had a little too much
to drink
from attacking me.
(2) a The teacher stopped the fight.
b She had just come in.
c I had punched this boy.
d He had punched me.

(Examples 6 and 7 from Labov 1972: 360; the cited examples are arranged as in the original.)

Unlike in Labov's examples above, a minimal narrative, as in Sacks' example cited before that, will have a sequence of two clauses that are temporally ordered: that is, a change in their order will result in a change in the temporal sequence of the original semantic interpretation (ibid.). As noted above, in Sacks' example, the 'mommy' picked up the baby after the baby cried – shifting the temporal sequence would alter the semantics of the narrative. Nelson and Horowitz (2001) and Thornborrow and Coates (2005) too describe a narrative in terms of temporal sequencing. For the former, a narrative is 'at least 3 propositions uttered in the same order as the past events they represent' (Nelson and Horowitz 2001: 307). For Thornborrow and Coates, the two criteria of the narrative form are as follows. (i) There has to be a sequence of narrative clauses (clauses containing a verb in the simple past tense or, sometimes, the historic present tense) whose order matches the real time order of the events described in those clauses, and which constitute the heart of the story or the narrative core. This narrative sequence, linked temporally and sequentially, is minimally two events represented in two narrative clauses. (ii) A story has to have a beginning, a middle and an end.

For Sarbin, 'to qualify as a narrative, a string of words would have to reflect a temporal dimension and also recognition of, if not the solution to, one or more moral issues' (Sarbin 2005: 24,) while for Gottschall, stories the world over follow the same master formula: 'Story = Character + Predicament + Attempted Extrication' (Gottschall 2013: 52). Gottschall calls this structure 'intensely strange' since all fiction – from children's makebelief to folktales to modern drama – is about trouble (ibid: 53). He surmises that stories universally are about trouble since 'the pattern of complication, crisis and resolution' they provide are actually opportunities for learning. 'I think that problem structure reveals a major function of storytelling. It suggests that the human mind was shaped *for* story, so that it could be shaped *by* story' (ibid.: 56).

This *moral dimension* is usually encoded in the 'evaluation' of any story, and this takes us back to Labov and Waletzky's (1967) formulation of the narrative form as comprising the following components: *abstract, orientation, complicating action, evaluation, resolution* and *coda*. Of these, an abstract is a brief summary that occurs at the beginning of a story, and orientation refers to background information on the who, where and when of the story. Complicating action and resolution – absolute essential criteria for a narrative – refer to the narrative clauses that describe the key events of the story. Evaluation is usually an explicit aspect of the story (for example, when the narrator exclaims something like 'It was hilarious!') and/or may be embedded within the narrative; finally, coda is an ultimate comment that comes after the resolution of the story – a sort of wrapping up of the story being narrated. As noted in Labov (1972: 370), each of these components of the narrative form can be seen as answers to underlying questions:

(i) Abstract: what was this about?
(ii) Orientation: who, when, what, where?
(iii) Complicating action: then what happened?

(iv) Evaluation: so what?
(v) Result: what finally happened?

To count as a story not all the criteria are essential, but complicating action and resolution have to be present in a narrative. Since the actual telling of a story takes time, the narrator usually announces that a story is coming up so that the others can take the role of story recipients, and consequently, their rights to hold the floor are suspended (Sacks 1995); it is the narrator who must hold the floor from the moment she or he starts the narration to the end. Nair (2003) postulates that stories typically have extended form as they cater to a maxim of conversation:[8]

> Why then are stories told at such great length? My solution . . . is simply this – since it is a maxim governing conversation that we do not tell people things they know already, story-tellers meet this conversational criterion by presenting general truths such as those expressed in idioms and proverbs – which they know their audience knows – in the form of specific accounts – the particulars of which are unknown. This 'manoeuvre' enables tellers to get their recipients to respond to the story by drawing out and stating the general 'moral' implied by the story, rather than announcing it themselves. They thus avoid *moral responsibility for an overt violation of the maxim which enjoins us to eschew 'redundancy'.* (Ibid.: 258; emphasis added)

Kitzinger (2002) in fact notes the 'story strategy' as one of the ways by which speakers accomplish long turns in conversation, and stories can potentially establish conversational dominance. What actually opens up the space for a story to be told are *prefaces* that often carry indications of what the story will consist of, when it will be over and what sort of things could happen. In elicited narratives (for example, in an interview situation) things are a little different as the storyteller does not have to negotiate space to tell her/his story by taking the floor but is invited to tell it by the interviewer. However, such narratives too begin with an abstract that gives a brief summary of what the story is about. Prefaces indicate the narrator's alignment to the story as well as appropriate reaction to it, setting up recipients back to real time (the conversational present). The narrator must then 'smoothe' the way back from the story world to the embedding conversation (Polanyi 1982: 164), which marks the transition from the imaginary world of the narrative that the speaker and listener have just shared to the real time and present conversation. This is done via a coda or what Jefferson (1978) calls 'exit talk' – for example, 'That was the funniest thing I ever heard.'

Before we move on to narrative function, we cite below one more example from Labov (1972) to explicate what is *not* a narrative form: the following material was given in answer to the Danger of Death question in Labov's study of Black English vernacular.

> (You ever been in a situation where you thought that you were gonna get killed?)
> Oh, yeah lotta time, man.
> (Like what happened?)
> a Well, like we used to jump off the trestle
> b and the trestle's about six-seven stories high
> c You know, we used to go swimmin' there . . .
> d We used to jump offa there, you know
> e An' uh-like, wow! Yaget up
> f An' ya feel like
> you are gonna die and shit, y'know
> g Couple a times I almost . . . I thought I was gonna drown, you know
> (Labov 1972: 361, example 9).

The events referred to in Labov's example above are in the general present, and because the clauses refer to general events which have occurred an indefinite number of times, they are not narrative clauses. 'Clauses containing used to, would and the general present are not narrative clauses and cannot support a narrative' (ibid: 362).

Narrative Function

Thornborrow and Coates (2005: 7) note that there are three important aspects of the narrative function: (i) the narrative as social identity, (ii) performance in narrative discourse, and (iii) narrative and cultural identity. Amongst these three aspects, as a marker of social identity and starting from bedtime stories for children to gossip tales and workplace narratives, the narrative establishes social norms via storytelling. Bruner (1990, 1991) has emphasized how the narrative holds a key position in a social and cultural world, while many other studies have examined the nature of society and individual lives which have been laid bare via the narrative. Armbruster and Meinhof (2005), for instance, have shown how three generations of people living on the German–Polish border have different ways of narrating 'what happened' to them to construct coherent socio-historical identities. The study found that there was often more similarity between accounts of same generation members than members of the same family. Thus, a social 'generational identity' is constituted through narrative form in the telling of their life story and their representation of historical experience. Gendered roles are also played out through the narrative and in line with so many studies on gendered talk we have discussed. Coupland, Garrett and Williams (2005) have shown that more than girls, boys tell stories about personal adventures, about risks to their own or others' well-being, about mishaps and damage, and about conflict with authority figures.

This brings us to the second functional aspect of narrative where people can 'perform' gendered worlds via talk. The view of 'performance' of identity and the social self originates with studies like Goffman (1971), and was later developed by Bruner (1990) and Butler (1990). As we saw in chapter 2, for Butler gender is a set of 'naturalized gestures' that are repeated through iteration; it is never static but is produced actively and in interaction with others every day of our lives. One may still wonder, however, how gender is accomplished in narrative structures. That is, how do naturalized gestures occur within narratives to perform masculine/feminine identities? An important perspective in this context of narratives performing gendered identities is provided in Coates (2005), who notes that heterosexual couples employ powerful linguistic strategies whereby they 'do' or perform their 'coupledom' in public. Amongst such features of what Coates calls 'collaborative narration' are:

(1) two narrators making contributions to the story which join together seamlessly: that is, there are a number of 'latched utterances' which indicate that turns follow each other seamlessly;
(2) frequent repetition;
(3) frequent rephrasing of each other's ideas using different words;
(4) shared construction of utterances; and
(5) frequent backchannel support to signal acceptance of the other's speech. (Coates 2005: 91–92).

That is, latched utterances, repetition, rephrasing, joint construction of utterances and overlapping speech are all symbols of collaborative speech in which the narrative floor is shared by two people thereby symbolizing the connection between them. Earlier research by Coates had shown that male speakers in single-sex groups prefer *solo narration*, while *collaboration* is typical of women's friendly talk (Coates 1997a, 1997b). However, joint storytelling by heterosexual couples, also called 'duetting', following Falk (1980), becomes a powerful display of their 'togetherness', and Mandelbaum (1987) notes that duetting also highlights the *performative* aspects of storytelling.

The very reasons that explain men's reluctance to collaborate in duetting with other men can explain their willingness to 'duet' with a female partner: heterosexuality is a key component of hegemonic masculinity, and in co-narrating with another male there is a threat in connection with the latter. By contrast, 'co-narrating a story with a female partner performs coupledom as well as heterosexuality, and so it is highly valued' (Coates 2005: 92).

This differential performance of the narrative – collaborative duetting in the case of heterosexual couples and non-collaborative solo narration in single-sex groups – also highlights the importance of *narrative context* in the telling of a story. Stories are different for different participants, and they manifest themselves differently in the public and private contexts. In this sense, the narrative is not simply a pervasive discursive form but a resilient and versatile resource through which speakers can accomplish many different social and cultural actions. As noted by Thornborrow and Coates (2005: 7), 'narrative form is inevitably shaped by the social context in which it occurs and . . . narrativity as a discursive mode is at the core of our social and institutional world'. They note that stories can be told to entertain (jokes, folktales, anecdotes), to justify and explain (accounts and descriptions of events), to instruct (the 'cautionary' tale, fables) and to establish social norms (gossip). But even more importantly, *stories tell us who we are: they are central to our social and cultural identity* (ibid.; emphasis added).

Blum-Kulka (2005) too emphasizes the contextual dimension of narratives in making the distinction between 'tale', 'teller' and 'telling'; while the 'tale' delimits the story itself (the narrative sequence of events) and the 'teller' is the narrator, it is the 'telling' that specifies the context within which the story is told. 'Tellings' thus are situated narrative events, each with its unique participation framework, and by virtue of being faithful human articulations of the lived social world, a telling or a narrative will function as a reflection of that world. For McAdams, on the other hand:

> . . . *life stories are cultural texts*. . . . these cultural texts come to the listener through the voice and the consciousness . . . of an individual narrator, an agential self (the I) who appropriates what the culture has to offer, selects and discards, modifies and personalizes in order to tell a story that aims, in some sense, to be true to lived experience. (McAdams 2005: 127; emphasis added)

Stories in fact give us the opportunity to straddle cultural worlds: 'of the many psychological boundaries that narrative teaches us to breach, one of the most salient is that between personal extinction and cultural preservation, between the teller's imminent mortality and her audience's immanent satisfaction' (Nair 2003: 14). In the context of our current exploration into how narrative identity emerges in situations of interlocution, a relevant idea to explore would be what sociocultural realities find expression in their narratives and what gendered identities get postulated in the process? How does a narrator relate to an 'other' in the telling of her/his tale? Would there be distinctions in the telling – like we predicted at the beginning of this book that *you* will narrate *your* life story differently if you were telling it to your long-lost friend as opposed to a stranger you met on a train?

In elucidating the functional aspects of the narrative structure, Nelson and Horowitz (2001: 310) claim that the narrative is distinctive interpersonally as well as grammatically because the speaker (i) invites the listener to be engaged in the story domain; (ii) explicitly testifies to the occurrence of these events in the speaker's past; (iii) sequentially displays the recounted events to the listener (Clark 1996; Traugott and Pratt 1980); and (iv) claims that the recounted events are relevant to the self and the interpersonal situation that instigated the story (Labov 1972).

Nair notes of the vicarious advantage that the narrative offered to us as listeners:

> Listening to a narrative . . . is a relatively inexpensive means of trying out patterns of living, situations and emotional reactions that one may never experience, or want to experience, in one's own life. The feelings, among others, of curiosity, awe, pity, sheer fun, and final reassurance that a narrative evokes – those indirect 'perlocutionary effects' of speech act theory – must occur in our minds, not just or even necessarily, within the story-teller's. (Nair 2003: 15)

When engaged in the story domain of the speaker, *the listener as the other* is construing an image (in other words, identity) of the speaker in her/his mind and moreover adds to the narrator's story in through her/his intervention (these could range from simple backchannels to signal understanding, and encourage the speaker to continue to proactive duetting that actually contributes to the making to the narrative). Further, as (ii) in Nelson and Horowitz (2001) above indicates, the fact that the speaker is recounting a tale will imply that she/he is placing herself/himself in a particular identificatory modality (Derrida 1998: 28) by portraying un/consciously a self-image. By sequentially displaying the recounted events to the listener, this un/conscious knowledge of the speaker guides the listener into, through and out of a cognitive representation or situational model of imagined events where language is actively involved in establishing and reifying that self-image. This aspect of the narrative foregrounds the role of intentionality in the individual, and one can ask if an individual self is completely autonomous in carving a self-identity out of her narrative or do the presence and contributions of listeners and other speaker(s) within the contextual setting affect this 'speaker positioning' within the narrative (as alluded to above)? Finally, as (iv) above claims, the recounted events are deemed to be relevant to the self and the interpersonal situation that instigated the story – the context of the narrative becomes immensely important. Labov notes that a story, whether spontaneous or elicited, will fall flat if it elicits the response 'So what?' from a listener (Labov 1972: 362) – the whole point of narrating a story hinges on the fact that the narrative of the floor-taker must be seen to be of value; it should not elicit the 'withering rejoinder' (ibid.: 366) from the listener, 'So what?' In terms of the narrative form, it is the evaluative component that will play a crucial function in the narrator's portrayal of the worth of her narrative.

In a narrative world where the speaker and listener 'jointly imagine' a fictitious cognitive world (Clark 1996), it is expected that the narrator will employ certain linguistic strategies by which the storied world will not only capture the real-life situation of the narrator but also underscore the value of her narrative. They would also only demonstrate their (un/conscious) portrayal of the self as well as the listeners' perceptions, stereotyping, subversion, co-creation of this self-image through interpersonal dimension of conversation in the actual communication situation. Further, given the Ricoeurian (1992) postulation that the 'ethical intention' animates each individual life in terms of the 'good life' that one seeks, this ethical dimension will expectedly be employed to justify a teller's 'telling'; it will help subvert the 'So what?' question as in Labov (1972). What remains to be seen is, around what possible plots with such pivotal ethical dimensions of the individual's lived reality can a narrative be woven? And finally, what would be the cultural stakes in the grounding of such an ethical dimension within individual narratives? We look briefly, below, at some such possibilities of the narrative plot.

Narrative Plots

In an earlier section of this chapter (see 'Narrating as Rewriting of the Self'), we discussed Ricouer's (1984) analysis of Aristotelian tragedy as a three-part mimetic process of pre-configuration, configuration and re-configuration. We also saw that stories, inevitably woven around a 'beginning–middle–end' sequence in terms of a plot, lend to each narrative composition an episodic dimension and configurational dimension. The former confers succession adhering to a linear representing of clock time in the story ('this happened and then that happened'), while the configurational dimension transforms the succession of events into a meaningful whole through a process of emplotment. It involves a different temporal movement that goes back in time to reconfigure varied aspects of the episodic dimension into a harmonious whole. Now, following from the notions of the narrative function that we discussed in the preceding section ('Narrative Function'), we come to see the narrative as real-time performance of a tale that actually draws on storytelling's functions as a reflexive tool for examining dominant cultural meanings. In drawing attention to the culture's system of signification and expression, a narrative will expectedly draw upon social anthropologists' and ethnographers' view of the telling of the story itself as a performance. Bruner notes that an important function of storytelling is that it allows us 'to present ourselves to others (and to ourselves) as typical or characteristic or "culture conforming" in some way' (Bruner 2001: 29), and, by extension, the way we (re)configure ourselves in terms of the events of our lives will also be culture-conforming in a major way. There is a 'nexus' of narration and culture in that even the boldest of stories are usually narrated according to the particular culture's dictations.

Thornborrow and Coates also add to this issue of a story's performance when they note that what makes a good story is the teller's 'prat avoidance' technique; this latter is defined as something which involves 'a high degree of control over the tale as well as a high level of reflexivity in the telling (e.g. the ability to stand back and laugh at oneself)' (Thornborrow and Coates 2005: 10). For them, also important in the 'performing' of a tale are *intensity* and *incongruity* where high levels of risk-taking and exceptional events are valued over more mundane, boring happenings. Polanyi (1985) and Bruner (2001) take similar stands with regard to story plots: for the former, what is tellable within a culture are stories that also involve 'deviations from the expected' (Polanyi 1985: 17); for the latter, though stories may establish us culture-conforming, they themselves must be culture-breaching so as to be 'tellable'. Telling a story thus explores the boundaries between the ordinary and the exceptional, and for a story to be tellable, it must involve a breach of what Bruner calls the canonical script – something on which the tellability of a story depends. It is in the light of this aspect of the narrative that one can also see the autonomy of the self – how a person tells a story about her life to make it culture-conforming as well as culture-threatening at the same time will depend on her usage of language. It functions as a tool in her hands to present an ideal self even while accomplishing what is being called here a breach of the canonical script.

Finally, establishing one's identity will then be concurrent with the narrating of the story thus making identities highly context-dependent; an individual's endeavour to tell an engaging 'culture-threatening' story will be concurrent with establishing a 'culture-conforming' idealistic/moral self through her position within that story. For an ethico-moral self 'aiming at the "good life" with and for others in just institutions' (Ricoeur 1992: 172), we contend that narratives will inevitably construct selfhood in relation to others via various plots.

> . . . stories revolve around a handful of master themes. Stories universally focus on the great predicaments of the human condition. Stories are about sex and love. They are about the fear of death and the challenges of life. And they are about power: the desire to wield influence and to escape subjugation. (Gottschall 2013: 55)

Do our lifestyles indeed revolve around such master themes and do plots of our narratives reflect these? In negotiating their various symbolic roles within the sociocultural setting, how will narrators' stories within talk-in-interaction carve their narrative identities? Such perspectives on the plots of narratives will help us understand how the Ricoeurian ethico-moral self operates and manifests itself in the narrative form, and how it configures its self-identity through its narrative self-understanding. An added dimension will come from Gilliganian theorizations that we examined in the second chapter: a question that it might help answering is, do women's narratives 'perform' 'care' ethics and do men 'perform' narratives emphasizing 'rights'? In the final section of this chapter, we briefly look at the framework and features that will be employed in such a study, namely Conversation Analysis.

Conversation Analysis to Examine Narratives of Interlocution

Conversation Analysis and Its Application to Study Narratives

Narratives presume a narrator. In the conventional sense of storytelling, the storyteller is to be considered the be-all and know-all of the story – it is she/he who knows what the story is about; who its main characters are, and what circumstances and problems they will face. While this may be true of cultural forms of storytelling – from fairy tales to folk tales to classics – in view of our discussions in the preceding chapters, we can surmise that it may not always hold true for the stories that emerge in the context of conversation which we are calling *narratives of interlocution* here. In the next couple of chapters we shall be looking at stories that emerge contextually in the midst of conversation; how and why narratives that emerge in the context of interlocution can reveal a contingent and unique narrative identity to a self. For this examination to work, we need a few tools with which to examine narratives and this section gives a brief overview of Conversation Analysis as a framework that is quite suitable for this purpose.

Conversation Analysis (CA) developed through a certain ethnomethodological concern of Goffman (1956), who showed that an understanding of social structures could be achieved through description and analysis without hypothesis-testing. 'It is the systematic analysis of the talk produced in everyday situations of human interaction: talk-in-interaction' (Hutchby and Wooffitt 1998: 13). The aim is to focus on the production and interpretation of talk-in-interaction as an *orderly accomplishment* that is oriented to by the participants themselves (ibid.: 14–15; emphasis added). There are three basic assumptions that underlie CA, namely:

(1) conversation is highly organized and orderly, with the consequence that features seem to recur in an organized fashion;
(2) talk is contextual;
(3) nothing is by chance.

In other words, talk '. . . exhibited orderliness . . . [and it] did so not only to us, indeed not in the first place for us, but for the co-participants who had produced them' (Schegloff and Sacks 1973: 230).

The two core questions in CA are:

(1) What interactional business is being mediated or accomplished through the use of a sequential pattern?
(2) How do participants demonstrate their active orientation to this business?

Sacks, Schegloff and Jefferson's (1974) classic paper on turn-taking proposes a model for conversation which seeks to explain the practices people use for ensuring – with systematic and orderly exceptions explainable by the theory itself – *how it is that people in conversation overwhelmingly speak one at a time*, i.e. how they take systematic turns in uttering the basic unit of conversation called a Turn Construction Unit (TCU) in Conversation Analysis.

Given that a narrative will typically be spoken over many lines, it is only to be expected that longer TCUs will be taken up by speakers. However, a speaker's narration may be redefined by a listener who may be 'back-channelling' as a way to signal to the speaker that she/he is attentive and/or encourages the speaker to continue, or offering genuine 'help' in narration through duetting or some other method, or may actually be disrupting the narration.

> The pauses, the ums and ers, wells and you knows, the lapses into silence, reformulations of utterances and the overlapping speech that we would automatically 'erase' from an ideal representation of our linguistic performance turn out to be really important in 'holding a narrative together', as well as in structuring the changeovers between speakers and hearers in a conversation. (Nair 2003: 253)

What determines whether such a turn is a genuine help to structure changeovers or an interruption is whether the significant turn was uttered at a Transition Relevance Place (TRP). Let us briefly look at such features of CA as turns, TRP, etc., that will be crucial in the analysis of narrative structures, after which we shall begin looking at the first of the narratives of interlocution examined in this work to understand how a self reveals itself in language.

Basic Features of CA

Floor: Turn-taking–TRP–Overlap–Interruption–Turn length/distribution

The concept of floor was introduced by Sacks (1972) and it refers to the right to begin to talk. It is a psychological framework which participants in a conversation share. When a speaker takes the floor either by *self-selection* (choosing to speak) or *other-selection* (being asked/requested to speak), she begins speaking what is known as a 'turn'. Ideally, it is when she has finished her turn that the other speaker takes over and begins his turn. The Turn Construction Unit (TCU) can be whole sentences, phrases or even words, but they must be recognized (in context) as constituting a complete turn as proposed in the Sacks, Schegloff and Jefferson (1974) model.[9] The turn is therefore a cardinal analytic unit since it identifies the current speaker who has the right to speak and hold the floor, and demarcates the next. In this sense turn-taking may have to do with the 'selection' of a speaker, and Sacks, Schegloff and Jefferson (ibid.) propose a simple set of rules to describe turn allocation at TRPs (Transition Relevance Place):

Rule 1

(a) If the current speaker has identified or selected a particular next speaker, then that speaker should take a turn at that place.

(b) If no such selection has been made, then any next speaker may (but need not) self-select at that point. If self-selection occurs, then the first speaker has the right to the turn.

(c) If no next speaker has been selected, then alternatively the current speaker may, but need not, continue talking with another turn-constructional unit, unless another speaker has self-selected in which case that speaker gains the right to the turn.

Rule 2

Whichever option has operated, rules 1(a)–(c) come into play again for the next TRP.

However, as Button says about this essentially ethnomethodological concept of rule – 'We do not get a turn *because* of the rules . . . the rule does not *precede* the action. Rather the rule is discoverable in the action' (Button 1990: 79; italics in original).[10] As such, these rules indicate the importance of turn-taking in speaker identification in conversation and underscore the importance of context in talk-in-interaction. An example is cited below of turn-taking and TRP from Hutchby and Wooffitt (1998: 56).

Host: Well did you – did you then explain that, you
understood that, you know dogs have the call of
nature just as er as people do, and they don't
have the same kind of control and so
the[refore, s-so[11]
Caller: [No, but dogs can be tr[ained
Host: [I haven't finished,
so therefore the owner . . . being there has the
responsibility . . .

The caller's overlapping turn in line 6 can be described, following Jefferson (1983), as a *transitional onset.* Although the host treats this as an interruption, it may be that the caller has identified and oriented to a possible completion point: a TRP in the current turn. Jefferson (1983, 1986) identified three major categories of overlap onset: (i) *transitional onset* (when the next speaker orients to a possible TRP); (ii) *recognitional onset* (when the next speaker recognizes what the current speaker is saying and can project its completion even before the end of the current speaker's turn);

and (iii) *progressional onset* (when there is some disfluency in the current turn and a next speaker suggests a completion to move the conversation forward).

In contrast to the overlap example above, an *interruption* is seen as simultaneous speech whose onset is prior to the last word that could be the possible boundary of a TCU. In Sacks, Schegloff and Jefferson (1974), the proposed model of conversation has the existence of TCUs which can be whole sentences, phrases or even just words, but which are recognizable (in contexts) as potentially constituting a complete turn. Each speaker is initially entitled to just one of these; then the second speaker, say Speaker B, has the right/obligation to speak next. Speaker B would be interrupting – and hence become a 'dominant' person in the interaction – if she/he starts speaking at a point which is *not* a TRP. A speaker with many TCUs may be deemed an interruptive speaker. However, as Hutchby and Wooffitt (1998) caution, one should not rush to label an utterance as interruption because the speaker may have uttered the sequence at what occurred to him/her as a TRP – i.e. the orientation of the speaker must be taken into account.

Given the description of turns, overlap and interruption, it is easier to appreciate how turns can be so orderly in most of our conversations. Turn-taking organization is not organized to be indifferent to the size of the turns parties take; rather, its 'underlying (though supercessable) organization is designed to minimize turn size' (Schegloff 1982: 73). Consequently, long turns with multiple and/or lengthy TCUs ought to be understood as 'achievements and accomplishments' (ibid.) which have overcome the inherent bias of the system – one that envisages turns to be of *minimal* size amongst co-participants. A narrative that emerges in the situation of interlocution may not be considered as an achievement or accomplishment since all listeners inherently understand the notion of story and hence can recognize the fact that a storyteller will need a longer TCU. Contrastively, however, if a speaker interrupts an ongoing TCU to enforce his story just to establish his right to speak and if the current speaker does not interrupt, then it can be deemed an accomplishment (see 3 below). Kitzinger (2002: 69) shows that long TCUs can be accomplished by any of the following strategies:

(1) using particular sentence structures (such as 'if/then' constructions)[12] which are hearably not complete unless the 'then' part is uttered;
(2) taking a big in-breath that puts hearers on the alert for a long possibly multi-unit turn;
(3) beginning a turn with a bid to tell a story ('Did you hear about . . . ');[13]

(4) using a list launcher ('Four things . . . '); and
(5) using markedly first verbs (like 'I thought . . .' or 'I tried . . .' which would require further elucidation).

Repair: Adjacency Pairs – Preference Organization

An important concept in the context of talk-in-interaction is that of *repair* which deals with turn-taking errors and violations. For example, if two parties find themselves talking at the same time, one will stop prematurely thus repairing the trouble. Thus, the party attempting or enforcing more repairs can be the dominated or dominating one, respectively. Repairs may be of the following types:

(1) *Self-initiated self-repair*:	Both initiated and carried out by speaker
(2) *Other-initiated self-repair*:	Carried out by speaker but initiated by recipient/co-participant
(3) *Self-initiated other-repair*:	Speaker tries to get recipient to repair the trouble, for example, trying to remember a name
(4) *Other-initiated other-repair*:	The recipient of the trouble source turn initiates and carries out the repair (what is conventionally understood as 'correction').

Adjacency pair (Schegloff and Sacks 1973) refers to a sequential pair in which talk is produced. The structure of such a pair is composed of first and second part in exchanges such as compliment–compliment responses, greetings, question–answer and so on. They are thus two utterance sequences which are:

(i) adjacent
(ii) produced by different speakers
(iii) ordered as a first and second part
(iv) typed, so that a first part requires a second part (or a range).

Preference organization refers to a phenomenon in which hearers have a dual choice – of preferred and dispreferred second choices. In invitations, for instance, the preferred second pair is an acceptance while the dispreferred second pair is a rejection. Further, requests/invitations and other first pairs can be preceded by sequences termed as pre-sequences (Schegloff 1990, 2007) which include pre-invitations ('Are you free this weekend?') or pre-requests ('Can I ask you for a favour?').

A CA Analysis of Narrative

From the discussion above of the basic features of CA, it is easy to see that the object of CA is to 'identify and describe the ways in which participants collaboratively produce recognizable action sequences which exhibit orderly structural and normative properties. Those sequences emerge from production of alternative turns by two or more participants in a conversation' (Hutchby and Wooffitt1998: 185).

In other words, the structural phenomena that manifest themselves in language are essentially *dialogical* in nature, while any elicited/spontaneous narratives of a speaker will result in stories that are essentially monologic. In a Bakhtinian vein, Nair notes that conversational structure is interventionist and 'is typically "alternating", with an *ABABAB pattern* that requires a constant relocation of the deictic centres of "self"' (Nair 2003: 6), while the narrative – 'often idealized as monologic' – is quite unlike conversation as it structurally sequentially displaying an *ABCDEF pattern*.[14] Moreover, the underlying organization of talk in conversation is designed to *minimize* turn size (Schegloff 1982: 73; cited earlier) whereas narratives are designed, and sometimes used, to maximize a turn size.[15] Finally, how does one apply a framework that looks at *micro* aspects of talk to analyse the *macro* feature of discourse which is the narrative?[16]

The foregoing discussion hints at an inherent contradiction in subjecting the narrative structure to a CA analysis: individual narratives are *monologic* data whereas CA principles have a *dialogic* foundation. How then can one resolve this seeming paradox? One way of resolving it is to acknowledge, as we did in our section on narrative function, that the narrator's story is always situated within a sociocultural set-up and in itself points at a 'dialogical' sense of creation of self. Sarbin says in this context: 'Our self stories are inevitably co-authored, most often unwittingly composed during dialogical interchanges whenever we have an "I", a "you" . . . is necessarily a part of the social context and ultimately enters into the formation of identities' (Sarbin 2005: 30).

Not only does this perspective afford to the narrative an inherent dialogic subtext, the narrative form itself can be remodelled to be dialogic.

> Our boundaries of self are both defined and extended when we meet with others through our narratives. As I suggested earlier, we communicating cogs may well have command over two basic kinds of narrative – *narratives of the self* and *narratives to the other*. Our centres may be created by the first kind of narratives, but our boundaries, our defences, are marked by the second kind. (Nair 2003: 23; emphases added)

Listeners thus are co-narrators as well co-constructors of meaning:

> Audience reactions, the twitters, chirps and trills of participation, are shown not just to influence a teller's story but to be structurally a part of the story. Hence, the story begins to emerge not just as a teller's show but rather as a joint production by narrators(s) and listeners(s), speaker(s) and hearer(s). (Ibid.: 32)

As co-narrators of the life story in the context of interlocution also, the listener is then involved in the *refashioning* of the self. We saw in a previous section, Coates' (2005) formulation of 'collaborative narrative' whereby couples performed their coupledom and, by extension, hegemonic patriarchy by jointly narrating stories. Within such a perspective, in the various interlocution settings described in this work, there may be a joint narrative in which one participant is narrating and another pitches in with some aspect of the narrative form. Another way of working around this conundrum is to see the ethical implication as encoding the dialogic dimension of the narrative: for example, since the ethical intention is the 'aiming of the good life with and for others' (Ricouer 1992: 172), how does the listener orient to the good life being projected and how does she/he contribute to it? An individual's narrative about some episode of his life may be given a configuration dimension by the listener in the dialogic: in doing so, she too becomes part of the discursive creation of a good self. Finally, what experiences are sequestered (within the contextual setting of the interview situation) individually/jointly by the individual narrating episodes from her life will also provide glimpses of how negative experiences (by being blocked out) actually sustain the 'good life'.

Let us now begin our analysis of narrative structures using the methods of CA in our endeavour to explore the revelation of self in language.

LIFE STORY 1:[17] *'They Brought It Out in a Big Way'*

Transcript Details:	[CASNS0403]
Participants:	A 20-year-old university student, female (N) and author (S); the student was being interviewed by the author as part of a study on peer groups.
Language of Interaction:	Assamese
Narrative Context:	The narrative occurs four minutes into the conversation. Before this, S was engaged in a discussion with N who was talking about herself; her hobbies; her family; her educational background; the difficulties she was facing in

	her chosen subject area and the medium of communication (English) which she was finding difficult to cope with. S then asks if she had had any memorable experience, to which N says that she was not liking it too much as her peers were not to her liking. She elaborates why she does not like them – they had all come from various places and had different mental orientation. When S asks her if this is in hostel, she replies it was not her friends in hostel (whom she liked) but it was her peers in her department. S's immediate turn prior to the narrative below is when she asks N is she is unable to have a dialogue with her peers or something else to which N says that 'their minds' do not match 'our minds'. By 'our' she possibly means her hostel mates. S asks her how this is so, and she says that they gossiped too much and could make up rumours (*kiba kibi* which literally means 'something or the other') over the smallest of things. S then asks if she could tell about any such incident, to which N initiates a clarificatory turn by asking whether she meant incident relvant to her or other. S responds by clarifying it could be related to her or something else, to which she responds with 'Yes. Something that happened with me. Mmm, Maam', and then launches into her narrative turn below. Her entire preceding discourse reported in detail here acts as the story preface now to her narrative.
Narrative Highlights:	*Exemplifies narrative form, function and plot.* N's story below posits her as the marginalized and her language performs this exclusion (Barua 2016b). However, as discussed below, it is her turns with S starting from line 11 onwards being currently analysed for the 'revelation of self in language' that enable her to graft a positive narrative identity who is above the gossip-mongering classmates.

Extract A[18]

1 N:	*>edmison*	*tu*	*mur*	*deri*	*ke*	*hoise*	*ma::ne* (.)<	*moi*
	admission	cl	I-gen	late	cpm	happen-pres	means	I

2	*>go::m*	*pua na::silu*↑↓< (.)	*ta::r*	*pisot*(.)	*seken*	*ba::r*
	know	get-neg-pst-1p	that	after	second	time

3 *>jetia hoisil edmison*(.) *tetia*↑↓*:: ahisu ma::ne moi*< {S:*acca:*}
when happen-pst admission then come-pres.1p means I-nom okay

'My admission happened late. I had not known. . . . After that, when admissions happened a second time, means it was then that I came.'

4 *>itimodhye kla::S hoi gol ma:ne*<(.)
meanwhile class happen go-pst means

→5 *taha::ti gutei khini tu log pa:*↑↓*lei a:ru* (.) {S:*aah*}
they-cl all pl dm meet get-pst-emph and Ah!

→6 *taha::ti nijor ma::jot fri: HOYEI gol*(.) {S: *buisu*}
they-cl self-gen between free happen-emph go-pst understand-1p

'In the meanwhile, classes had already started. All of them had already met up. They were already free between themselves. (S: I understand.)'

→7 *ta::r pisot* (.) *a:ma::r lora:: DUTA:I hoi ma:ne* {S: *a::*}
then after we-gen boy two-only cop means Ah!

→8 *>edin ma::ne moi eta lora:r logot*<(.) *ma:ne*(.)
one day means I-nom one boy-gen with means

9 *<ene::i aru> godhuli xomoyot khu*↑*:j karhisilu* {S: *a:*↓*:*}
just and evening time-in step walk-pst-1p Ah!

10→ *>@TA::KE DEKHI ma::ne taha::ti bohu::::t besi*
that-emph see means they-cl lot much

→11 *uliyai dile ma::ne-*< @ (.)
bring-out give-pst means ((S laughs))

'And then . . . we have just two boys (in our class). One day – means – I just took a walk with one of the boys in the evening. . . . Seeing that they just brought out a lot (of news/rumours).'

→12 *>zit<u>::u</u> ma:ne moi ajileke bhugiasu ma::ne* < *.hhh*{S: *acca*↑↓*::*}
that means I-nom today-till suffer pres means okay

→13 (0.3) *ma::ne*↑ *<u>xeitu</u> karo::ne >muk ma:ne <<NAMA::TA*
means that because I-acc means neg-call

→14 *hoi goisil °taha::ti° maa:ne*>(.)
happen go-pst they-cl means

'(For) which . . . I mean . . . I am suffering till today. I mean for that reason they had even stopped talking with me . . .'.

15 S: [*ahh… maane: clasot?*
ah means class-loc

'Means . . . in class?'

16 N: [*clas↓ot* =

17 S: *=o:: xeitu mane beyake uliyae disile?=*
yes that means badly bring give-pst
'Oh! So, that . . . means . . . they had brought out in a bad way?'

→18 N: *=bohu::t beyake uliyai dile*(.) {S: *acc(ha)ha*}
very badly bring-out give-pst okay

19 *<bohu::t BES(hehe)I uliyai dile ma::ne>=*
lot much bring-out give-pst means

'Yes . . . means they brought that out in a big way. They brought it out too badly . . . they brought out too much.'

20 S: *ach(haha).* (.) *khaali kothapatar ka:rone? ba: okoman=*
okay only talk- do-gen because or little

'Only because of talking? Or little . . . '

21 N: *>=@okoma:n ma:ne*(.) *soppin kompleksot lohg pa:lu<*, {S: *o::*}
little means shopping complex-in met get-pst

22 *>ekkeloge hosteloloike ahilu khujka:rhi<* {S: o::}
together hostel-till came-1p step walk oh

→23 *xeTTUwe maa:ne*(.) *bohut uliyai dile a:ru@ °kiba kibi°*
that-emph means lot bring-out give-pst means something or other

'Little . . . means, I met (him) at the shopping complex and walked back together to the hostel. It was that which they brought it out in a big way . . . something or the other . . .'

24 S *>ta:r pisot tumi kenfrant nokorila a:ru<?*
that after you confront did not and

'And you did not confront them after that?'

→25 N: *ae*[19] *na:i kora aa:ru↑*, {S: *accha*} *>koi laa↑↓bh na:i tahatok ma:ne* <{S: *o::*}
edm. not do and okay say gain neg them means oh

26 *eNEKU↑↓waye taha:ti=*
like this-emph they

'Eeh! No, I did not – there is no point telling them. They are like that only.'

S: *=buisu*

'I understand.'

The abstract of N's narrative can be seen in the context cited before the narrative – she is talking about her peers who can gossip a lot and the orientation of the story begins when she tells about her late admission and about how she began attending classes only after the second round of admissions. Her delineation of her classmates as 'other' begins in line 5: her use of the word *taha::ti*[20] (they-classifier) who had already met up as classes had already started and become 'free amongst themselves' is pertinent because *it signals the distancing of the classmates as the 'other'* which becomes slowly apparent in her speech as her narrative progresses. Her repetition of *taha::ti* in line 6 and her speech in lines 6 and 7 underscore this linguistic distancing through her portrayal of the classmates as already friendly and familiar and quite free with each other even before she joins class and she, as the late comer, is alienated. Her orientation sets the stage for her narrative identity as the *marginalized self* – her narrative implicates how the classmates already treat her as the *outsider* in the group.[21] She crucially uses a discourse marker *tu* in line 5 (line marked with '→') to justify her classmates positioning vis-à-vis the story being recounted. N's speech through lines 7–11 where she tells about the boy classmate (with whom she had one day taken a stroll) is the 'complicating action' of her story and it immediately adopts a *defensive tone* signalled by her extensive use of the filler *maa:ne* ('means') in line 7 and fast speech >*edin ma::ne moi eta lora:r logot*< with which line 8 begins. Her use of *ma::ne* ('means') as many as fifteen times during the narrative suggests that she is using it as a filler to properly orchestrate her story so that it would earn her the sympathy of the listener[22] – it establishes her narrative identity as the victimized self who has had it rough because her peers are gossipmongers. Further, her use of animated speech in lines 10–11 (signalled by '@ …@') also serves to aggrandize her *incredulity* at the classmates' reaction to the sighting of her taking a walk with a boy: they had gossiped about it and 'let it out in a big way' (line 10–11).[23] Although she never mentions exactly *what* her classmates said about her in this stretch of her narrative, the fact that she repeats that was 'let out in a big way' many times over during the next few lines speaks of a sense of marginalizing by the classmates' gossip. This repetition of her phrase *bohu:t BESI uliyai dile ma:ne* (lines 10–11) 'they brought out too much (rumours)' is actually a euphemism for the kind of injurious effect that group's vicious gossiping had had on her.

Lines 12–14 are the evaluation and resolution of N's narrative and reveal the trauma she underwent on account of the vicious response of her classmates. Not only did the latter misrepresent the facts and spread rumours about her, they also totally ostracized and alienated her. She confesses in line 12 that she had suffered and was suffering till that day as a consequence of that gossip-mongering amongst her classmates. The sense of being isolated is conveyed in her words in line 13 where she says that her classmates had in fact stopped talking to her altogether. This 'silent treatment' and ignoring of her by her classmates not only constitutes her subjectivity but her silence in line 13 performs the marginalization regarding which I have noted:

> There is a double silence involved in N's narrative voice: one which *reports* the silence of the classmates via which the social ostracizing of N is accomplished and secondly, the silence of N herself about the details of the incident which performs and appropriates the damage done to her character as a 'consequence' of having taken a stroll with a boy classmate In this sense, *the marginalizing of the marginalized here is being accomplished within the speech of the marginalized herself.* (Barua 2016b: 58; italics in original)

What is important in the current context of understanding narrative identity as emergent in conversation and the impact of the self–other dynamics is the building up of the narrative in the turns by N and the author. To be honest, when I first examined the initial part of the narrative for analysing the marginalization and the power of social groups like the peer group to exclude, the turns of the speaker had excited me no end but I had not paid much attention to my own turns as a listener and co-participant of N's narrative. When I revisited this narrative for this book, the self–other dynamics that N and I are engaged in and our TCUs in the resolution and coda of the above narrative revealed stupendous examples of contingencies of selfhood and language. My earlier (Barua 2016b) analysis stopped at an examination of the *marginalization of the self* but it is evident that there *was resurrection of the narrating marginalized self* that is N and, surprisingly, I realize that this owes to a lot of my turns as her *listener*. When N first reveals that her being sighted with a male friend was 'brought out' (to mean to spread rumours about) 'in a big way' by her peers, S – the interviewer, listener and current author – crucially laughs (line 11). It is only when N continues to narrate and reports suffering a lot on account that the listener initiates a repair – evidence by the intonational changes in {S: *acca*↑↓::} in line 12, S realizes that her laughter was potentially damaging to the narrator's story and her own presented face[24] and hence the intonational change signals a change in orientation as a more *sympathetic* listener to N's ongoing story – the listener has to care for the speaker's narrative, bound as they are by social relations.[25] The trauma is driven home in the pause that N takes in line 13 after which she launches into the resolution of her narrative – her peers had stopped talking to her altogether. S's turn in line 15 is clarificatory when she asks if this was in class, to which N has a preferred adjacency pair of a confirmatory answer that it was indeed in class (line 16). S's next turn is a progressional onset of a different kind in that she categorically asks if it was brought out 'badly', to which N takes the floor to confirm that it was indeed brought out badly. The next TCU of S is where she asks if all this was only because of walking with a male classmate – N expands on the narrative orientation again; she gives specifics of where she had met the guy and till where they walked. And they, her peers, brought out '*kibakibi*'.[26] S's next turn in line 24 is again a progressional onset – when N is asked if she had not confronted them regarding this, she says (lines 25–26) that she did not as there was no point to it and they were 'like that only' – a point emphasized by her intonational changes in the word *eNEKU*↑↓*waye* (like this). This TCU of N gives her an opportunity to redeem her moral position – they are like this (gossipers) and hence there was no point in confronting them.[27] It restores to an extent her 'good' self and even though her narrative had been momentarily challenged by S's laughter in line 11, the social dynamics of the narrating self and narrated to other take precedence over other social relations – N was after all a student who was enrolled in one of the courses the author was teaching at the university.[28]

It was discussed in Barua (2012b)[29] that two things stand out in N's narrative above. First, her narrative never really explicitly states *what* exactly was spoken about her by her gossip-mongering peers. Although it is inferred from her narrative that her classmates had spread rumours about her going around with the boy/classmate with whom she had taken a stroll, the exact content of the rumours is sequestered. Even though she has trusted the interviewer, a teacher of one of the elective subjects, with her life story, the exact nature of the rumour is not let out by her – she uses euphemisms instead '*besi uliyai dile*' (they 'brought it out' too much). This perhaps is a *self-preserving principle* running through her narrative because to repeat the rumour would be tantamount to bringing upon herself the 'slur' of being someone's girlfriend, someone easy enough to be approached by boys, or some other identity that could be potentially damaging. Secondly, N's extensive use, as many as fifteen times, of *ma::ne* ('means') in her narrative above is extremely important; this is an example of a *ritual utterance* (Labov 1972). As noted in Barua (2016c: 204):

> Structurally, this is an example of a *ritual utterance* defined in Labov (1972, p. 380) as 'unexpressive utterances that do not contain any overt markers of emphasis' but play an evaluative role within a narrative. However, from a theoretical perspective of hedges,[30] the double instances of *ma::ne* in each of lines 2, 4 and 5 (marked with '→') . . . can be called *face-saving fillers.* (Italics in original)

Each instance of *maa:ne* in N's narrative serves to explicate her behaviour and her classmates' unjust reaction to her simple gesture of taking a walk with a (boy) classmate. The extenuating tone and the use of a phrase such as *<ene::i aru>* ('Just like that' in line 9 above) accompanying each instance of *ma:ne* in N's first few lines establish these as face-saving fillers. 'Face-saving' typically refers to a speaker's attempt to avoid having other people lose respect for one, as well as being 'the public self-image that every member wants to claim for himself' (Wardhaugh 2010: 292). N here wants to save her image in front of her teacher (current author) and lay the blame for her total isolation on her peers: she was unfairly 'held guilty' of going around with one of the only two boys in her class. Labov noted that intensifiers like expressive phonology, gestures, quantifiers, repetition and ritual utterances act as internal evaluative devices which select a narrative event in order to strengthen or intensify it (ibid.: 378–79). In N's case, her nervous use of *maa:ne* extensively marks the constitution of a fragile self in a fragile narrative space.

Nair says that our problem 'as researchers is to find observable correlates for the complex processes that we "know" must go on out of sight during and after the telling of a story' (Nair 2003: 15). As seen from the analysis of the narrative above, the minutest contours of language give evidence for cognitive assessment of the narrative situation – the narrator must be aware of the ongoing challenges of her identity that may emanate intentionally or otherwise from the listener, and in the course of her storytelling, she must undergo a resurrection of narrative identity where it becomes possible to be acknowledged as a self-affirming good individual in the context of the interlocution.[31] In the case of Life Story 1 reported above, contingent TCUs that could *not* have been predicted at the beginning of the narration both challenge as well as redeem narrative identity in terms of a moral self. As a framework that reveals the minutest of speech in the service of narrative analysis, Conversation Analysis thus provided observable correlates in the extract above for the complex processes that speakers and listeners of narratives 'know' are ongoing during the telling of the story. As such, the CA model proves a worthy micro ally in revealing macro issues of identity at intersections of the self, other, language and discourse. In the next chapter, we shall look at the implications of a gendered self and other in terms of the narrative structure; and in the following chapter, we shall look into strategies that narrators employ to protect their narrative identity through a discursive narrative device that I call the *ancillary narrative*.[32]

Notes

[1] 'Meaningful action is an object for science only under the condition of a kind of objectification which is equivalent to the fixation of discourse by writing' (Ricouer 1981a: 203).

[2] 'In the same way that a text is detached from its author, an action is detached from its agent and develops consequences of its own' (ibid.: 206).

[3] '[A] meaningful action is an action the importance of which goes "beyond" its relevance to its initial situation' (ibid.: 207; italics in original).

[4] '[T]he meaning of which is in suspense' (ibid.: 208).

[5] In our Story A in chapter 1, for example, the linearity of time is suspended till the end and the configurational dimension is achieved when the reader/film audience grasps (and gasps!) that the psychologist himself was also a ghost. In Story B, the time dimension is apparent even though the story progresses in the simple present tense. The configurational function occurs when the reader/film audience grasps that the friend, his nephew and the person who hired him for top secret work were all ghosts of his own mind – in other words, his hallucinations.

[6] You may recall we discussed this point earlier in chapter 1 – how in a sense we do not know so many aspects of our own lives, for example, those people or events involved just prior to our birth or even later that might have moulded our lives without us ever knowing about it.

[7] See discussion in first section of chapter 1, 'How and Why Do Humans tell Stories?'

[8] Grice (1991) postulated four other categories – quantity, quality, relation and manner – each having its own specific maxims and sub-maxims. Of these, the category of quantity dictates that the speaker's contribution should be as informative as is required for the current purpose of the exchange; the category of quality states that speaker should not utter what is false or for which there is no evidence; the category of relation dictates that one should be relevant; and the category of manner states that one should avoid obscurity and ambiguity, and be brief and orderly. Since narrating a story intra-conversation violates many of these categories and maxims, the narrator often has to 'manage' the narrative situation. Conversely, the listener's backchannels signify that they are 'okay' with the narrator violating these conversational maxims

[9] In the context of this work, a TCU can be seen as an entire narrative of interlocution (life story), as we shall see in the next section and subsequent two chapters.

[10] The rules of the game change when it comes to narratives of interlocution – so for any narrative that begins as a result of the listener or in this case current author/researcher type of questioning (for example, 'Do you remember a time when life was especially hard for you?' or 'Do you remember any particular fun time you had with friend?'), the narration may be more or less elicited. However, there may be narratives that emerge on account of other people's interventions in the situation of interlocution. In each type of context, the narrator will have to refashion a self based on the context of interlocution: the listeners at hand and in relation of the narrative positioning she/he wants. It is the use of language with a back calculation of all the presuppositions and possibilities that make the narrative being spoken a 'linguistic selfie' (Barua 2016a).

[11] The square bracket indicates beginning of overlap. See pp. xvii–xviii for transcription symbols.

[12] An example of an if/then construction: '*If* you invest in this scheme, *then* you can be assured that you will reap rich dividends later on and you can also re-invest your money at your own discretion at some later point in life.'

[13] The topics on which a speaker will narrate will show what issues hold salience for her in the context of her life and since 'hierarchy of salience of the identities held by an individual represents a unique characteristic of that individual, making him/her different from others' (Burke 2003: 3), a narrative will be representative of selfhood.

[14] See subsection titled 'Narrative Form' above.

[15] Strategies of maximizing long TCUs as noted in Kitzinger (2002; cited in last section)

[16] 'Narrative has the same psychological validity as the sentence. It is as central in cognitive processing. While the sentence is accepted, however, as perhaps the most significant of grammatical universals, the narrative has still to win its spurs as a discourse universal' (Nair 2003: 31).

[17] This extract is from a university student 'N' who was interviewed by the author while she was working at the Centre for Assamese Studies at Tezpur University in 2012. N was a young adult female of twenty and she had just joined her course that semester. She had signed up for an interdisciplinary elective course under the author and had volunteered to be part of a study that the author was engaged in at that time. N's life story reported here has been analysed in Barua (2016b) with part of the data cited here (up to line 14) included as Extract IA, Extract IB and Extract IC (ibid.: 54–55, 56, 57, respectively). Lines 7–14 of this extract are discussed in Barua 2016c: 202–03, for an analysis of N's filler *ma:ne*. Line 14 onwards is a continuation of the narrative being cited here for the first time, and has not been analysed in previous work. The current analysis focuses on N and the author as co-narrators, especially line 11 onwards, and this deepens the analysis of the self whose narrative presents her as marginalized by the other (as presented in the earlier work; see Barua 2016b).

[18] See pp. xvii–xviii for all the transcription symbols used in this work.

[19] There is no English equivalent for this expression. It can be interpreted as a discourse marker that encodes emotional responses for which we may need recourse to cultural knowledge for interpretation. At best these may be deemed 'emotive discourse markers'.

[20] *taha::ti* is a dialectic variation of *xihote* (they).

[21] Peer groups are very strong social groups in young adults and can impact one's identity through their inevitable in-group/out-group (see, for example, Gay 1992; Goodwin 2002; Pascarella and Terenzini 2005; Warrington and Younger 2011).

[22] The use of *maa:ne* as a filler in Assamese has been analysed in Barua (2016c).

[23] Her animated speech here marks the *incongruity* of the situation that makes for an appealing story in the sense of Thornborrow and Coates (2005; cited earlier).

[24] Way back in the 1950s, Erving Goffman defined a presented face 'as an image of self delineated in terms of approved social attributes' (Goffman 1955: 213). The

'presentation of self' means: 'How each individual ought to handle himself with respect to each of the others, so that he does not discredit his own tacit claim to good character or the tacit claim of the others that they are persons of social worth . . .' (Goffman 1981: 16).

25 A narrator's 'claims to identity, to a place within society, can result in mental death through a negative evaluation of her stories. In this respect, a kind of "care of the self" – its protection and projection as it is achieved through narrativization – becomes an important concern' (Nair 2003: 19).

26 Roughly, this translates to 'something or the other' – something indefinite.

27 This indicates a sort of second-order desire in N (Frankfurt 1971; cited earlier), in which she does not want to be identified as being alike with her peers

28 N's admission of this whole episode needs some elaboration here. As a student, it could not have been easy to confide in S regarding this life story since narrating an incident in which her peers gossiped about was potentially damaging – as a listener who was her teacher, I could form some opinion about her. That she narrates about this incident shows her as punching the boundaries of academic culture in which affairs between students are not usually reported to teachers – they fall in the realm of personal inter-relationships. N's narrative however has its advantages – due to contingencies of the situation of interlocution (starting with S's laughter which could have been damaging but turns out not to be so), N's narrative ultimately positions her on moral high ground in front of her teacher who was also the interviewer, the listener and ultimately the co-creator of *her narrative identity which ends up marginalizing the ones who had marginalized her in the first place* – 'they' are like that only and *she* was different from these gossip-mongers.

29 See Barua (2012a).

30 Hedges are linguistic elements that are 'parts of the system of epistemic modality in language; they add a judgment of truth or probability to referential information' (Crismore and Kopple 1990: 49). In the context of N's extensive hedging in the narrative above, hedging seems to enforce a certain cognitive assessment of the narrative situation in which any potential threat to her face is mitigated. 'The *mitigating* role that hedges play in conversation make them more than just chance fillers in conversations; their role in the epistemic modality of a person's communication strategies hints that hedges can actually be important cognitive devices that facilitate conversation in more ways than one' (Barua 2016c: 196). N's hedges here can thus be seen to facilitate the ongoing conversation with the teacher/author within which this narrative was being embedded.

31 'The effort and desire involved in communication *provoke a self that is new to oneself, specific to that encounter*' (Henriques *et al.* 1998, xvii; cited earlier; emphasis added).

32 '. . . the human self at an unnatural time, a time of crisis, responds by weaving extra self-protective shells of narrative' (Nair 2003: 17).

4

Let *Me* Tell *You* a Story

Self–Other Dynamics in Narratives

We started this exploration of selves and narratives by first delving into the question of who we are as a species and why we have the primordial propensity for storytelling, after which we took a philosophical detour to understand the concept of self, other and goodness around which our life stories get structured. We then undertook a more nuanced look at the concept of self and other from a gendered prism and it threw light on psychosocial aspects of gendered selves as well as gendered ethics, following which we tried to see in reasonable detail what the narrative actually is – what may be its forms, functions and plots to tell. We examined various formulations of the narrative structure and looked at some of the features of Conversation Analysis. We also analysed an extract with tenets of CA and it threw up startling insights into how an individual can project her identity in a narrative context and how others/listeners too contribute to the refashioning of the self in the situation of interlocution, and how the self-preserving principle may occur to actually sequester aspects of our life stories that may be too painful to recount. It is time now to examine more ways in which our selves actually manifest in our life stories narrated while in conversation with others. We live through our narratives, and the images we make of ourselves in our narratives are the ones that circulate in perpetuity. *So what kinds of images of ourselves can we discover in our narratives*, past and present? (Nair 2003: 17; emphasis added).

Life Story 2:[1] *'One by day and (at least) half by evening'*

Transcript Details:	[MNK A10057]
Participants:	M, his wife N, their three children the eldest of whom was studying in Class II and the current author
Language of Interaction:	Hindi
Narrative Context:	The interview has just begun with M and N following interaction of S with M and N's children who recite numbers and poems for her. M had an easy everyday familiarity with the author who was then a PhD researcher and he was employed at her hostel as a cleaning-staff member. He used to address her as 'Guruji' or 'Sir' affectionately – the terms having a significance in the narratives about to be cited here (see notes 2 and 11). The former's first line in his Turn Construction Unit (TCU) is in response to a request to tell something about where and how they got married.
Narrative Highlights:	M's narrative brushes aside the main question of how he got married and rather he showcases the good life he aspires which his job has ensured. His narrative identity surfaces through contrasting narrative pseudo-event regarding how he/they were raised by their own parents.

Extract B

1 S: *kuch::* *wo* *bata:iye* *bhaiyya*↑ *>matlab<*
something that say-hon brother means

2 *SHA:DI::* *kaha* *pe hui*↑ *kese*↑ *hui* *a:pki?*
wedding home loc happened how happened you-hon-gen

→3 M: *sha:di::*↑ *ghar* *pe* *hi* *hui* *thi,* ↑*gao* *me* *hi*↑ {S:*hm:*}
wedding home loc emph happen pst village loc emph

→4 *kyuki*↑ (.) *ghar* *me:::* *esa:* *kuc* *nahi* *hæ* *guruji,*[2]
because house loc like something neg pres ((M's TA for S))

5 *ke* *matlab*(.) *ye* *ho* *ke*
that means this happen that

((Three lines deleted. S asks for fan to be switched off as it is too noisy))

→9 M: *esa:* *kuc* *nei* *hæ* *hama:re* *yaha:* *ke*(.) *matlab* *larka:* *dekhe*↑
like something neg pres our here that means boy see

10 *ya* *larki* *dekhe*↑ {S:*ha:*} *jo* *ghar* *wale* *kar* *dete* *hæ*
or girl see yes what home pl do give pres

11 *wehi* °*wo*(.) *hota* *hæ*°=
that-emph that happen pres

'Wedding had happened at home only. . . . in my village. Because at home there is no such thing as that means . . . this happens that . . . Nothing like this happens at our place that one sees the boy or the girl. Whatever the family decides is that . . .'

→12 S: =*fiks* ?
fixed?

13 M: *fik*[*s*
fix

14 S: [*ha:*=
yes

15 N: =*jo* *ma:* *ba::p* *kar* *dete* *hæ* *wahi* [*hæ*
what mother father do give pres that-emph pres

'Whatever parents decide is it.'

16 M: [*bas*↑
only

17 *esa:* *kuc* *nahi* *hæ* *ki::* *ham* (.) *gaye*↑, *larki* *ko* *dek*↑↓*hke*
like something neg pres that we went girl dat see-cpm

18 *a::* *ga*↑↓*ye* {S:*hm::*} >*ya:* *larki* *dekhke* *a::* *gayi*< <*a:j*
came went or girl see-cpm come went-fem today

19 *kal* *jese* (.) *hota:* *hæ*> {S:*hmm*} *hame* *bhi*(.) *hama:re*
tomorrow like happen pres we-acc also our

→20 *udhar* *bhi* *ho* *raha:* *hæ:* *a:j* *kal* *esa:* *kuc*
there also happen prog pres today tomorrow like something

21 {S: *accha:*} '*dishtrikt* *me* *bhi* *or* *gao* *me* *bhi* {S:*ha:*}
okay district loc also and village loc also yes

→22 *esa* *kuc* *nahi* *hæ* {B:*papa*↑}= ((Here on the child keeps calling
like something neg pres M or talks with N in between))

'It's nothing like this that we went and saw the girl; or the girl went and saw like it is happening nowadays . . . at our place also something like this has been happening – at the district and also in my village. Nothing like that.'

→23 =*gao* *me* *sha:di* *hui*↑, {S:*ha::*} *gao* *se*
village loc wedding happened yes village from

24 *phir* *paresha↑↓:n* *hue↑* {S:*ha::*} >*ki* *bhei*< *kha:e* *kya↑:* *kama:ye*
then troubled were that brother eat1 what earn

25 *kya:↑* {S:*ha:*}*phir* *idhar* *a:ye* *di↑lli* {S:*ha::*} *tab* *esa:*
what yes then here came Delhi yes then like

'The wedding happened at my village, then I was troubled at the village – as to what to eat and what to earn: then I came here to Delhi. Then something like . . .'

→26 *kuc* {S: °*ha:*°} >*nokri* *kar* *rahe* *hæ* *ab*< {S: *accha:*}
something yes job do be-impf pres now okay

'Doing a job now.'

27 >*apna:* (.) *philha:l* *to* *yei* *soca:* *hæ:* *ki* *bacco* *ko* *likhao*
self now dm this-emph think pres that children dat write-2

28 *parhao* *acce se* *apna↑*< {S:*hm:*} *PHÆMILI* *KO*(.) *har* *sambhav*
educate-2 well with self family dat every possible

29 *matlab* '*sukh* *dekhna:* *ca:hte* *hæ:* {S: *ha:↓*} *ki* *bhei*
means happiness see wish pres yes that brother

'As of now what I have thought is that children should be educated well. The family should be able to experience happiness . . .'.

30 *har* *praya:s* *ye* *ho,* *ki* *phæmili* *sukhi* *rahe* {S: *ha:↑↓*} (.)
every effort this be that family happy be-impf yes

→31 *jese* *hama:re* *ma:* *ba::p* *ne* *hame* *jese* *bhi* *pa:la↑:*
like our mother father erg us like also brought-up

32 *hame* *pata:* *hæ↓:* {S: *hmm*} >*ki* *bhei*< *sube:* *kha* *liya*
we-dat know pres that brother morning eat take-cpm

33 *to* *sha:m* *ka* *pa↑↓ta:* *nei* {S:*hmm*} <*e:sa* *nei* *socte* *rehte*
then evening of know neg like neg think-impf be-impf

'Every effort should be so that the family stays happy. The way our parents have brought us up we know – that if we had food in the day then we don't know about the evening. We do not keep on thinking like that . . .'.

→34 *ham* *log*> >*ham* *YE* *SOCTE* *↑HÆ:*<*ki* *bhei*(.) *sham* *ko* (.)
we people we this think-impf pres that brother evening dat

35 *agar* *sube* *ek* *khayi* *hæ:* *to* *sham* *ko* *a:dhi* *to*
If morning one eat pres then evening dat half dm

36 *mile* *hi* {S: *ach(haha)ha*}
get emph okay

'We think that if we get to eat full in the day, then we should have at least half for the evening.' ((One line deleted))

38 M:	*is*	*cakkar*	*me*	*[hæ*
	this	circle	loc	pres

'We are striving for this.'
(Literally: 'We are in this circle.")

39 S:	*[wa:h*	*sahi*	*soce*	*hæ*	*hehe*
	wow!	right	thought 2	pres	

'Wow . . . that's well thought. Hehe!'

40 M:	*>is*	*cakkar*	*me*	*ham*	*thora*	*sa*	*hæ:↑↓<*	*ki*	*matlab*	*kya*	*hæ:*
	this	circle	loc	we	little	cl	pres	that	means	what	pres

' In this (circle) . . . we are a little . . . means'

M's first line in his TCU (line 3) above is part of an *adjacency pair* – he narrates the story in response to the author's request to say something about his marriage. It is also the *abstract* of his story – his wedding was solemnized at his home in his village. He continues with a rather elaborate orientation through lines 4–22 in which he gives the background information of the process of fixing weddings at his village – one where what the family decides is final. He even postposes the subject position in line 9, possibly marking the cultural set-up vis-à-vis arranged marriages at his native place. Significantly, although the author had asked him about his marriage – how it had happened and where – M's answer is a discourse on how marriages are solemnized at his native place, it is a matter in which parents fix everything.[5] His turn in lines 9–11 ends at a Transition Relevance Place (TRP) and S's turn in line 12 is a *progressional* onset where she offers 'fixed' as an alternative that M accepts in his next turn, thereby making it an other-initiated self-repair (S being the other and M the repair-accepting self). His use of *esa: kuc* ('something like this') in lines 4, 9 and even later in 17, 20 (where it is postposed to final position for dramatically highlighting the situation) and 22 is pertinent: the implication is that because the wedding is solemnized as per the family's wishes it takes place at home (line 4). His *esa: kuc* becomes a free-floating stock phrase (what Labov 1972: 380 calls a 'ritual utterance'), which he repeats in line 9 to maintain narrative continuity following the break (in lines 6–8 about the noisy fan) and also to highlight the subtle moral issue at hand – *the wedding is never by personal choice*. His wife N subsequently takes the floor at this TRP – since there is a slight break in the conversation, she uses it to take the floor and rephrases M's statement in line 15. This could be a way for 'duetting' with her husband in his narrative but M ignores it and assertively takes back the floor from her in his TCU in line

16 by launching into further elaboration of his orientation with longer TCU.

M's use of *bas* ('only') in line 16 is crucial: it can be interpreted as *support* for N's previous TCU as well as an indication for her to stop. M makes a self-initiated self-repair in line 19 where he uses *hama:re udhar* to indicate new trends at his native place of 'seeing' the prospective groom of a bride in advance. His village and the district have 'caught up' with the times but he had been married as per what his parents had fixed. He also uses '*ki bhei*' as another stock phrase in his TCU (lines 24, 29, 32), as possibly a discourse strategy for establishing familiarity. M repeats his abstract in line 23 to maintain the floor and his narrative continuity that it was at his village that he got married. His narrative then reaches the complicating action through lines 23–25 which have the three temporal sequences linked by 'then' (*phir*) constructions and ends with the evaluative *nokri karrahe hæ ab* in the second part of line 26 where he says that he is presently doing a job. This is a significant turn because M has given new direction to his narrative – the bad times that he faced after marriage in his village about which he hints in lines 23–24 are glossed over[6] – '*kha:e kya↑: kama:ye kya↑*' ('what to eat and what to earn' in line 25) – and he ends that TCU with the fact of his doing a job now.[7] Line 23 which comprises part of the narrative clause of the *complicating action* is open to interpretation; since M says he did not know what to earn and what to eat (lines 24–25), his use of *se* might imply that he was troubled by the village rather than in the village and as such it is the village that is responsible for his having to come to Delhi in search of better prospects (line 25). His evaluative statement *tab esa: kuc* occurs in line 25 and he extends it by saying he is now working. Lest his narrative be construed as not being too narration-worthy, he gives what Labov (1972: 371) calls an *external evaluation* for his narrative. He forwards new information in lines 27–30 about what he wants for his family and attributes it to the fact that he himself was not raised under the best of circumstances by his parents who sometimes could not afford to feed their children two square meals a day (lines 32–33). He reiterates that his own philosophy is unlike that of his parents and his lookout is that he ensures at least half a meal for his children in the evening if they have had a full meal in the day (lines 34–36). This explicit and extended resolution of his life story is a pseudo narrative in which he delineates (lines 31–33) how he/they had been brought up by his/their own parents.

M's TCU (lines 30–36) lays out his attempts at reaching for *a good life* where he can experience all happiness with his family by contrasting it with the way he/they were brought up in abject poverty when they had one square meal in the day but were uncertain of what they would get to eat in the evening.

His lines 30 to 36 are a potentially risky strategy; he gives a *negative view* of the way he was brought up, which does not portray an ideal upbringing since the parents were not good providers. However, through this negative portrayal of parenting that he had to face, he highlights *his/their* achievement as parents; he at least ensures half a meal for his children where his parents could provide none (lines 34–36). The subject position of line 33 is inverted and postposed to line 34 (*ham log*) as a *contrastive* feature to establish this positive aspect of his/their own parenting responsibilities. Line 34 also has a self-initiated self-repair – he starts by saying *sham ko* ('in the evening'); pauses and starts line 35 by saying *if in the day they have one (full meal), then in the evening they should have at least half.* The self-repair is successful as it elicits a backchannel from the author who says *accha* (okay) in line 36 while laughing at his candour indicated by *haha* within the word for 'okay'; she also takes the floor to compliment him on that thinking (line 39). M's evaluative lines 30–33 where he talks about how his parents raised him are also important from another perspective. These lines serve as a detour or a *narrative pseudo-event* (Labov 1972: 375), which enables him to project his narrative's resolution more forcefully in line 34 (see his use of the emphatic *ham YE SOCTE HÆ*). This strategy successfully establishes M as a master storyteller – one whose narrative identity is established as a successful individual and parent duo along with N who can provide at least half a meal to their children in the evening if not a full one.

Lines 30–33 are another external device that *suspends* the action in order to highlight the resolution of M's narrative; he thinks that he should be able to ensure at least one meal for his children. The juxtaposition of the negative clause which he attributes to his parents' thinking (line 33) with the positive clause in line 34 to their own thinking foregrounds the *moral issue* at hand: parenting is a responsible job and where his parents failed, he and his wife succeeded. His extended narrative ends with twin codas when he says in lines 38 and 40 that he is in this '*cakkar*' – meaning 'striving towards this end' – and this comprises his 'exit talk'. It smoothens the way 'from the story world to the embedding conversation' (Polanyi 1982: 164) and he initiates the discussion back to the conversational present (the interview situation). What is also important to perceive in Life Story 2 is that others contribute to M's narration – his wife N's TCU (in line 15) possibly supports and reiterates her husband's point regarding the sociocultural set-up in their village where whatever parents decide in matters of marriage is the ultimate decision one has to live with. The author's continuous backchannels (*hmm . . ., ha: . . .*) are also important since they signal to the narrator that she is interested in his life story. Her evaluation statement at the end of his narrative when he mentions that they strive for at least half a meal in the evening if they have had one in the day appreciates his thought and reiterates the value of his narrative. He thus performs his exit talk in line 40 to bring his listeners back to the conversational moment.

M's narrative above accomplishes many things. (1) It shifts focus from the specifics of his marriage to tell how he had an arranged marriage that was pre-decided by elders in the family (lines 3–11). (2) It provides background information about sociocultural aspects related to marriage where arranged marriages fixed by parents are the norm, even while it acknowledges the changes that have come over his society in recent times (lines 16–22). This strategy is an extension of the sociocultural imaginary since he tells his listener that things are changing in his village and his district. (3) It underscores the importance of a stable job that can sustain family life (lines 23–26) – he notes that he is doing a job now in line 26. (4) It projects his outlook for a 'good life' where he can educate his children and see all possible happiness (lines 27–30), and also to establish that their outlook of a good life is to not let their children go hungry: if they have had one meal in the day, there should be at least half a meal in the evening. (5) It manages to establish the importance of his narrative (avoids the 'So what?' question) as it draws a compliment from his listener. (6) It contrasts his life's perspective with that of his parents (lines 31–36), and thereby his narrative identity as a successful individual and parent is established.

In short, M's narrative as presented in Life Story 2 exemplifies all aspects of the Ricouerian 'good life' as manifested at four levels of praxis: (1) in standards of excellence, (2) in 'life plans', (3) in self-interpretation, (4) in the evaluation of a good life (Ricoeur 1992, discussed earlier). We end this chapter with two more narratives by M which encode his reflexive good life prominently. In this extensive narrative of M (running to nearly 150 lines of data in the transcript, lines 69 to 190 of the original transcript)[8] – following a question as to what he did right after coming to Delhi and before working at the hostel – M narrates about his first job at a 'biscuit factory' (lines 69–88). The extensive orientation of his narrative sees him reliving the days when he worked at the biscuit factory. This is followed by two major temporal sequences having multiple 'looped' narratives. The first involves a description of his stint as a sweeper at 'Stephen Hospital' where he used to earn more but had a difficult family life because of irregular working hours (lines 101–32). This section of the narrative also showcases N's 'duetting' with her husband in his life story. Using long TCUs to hold the narrative floor, M then narrates about his current job where he finds satisfaction because his duty hours as well as the people are good. This job also enhances his *self-esteem because others consider it a good job*. He winds up his long narrative in a coda by stating that, since he had a steady income as well as earned extra money by doing menial jobs for people, he really liked his current job. The different segments of his continuous narrative correspond to the three jobs: first at the 'biscuit factory' (where he saw 'good times'), second at a hospital (where his job did not give him a good family life), and finally at the current job of sweeper at a hostel (where he found stability and respectability in the company of 'good people').[9]

It is important to note that throughout these long narratives of M, his life is seen to be structured around his job – it points to the importance, and hence the *salience*[10] (Burke 2003), that he accords to his work which determines his lifestyle and life-chances. The reflexive good life becomes encoded in the metaphor of biscuits which he used to bring home from work – it was a time of plenty when the overflowing availability of biscuits became an indicator of 'the good life'.

Life Story 3: '*Biscuit Full of Life*'

Transcript Details:	[MNK A10327]
Participants:	Same as in Extract B (M, his wife N, their three children and the current author)
Language of Interaction:	Hindi
Narrative Context:	The interview with M and N continues from Extract B; S asks M in which year he came to Delhi and what he did before the current job at the hostel.
Narrative Highlights:	Showcases M's idea of the reflexive good life and N's duetting with her husband in his narrative

Extract C

69 M: *>usse pehle mæ codha so rupæ ki nokri karta tha:*
that before I-nom fourteen hundred rupees gen job did pst

→70 °sar °11↑< {S:*accha:*} *or YE LAGA LO mæ* *__itna__*↑ *>matlab< khush tha:*
sir okay and this add take I-nom so means happy pst

71 *usme*↑ {S:*ha:*} *>ye sæl mæ nehi karta tha<* (.) *biskit ka ek*
that-loc yes this sale loc neg did pst biscuit gen one

72 *wo tha*↑:= (.)
that pst

'Before that I did a job for fourteen hundred rupees, Sir. And take this that I was so happy there. I did not do sale. It was biscuit that . . .'.

73 N: =°*fækteri*°=
factory

74 S: =*fæktri?*=
factory

75 M: =*biskit ki fæktri thi, cota mota ek DISTRIBU- distribyutar*
biscuit gen factory pst small fat one distributor

76 *jisko kehte hæ*↑, {S:*accha*} >*wo*↑ *tha:*↓< (.) *uske pa:s ka::m karta*
rel pro say pres okay that pst there near work did

→77 *tha mæ co*↑↓*dha so rupæ me.* {S:*accha:*} (.)
pst I-nom fourteen hundred rupees in okay

'It was a biscuit factory – what you call a distributor. It was that – and I worked there for fourteen hundred rupees.'

→78 @*mæ sach me bata: raha: hu ki*↑ *wo din mujhe*↑ *guruji*↑
I-nom truth in say prog pres that those days I-dat TA

→79 >*kasam se sar*< *<u>itna:</u> ya::d a:te hæ*↑: {S:*hmm*}
swear with sir so remember come pres

80 *ki* (.) *codha so rupæ me <u>pac</u> so rupæ ghar*
that fourteen hundred rupees in five hundred rupees house

81 *ka kiraya: deke ham mia: bibi ITNE ACCHE SE DA:L*
of rent give-cpm we-nom husband wife so good with pulses

82 *roti khate the* {S:*hmm*} >*BARA: ACCHE SE*< {S:*ha:*}@
roti eat1 pst very good with yes

'I tell you truthfully, those days I remember so much that out of fourteen hundred, after paying rent of five hundred rupees we husband–wife would have our daily food so well – really well.'

83 *or A:J*↓ (.) *kama:*↑↓*te hæ: <u>ti:n</u> haza:r*↑ {S: *ha:*} *phir*
and today earn pres three thousand yes then

84 *bhi woi rona:*↓{S:*accha:*} *a:j pe*↑↓*se hi nei hæ*↑ {S:*accha:*}
too same crying okay today money emph neg pres okay

85 *kal a:*↑↓*ta: khatam ho ja:yega:*↑ {S: *ha:*} *parso ye*
tomorrow flour finish happen go-fut yes day-after this

86 *ho(hh) jayega:*↑ *sach me wo din itna ya:d a::te hæ, ki*
happen go-fut truth in those days so remember come pres that

→87 *jamke to <u>biskit</u> kha:te the* {S:*acch(ha)a:*} >*itne itne la::ta:*
full on dm biscuit eat pst okay so much so much bring

88 *tha: mæ ghar*< ((gestures))
pst I-nom home

'And today, I earn three thousand and yet it is the same sobbing (complaints) – today there is no money; tomorrow the flour will be over, day after something else will happen. Really, I miss those days so much – we used to eat biscuits to the brim. I used to bring this much home.'

((Lines 89–100 deleted; M is asked for specifications as to when he worked where.))

[MK A10441]

101 M: ↑*or*(.) ↑*or* *iske* *ba:d* *mæ* *stephan-a-apne* *hostel* *se* *pehle* *mæ*
and and this-gen after I-nom Stephen our hostel from before I-nom

102 *stephan* *hospita:l* *me* *pa:nc* *sa:l* (*mæ* *laga:* *tha*)
Stephen hospital loc five years I-nom join pst

'And . . . after this – before our hostel, I was engaged at Stephen Hospital for five years.'

((Two lines deleted; N asks child to take away refreshment bottles.))

→105 M: <*ca:r* *se* *sa:re* *ca:r* *haza:r* *rupæ* *mahine* *kama:ta:* *tha:*>↑,
four from half four thousand rupees monthly earn1 pst

106 {S:*accha:*} *ek* *rupæ* *jeb* *me* *nei* *bacta* *tha*↓: {S:*hmm*}
okay one rupee pocket loc neg spare pst

107 °*agli* *tankhwa:* *tak*° {S:*acca*} >*pata:* *nei* *kaha:* *cale* *ja:te* *the*↑<=
next salary till okay know neg where go go pst

'I used to earn between four and four and a half thousand – there would not be a single rupee in my pocket till the next salary – I never knew where they went.'

((Three lines deleted; S asks if it wasn't a better job since it paid more.))

113 M: (.) *ISSE* *ACCHI::?* *ki* *matlab* *ghar* *ka* *ye* *pata* *nei*
this-from good that means home gen this know neg

→114 *rehta:* *tha* *sar* *mæ* *ki* *kab* *a:ya*↑↓, {S:*ha:*} *or* *kab*
stay pst TA I-nom that when came yes and when

115 *gaya*↑: {S:*ha:*}=
went yes

'Better than this? I would never know "Sir" when I would come home or go (from home).'

→116 N: =>*yei* *PATA:* *hi* *nei* *hota* *tha* *ek* *ek* *hapta* *ho*
this know emph neg happen pst one one week happen

117 *ja:ta* *tha* *dyuti* *karte* *ghar* *pe* *hi* *nahi* *a:te* *the* *ye*↑<
went pst duty doing home loc emph neg come pst he

'It wasn't known – it would be one whole week while doing duty – he wouldn't even come home.'

118 S: *he*↑:::?=
Q into

'Is it?'

→119 N: =*WAHI pe dyuti karte rehte the*=
there loc duty do-inf stay pst

'He would be there only doing duty.'

120 M: =*esi nokri thi wo*
like job pst that

'It was such a job.'

((One line deleted.))

→122 N: *koi PHO:N nei koi kuc nei karte ye*=
some phone neg some something neg did he

'No phone calls – nothing he would do.'

((One line deleted))

→124 M: =*jab to PHON THA HI [NEI MERE PA:S*
then dm phone pst also neg I-gen near

'Then I didn't even have a phone'.

→125 N: *[pho:n bhi nei tha*
phone also neg pst

'There was no phone too.'

→126 M: *ek to PHO:N bhi itne m(h)enge the >ki bhei< le*
one dm phone also so costly were that brother take

127 *nei sakte th*↑*e*, {S: *ha:: ha::*} *ab to PHO:N itne [kam- saste*
neg can pst yes yes now dm phone so less cheap

128 *hæ to le sakte hæ*
pres then take can pres

'Then phones were also so expensive that one couldn't buy them. Now phones are so cheap that one can buy them'

129 N: *[ek ek hapte nei a:te the*=
one one week neg come pst

'He wouldn't come for one whole week.'

130 S: =*accha to pare<u>sh</u>a:ni hoti thi?*=
okay then trouble happen pst

'Okay – so that was troublesome.'

131 N:	*=ha:,*	*ek*	*haphte*	*dyuti*	*karni*	*hai*	*to*	*karni*	*hæ*	*ghar*	*pe*
	yes	one	week		do-inf	pres	then	do-inf	pres	home	loc
132	*nei*	*dekhna*	*hæ?*								
	neg	see-inf	pres								

'Yes – duty of one week had to be done then it had to be done. The children were not to be looked after?'

M's TCU starts with the abstract of his story in line 69, and his phrase *YE LAGA: LO* in loud speech in line 70 acts as a discourse marker to highlight the 'good life' that he is going to speak about (he had used a similar stock phrase *esa: kuc* in his earlier narrative to emphasize significant portions of his speech; see Extract B earlier in this chapter). M accepts the other-initiated self-repair in line 75 (both his wife N and the author S suggest the word 'factory' when M is unable to retrieve the word). He accepts the same and clarifies that it was more of 'a small distributor' than a factory. His emphasis on happiness with the new job (line 70) and nostalgia for bygone days (lines 78–79) perhaps have more to do with finally finding some stability and setting up an establishment rather than being able to live well in terms of monetary stability[12] – these lines of his narrative are marked by *affective pitch variations* indicated by '↑↓' in the transcript. Significantly, he keeps repeating how much he remembers the days (lines 78, 86) when he worked at the biscuit factory and emphasizes how good those days were (lines 81–82). He even repeats how much he earned (*codha: so rupæ* – 'fourteen hundred rupees') in line 77, probably to highlight that happiness had nothing to do with money – less money was enough to keep him and his family happy. As such *his idea of happiness and establishment gets symbolized in the image of 'biscuits' which he used to bring home* (lines 87–88) and eat in plenty. It takes on metaphoric implications of the 'good and carefree life'. This 'good life' is contrasted in the next segment of the narrative which has the complicating action in the temporal clause in line 101. Here M talks about his subsequent job at 'Stephen Hospital' where he earned more but was less happy. This extract also marks N's co-narration when she gives the embedded evaluations of M's narrative in her turns (lines 116–19, 122, 131–32).

M uses very marked structure in line 114 and fronts the subject position before the complement (*ki kab a:ya . . . or kab gaya*) to emphasize how troubled he was with that job's erratic timings. His turn is followed by N's co-narration above when she evaluates M's narrative in terms of the problems they faced because of erratic timings (N's TCU in lines 116–17, 119). It also leads to a potential difference of opinion – using a progressional onset she says in line 122 that he would not even call from work when it used to get late. To this, M points out in his next turn (line 124) that he did not own a phone at that time, to which N agrees (line 125). N's evaluative TCU also threatens his narrative floor, and he uses emphatic and loud speech to take back the floor and make his point (line 124). M quickly diffuses a possible counterpoint by adding that they could not afford a phone those days since they were expensive (lines 126–28). His TCU also serves as an indication of their changing lifestyle. The potential difference of opinion is converted by highlighting the economic situation and it leads N back to her original position that M would not come back home for a week at a stretch (line 129). Following S's turn in line 130, it gives her the lead to use a *comparator*[13] (a question) to launch another wave of evaluation through lines 131–32, and she asks retrospectively, if he had to work he had to work – was it not important for the children to be looked after?

Following another question by S when M is asked if he got his current job after that stint at Stephen, M answers in the affirmative and through lines 136–41 (not cited here) gives the actual dates when he did the jobs. He finally narrates about how he got his current job following a chance opening caused by the termination of service of someone who used to get drunk and come to work. In line 159 below, he mentions that the engineer's office removed him (without explaining why he was removed) – and his elaboration on why he likes the current job (lines 161–64) again prompts N's co-narration in line 173.

Life Story 4: *'Everyone Feels that He Has a Job'*

Transcript Details:	[MNK A10603]
Participants:	Same as Extracts B and C (M, his wife N, their three children and the current author)
Language of Interaction:	Hindi
Narrative Context:	In continuation to Extract C
Narrative Highlights:	Story strategy in which M gives looped stories one after the other; also showcases N's duetting; episodic and configurational dimensions of duetting; also showcases others' perception of his narrative identity

Extract D

145 M: *'agast do haza:r sa:t(.) ca:r me mæ dairek inji:nier ofis*
August two thousand seven four loc I-nom direct engineer office

146 *me a:ya, yuniversity me*↑ {S:*accha:*} *or INJI:NIER ofis se*
in came University loc okay and engineer office from

147 *mæne aplikæshen da:la: yaha*↓*:* {S:*acca:*}(-) *hostal me* {S:*ha:*}
I-erg application give here okay hostel loc yes

'In August 2007 . . . '04, I came to the engineers' office in the university and from the engineers' office I gave my application here – at (-) hostel.'

→148 *to yaha: jageh nikli thi ek larka: da:ru pi:ke ka:m*
dm here place come-out pst one boy alcohol drink-cpm work

149 *karta tha* >*ra:mti nei hæ apni?*< {S:*hmm hmm*} *jo æ blok me*
did pst Ramti neg pres our 1rel pro A block loc

150 *ka:m karte hæ*↑ {S:*ha:*} *unka larka: tha: wo da::ru*
work do pres yes her-hon-gen boy pst he alchohol

151 *pi:ke a:: ja:ta tha:* [*sha:m ko*
drink-cpm come go pst evening at

'So there was an opening here – one boy used to get drunk and come to work. You know our Ramti who works in A block? Her son would come drunk to work in the evening . . .'.

((Three lines deleted; S identifies person in question and M says it is indeed him.))

→155 M: *to unko wa:rden mæm ne nika:la*↑ {S:*achha*} *mæne itne me*
so he-hon-dat warden madam erg threw okay I-erg this in

156 *apni æplikæshan DA*↑↓*::L di* {S:*accha:*} *to us jagah pe*
self application throw give okay then that place loc

157 *phir mereko rakh liya*
then I-gen-dat keep take

'So Warden Ma'am threw him out and by this time I had given my application. Then I was appointed at that post'.

((One turn deleted.))

→159 M: *=to inji:nier ofis ne mujhe hata: dia:,* {S: *hmm*} *phir*
dm engineer office erg I-dat remove give then

→160 *mæ apna: 'idhar jam ga*↑↓*ya:* {S:*accha*} *ab* <u>*isko*</u> *chodne*
I-nom self here join went okay now this-dat leave-inf

161 *ka vica:r NEI banaya*↑*:* {S: *accha:*}>*ki bhei*< *kya: karna: hæ?,*
gen opinion neg made okay that brother what do pres

'So I was removed from engineers' office and then I joined here. Now I have thought not to leave this place – what else to do?'

→162 *kyuki acce log hæ*↑ {S: *hm:*} *accha*(.) *matlab*(.) *phæmili si*
because good people cop good means family like

→163 *rehte hæ apna*↑*:* {S: *hmm*} *sab* >*bha:i behen*< *ke usse*
stay pres self all brothet sister gen that-with

164 *rehte hæ* {S:*hm:*} *ishtudent bhi acche hæ or ba:ki sab log* (.)
stay pres student also good cop and other all people

'Because the people are good, they stay like family. Everyone stays like brothers and sisters. The students are also good and so are the other people…'

165 *afsar bhi acche hæ,* >*koi ye nahi ki ye tang karta:*
officer also good cop someone this neg that this trouble do

166 *hæ ki wo tang karta: hæ:*< (.) *dyuti bhi apni thi:k hæ*=
pres that s/he trouble do pres duty also self good pres

'The officers are also good. There is nothing like this person troubles or that one troubles. My duty is also good enough'.

((Six lines deleted: to a question by S as to which job M likes the best, the latter replies it is the current one at a hostel. N again takes up to co-narrating with M when she uses overlapping speech in line 173 to take the floor and explain why this job is better than others and M also duets by rephrasing N's TCU))

[MK A10707]

173 N: [*ghar pe a:na:, taim se ja:na: taim se a:na:*=
home loc go-inf time with go-inf time with come-inf

'To come home . . . go on time, come on time . . .'

174 M: =<*ja:[ne ka: bhi taim hæ*↑*, a:ne ka: bhi taim hæ*↑>
go-inf gen also time pres come gen also time pres

'There is a time for going, there is a time for coming . . .'.

175 N: [*bacco ko bhi dekhna*=
children dat also see-inf

'To look after the children too . . . '.

176 M: =*bacco ko bhi dekh sakte hæ,* {S: *ha:*} (.)
children dat also see can pres yes

→177 *or sabko ye lagta hæ ki* >*ha: bhei*< *nokri hæ*↑ {S: *ha::*}
and all-dat this feel pres that yes brother job pres yes

178 *or hame bhi ye lagta hæ ki nokri hæ*↑ {S:*ha::*}
and I-acc-hon also this feel pres that job pres yes

'And I can look after the children too. And everybody feels that "Yes – he's got a job". And I also feel that "Yes I have a job . . ."'

((Eight lines of M's turn deleted; he repeats the problems he faced at Stephen. It serves as a contrast to the lines above. He then continues his narrative with his evaluation in line 186.))

→186 M:	*to*	*is*	*kar*	*ke*	*yaha:*	*bohot*	*accha:*	*lagta:*	*hæ*	{S:*ha::*}
	so	this	do	cpm	here	very	good	feel	pres	yes

187	*ti:n*	*haza:r*	*rupe*	*mil*	*ja:te*	*hæ*	*mahine*	*me*	{S: *hmm*}
	three	thousand	rupees	get	go	pres	monthly	loc	

'So that is why it feels very nice here. I get three thousand rupees monthly . . .'.

→188	*or*	*idhar*	*udhar*	*ki*	*camca:giri*	*karke*	*so*	*paca:s*
	and	here	there	gen	servant-noz	do-cpm	hundred	fifty

189	*rupe*	*kama:*	*lete*	*hæ*	{S: *hmm:*}	(.)	*thik*
	rupees	earn	take	pres	yes		right

190	*apna*	*da:l*	*roti*	*nikal*	*ja:ta*	*hæ*	{S: *hm:*}
	self	lentils	chapati	come	go	pres	yes

'That is why I like it very much here. I get three thousand rupees at the end of the month and by working here and there, I earn hundred or fifty rupees – it takes care of our food'.

M's lines in his TCUs in lines 145–90 are crucial as they hinge on life opportunities and presentation of a good life as defined by others: he got a job at his then current place of work as one of his colleague's son who was temporarily engaged as cleaning staff used to come drunk to work. As that person was removed from the job, M got in. Line 160 in his TCU could have been a TRP since it ends with well-defined pitch variations ('↑↓') when he says with finality that he joined his current job. But following the author's backchannel in line 160, M continues to hold the floor and proffers new information that he has no intention of leaving the current job: lines 162–66 explain the reasons behind it – at the place of employment the people are good; they are like a family with filial bonding (*bhai behen* [brothers and sisters]); the resident students are good as are the officers; and nobody really troubles him and his duty hours are also okay. S then asks him where he liked it best till then and M says with a smile that it is at the hostel (these lines have been deleted in the extract above). N then takes the narrative floor unexpectedly in line 173 to state that M's current job ensures routine and he is able to look after the children too. However, this potential usurpation of narrative floor is thwarted as M uses emphatics in line 174 to reformulate N's evaluative turns and take back the narrative floor to further elaborate the self-esteem that others' recognition of his job gives to him (line 177): everybody feels that he indeed has a job and it makes them feel that way too. He uses emphatic speech in lines 177–78 (indicated by an underline) to reiterate that others' acknowledgement of his job also makes him/them feel he has a regular job where he needs to go on time. In the eight lines between 178 and 185 (not cited), he explains again that in the earlier (hospital) job, while he always knew what time he was supposed to report to work, there was no guarantee when he would return. In a highly idiosyncratic manner, he uses *is karke* (instead of *isliye*) in line 186 to wind up his long job-related narratives in which his social worth is highlighted: he gets a steady income of Rs 3,000 per month and by doing menial jobs for others he gets a few bucks extra. That he knows he has to work his way up the social ladder by doing menial jobs for others in a sycophantic way is underscored by M himself (line 188). He uses the term *camca:giri* to signify this extra income – *camca* is a Hindi word that can mean a servant or an ingratiating or obsequious person, one that curry favours his way into social existence. Here, his *camca:giri* is limited to financial gain through which he pockets some extra money. Still, the fact that he does this *camcagiri* at a place of social standing (a big hostel of a renowned university) where 'students are good, officers are good and all stay as if in a family', is enough to make him feel good (line 186) and for him to earn his livelihood (line 190).

The 'story strategy' (Kitzinger 2002: 69) that M uses in Extracts B, C and D is very important – not only does it ensure him long TCUs when he gets to continuously hold the narrative floor, it establishes his narrative identity as a gregarious, convivial and positive person whose verbose anecdotes and story-within-story strategy (looped narratives) pays off to prop up his narrative identity: he is the good parent who ensures at least half a meal in the evening too where his own parents could not (Extract B); he is the 'provider of plenty' who ensures that his family came first (Extract C); he is a good worker unlike the drunkard he replaced and he is a person of social standing whose workplace treats him like a member of an extended family because of which others also give him social recognition (Extract D). M's style of speech is indeed episodic while, significantly, N's TCUs give a configurational dimension to M's episodic narration about his various jobs (e.g., her lines 116–17, 122, 131–32, 173, 175 in Extracts C and D). N's interpretive aspects to her husband's narratives lend not just the evaluative components, but also crucially add to the narrative identity of her husband and, by extension, herself.[14]

Both M's and N's TCUs seem to emphasize the impact that the former's job has had on their life chances and lifestyles, and as such these point to the salience they accord to M's job in terms of their good life; the salience also underlines the importance they accord to family and children. Further, throughout these long narrative sequences of M, what stand out in a meta-theme of life chances and life plans are his notions of responsibility and commitment towards his family, his attempt to ensure their happiness and well-being, and to rise above his station in life (lines 23–36) – the *idem* aspect of his identity is revealed in the steady characteristics that define him (family man/provider), while the *ipse* aspect is showcased in his ability to move up the social ladder through ingratiation. The apparent ordinariness of his life and existential anxieties are averted through nostalgia for good bygone days (for example, in the metaphor of biscuits that symbolize a carefree and secure life in lines 87–88). Though he knows that money is important, he realizes that it cannot buy him peace, as is evident from his stint at 'Stephen Hospital' where he earned more than Rs 4,000 but the money never stayed with him; further, there was the additional problem of erratic timings that disturbed his family life (lines 101–32).

M is a 'smart' narrator using unique strategies such as juxtapositioning of two negative–positive sentences in his narratives to contrast elements within his narrative and keep the listener hooked, so to speak.[15] While the above narratives of M do establish the wish for the good life and the inherent morality in living it, the fact that N was seen to provide the configurational dimension to M's narrative about his job at various places makes one appreciate how they perform their coupledom and their marriage in their mutual concern for the children, the family and even M's job, which though crucial to their emancipation, was not worth it if it compromised family life. It leads us to also question if narratives may be indeed encode different orientations of men and women to their narratives. In the next chapter, let us look at a couple of narratives to examine the gendered aspect of narratives and also whether these can be attributed to cultural roles that women and men play in society.

Notes

[1] This extract is from an interview that this author has taken as part of her PhD research (Barua 2012a). At the time of the interview, M, then aged about twenty-six, had been engaged as a contractual sweeper in a hostel of the University of Delhi. He and his wife N belonged to a low socio-economic group (defined in the study as earning less than Rs 15,000 per month) and had migrated from Uttar Pradesh to Delhi. They had been married for ten years (possibly married before the legally prescribed age for marriage) and lived in a single room of a *basti* (low-income

community neighbourhood) in North Delhi. The couple had three young children, all of whom were present at the time of the interview. They spoke Hindi, but when interacting with extended family members, they said they spoke Gamaru. At the time of the interview, M had explained to the current author that Gamaru was a language variety spoken in their native village. However, recent interactions of the current author with native speakers of varieties of Hindi such as Maithili, Bhojpuri, Magahi and Angika have revealed interesting insights. According to some speakers, Gamaru is possibly a variant of '*ganvaru*' which means 'rustic' or 'villager' (the English equivalent could be 'joskin' or 'bumpkin'). It means 'the native's tongue' – possibly an endogamous reference to a language variety spoke in a particular area or by a local community. According to one speaker, all languages and people from Bihar are alluded to as 'Gamaru' to imply the native connection. The Rekhta Dictionary gives the meaning of '*ga.nvaaruu*' as 'rustic (taste or fashion), the villager' with extended ascriptions as 'clownish, boorish, rude, rough'. The feminine equivalent is listed as '*ga.nvaari*', 'rustic woman, village belle, feminine of *ga.nvaar*'. The associated linguistic feature is described as 'rustic language or speech, provincial brogue or *ganvaariboli*'. Sources: for '*ga.nvaaruu*': https://www.rekhtadictionary.com/meaning-of-ganvaaruu?keyword=ganvaru; for '*ga.nvaari*': (https://www.rekhtadictionary.com/meaning-of-ganvaarii?keyword=ganvaru), accessed 18 September 2022. I am particularly thankful to Professor Rajesh Kumar, Dr Om Prakash, Dr Vibha Pandey, Santosh Kumar Choudhury, Abhishek Singh, M. Pandey and Punit Mishra for their insightful comments and discussions on the etymology and implication of the term 'Gamaru'.

2 M used to address her as 'Guruji' or 'Sir' affectionately, the terms having a significance in the narrative cited here – since he uses the term Guruji (*ji* being the deference marker in Hindi) at the beginning of his story, it establishes his familiarity with the author. It is significant that if M was to meet the author today and narrate his life story after so many years, he would narrate it differently and I, as his listener, would possibly react to it differently. Thus narrative identities are fluid, hinging precariously on memory, language, self and other.

3 English words that are uttered as code-mixed with Hindi have been transcribed phonetically; where code-switching occurs, the English spellings have been retained and transcribed accordingly.

4 A non-literal reading of this line would be, 'This is what we are striving for.'

5 Recall the Foucauldian position that 'the subject is constituted through practices of subjection . . . on the basis, of course, of a number of rules, styles, inventions to be *found in the cultural environment*' (Foucault interview in Kritzman 1988: 50, cited earlier; emphasis added).

6 The fact that he was troubled by poverty in the village falls short of being explicit. He thus *sequesters* this phase of his story.

7 M had left his village and migrated to Delhi in search of better livelihood prospects.

8 Since the narratives in Extracts C and D occur just after the above narrative in Extract B and are in continuation to M's discourse about his various jobs, the original transcript line numbers are retained in Extracts C and D to give the reader an idea of where the narratives occur. In the case where multiple extracts from the

same individual/s or interview have been cited, the original transcript numbers have been retained in this work so as to give the reader an idea of when the particular narrative has occurred in the conversation. For an average transcript of about 1,000 lines, if the lines are numbered 69–132 as in M's Extract C here, then the narrative occurs early on in the interview. I's narrative (Life Story 9 of this book) occurs very late in the original transcript lines but since there is no other narrative by that speaker from that interview in this book, the original transcript number has been done away with for that particular life story.

[9] Of these looped narratives, the life stories in the biscuit factory and 'Stephen Hospital' are given in Extract C, and the one with his then current job at the women's hostel where he found stability is given in Extract D.

[10] 'The hierarchy of salience of the identities held by an individual *represents a unique characteristic of that individual, making him/her different from others*' (Burke 2003: 3, cited earlier; emphasis added).

[11] It has been mentioned earlier (see note 2 above) that M often refers to the author as 'Sir' or 'Guruji'. His explicit addressing of the author in his narrative is significant – although he is aware of the conversational present in which he was talking to me, his consistent use of these special terms of address in lines 70, 78 and 79 enable him to hold his positive face of interaction. At the same time it invites the listener to join in the story world he is leading into – one where he was so happy with the lots and lots of biscuits he used to bring home and he and his wife used to feast on. Further, that he bypasses gender considerations in his choice of lexicon is important. M consistently prefers the masculine term 'Sir' over the feminine equivalent 'Madam' for the current author, which hints at a socio-cultural implication: his social superiors are often male.

[12] Recall that in his earlier narrative (Extract B), he has already spoken of how he was troubled at/by his village and finally came to Delhi in search of better prospects

[13] For Labov, comparators include 'negatives, futures, modals, quasi modals, questions, imperatives, or-clauses, superlatives and comparatives more or less in increasing order of syntactic complexity. . . . A comparator moves away from the line of narrative events to consider unrealized possibilities' (Labov 1972: 387). It is a clause-internal evaluative device.

[14] In Nair's words, 'Since we cannot, in fact, ever manage to produce any narrative, simple or complex, entirely on our own, it follows that "care" of narrative "selves" should be a shared onus' (Nair 2003: 22).

[15] For example, M uses this strategy in Extract B also (lines 31–36) when he compares his parents' outlook with his own; they could not provide him two square meals a day whereas he would provide at least half a meal for the children if they had had a full meal in the day. This strategy is similar to what Kitzinger (2002: 69) calls 'if/then' constructions that accomplish long TCUs. In 'if/then' constructions, the sentence structures are hearably not complete unless the 'then' part is uttered. In M's juxtaposition of the 'negative/positive' clauses also, the negative part is not hearably complete until the positive counterpart is spoken. Such strategies also partly explain M's high quantitative dominance in his storytelling.

5

How *She* Defines *Me*

Gendered Self and Narrative

We saw in our discussions earlier in this book that narratives can have a sociocultural aspect as well as a performative aspect; they can establish social/generational identities (Thornborrow and Coates 2005; Armbruster and Meinhof 2005; Bruner 1990, 1991) or gendered identities (Coupland, Garrett and Williams 2005; Coates 2005), and can act as cultural texts (McAdams 2005). In this section, we discuss two such extracts that reflect sociocultural realities as well as establish gendered identities. Of these, the first extract exhibits characteristics of 'duetting' or co-narration not only in the sense of Coates (2005) but also in terms of the narrative form. In the extract below, D and J, an elderly couple the author interviewed for her PhD (Barua 2012a), reiterate/rephrase each other's turns, complete each other's turns at relevant TRPs and even consult each other to confirm facts such as dates, etc. These linguistic strategies become powerful tools whereby they 'do' or perform their 'coupledom' in public, and are features of what Coates (2005) calls 'collaborative narration'. The way they share the floor in this co-narration symbolizes the connection between these two people as husband and wife.

Life Story 5:[1] *'There Are Good Days and Bad Days . . .'*

Transcript Details:	[JDS B1 0054]
Participants:	J, D and the author
Language of Interaction:	Hindi
Narrative Context:	J and D's interview has been on for over thirty minutes.

	Asked to talk about a time/an incident when they found strength in each other, it is J who takes the floor – though the question was directed to both – and starts his TCU in line 656 with a latched utterance
Narrative Highlights:	Showcases extreme duetting in narrative form; salience within narrative and gendered identity; cultural notions of goodness

Extract E

656 J: *=>nei< wo shtrent to esa: hæ::↑* {S: *ha:*} *din bure bhi aye:*
neg that strength dm like pres yes days bad also come-pst

→657 *hæ*{S: *ha:*} *ab ye* (.) *waif ne*↑*:: phir ye wo ye sa-a:pna: do-'do:r*
pres yes now this wife erg also this that this self door

658 *tu dor*(.) {S: *hmm:*} *wo SE:L perce:j ka: bhi kara: tha:*
to door yes that sale purchase gen also do pst

'No – for strength . . . it is like this. Bad days had also come. Now this . . . wife had also done door-to-door sale purchase.'

((One line deleted: S asks when this happened.))

660 D:: *ye?=*
this

661 J: *=ye sa:l raha: sa:l bhar=*
this year prog year full

'This was for a year.'

662 D: *=derh do sa:l=*
one and half two years

663 J: *=derh do sa:l=*
one and half two years

((One line deleted; S asks to specify the year.))

665 D: *ye::? e:tisev- >maka::n e:ti for me ba[na: hæ?<*
this eighty sev- house eighty four loc make pres

'This? '87 – The house was made in '87?'

666 J: *[nainti=*
ninety

667 D: *=NEI NEI nice ka↓: >tab(.) tab mæ karti thi <dor tu*
neg neg below gen then then I-nom do-fem pst door to

668 *dor ka↑:?*
door gen

‘No – the one below. That is when I did door-to-door.’

669 (0.6)

670 J: *ha: e:ti for=*
yes eighty four

671 D: *=ha: e:ti for* (.) *ha: e:ti for* {S:*hm*} *ei:ti fo:r me*
yes eighty four yes eighty four eighty four loc

‘Yes. In ’84. Yes – in ’84.’

((1 line deleted.))

→673 J: *ha:: tab ga:riyo gurio ka: khatam ho ga:ya tha: e:ti for::*
yes then cars ec gen finish happen go pst eighty four

→674 *e:ti sevan <e:ti sevan> me toga:rio gurio ka: ka:m <u>khatam</u>*
eighty seven eighty seven loc dm car-pl ec gen work end

675 *ho gaya: Tha=:* {S: *hm:*}
happen go-pst pst

‘Yes – by then in ’84, in ’87, the car business had ended.’

676 D: *=tab tha↑:*
then pst

‘It was then . . .’

→677 J: *GA:RIYA: THI↑↓ kaba:riyo kuboriyo ko beci: phir*(.){S: *hm*}
car-pl pst scrap-dealer ec acc sell then

→678 *wo ka:m manda: ho gaya: tha:* {S: *ha:*} *>phir co:t put*
that work ruin happen go-pst yes then wound ec

679 *lag gayi↑↓<* {S:*ha:*} *phir Uske ba:d* (0.2)
join go-pst yes then that-gen after

‘The cars were there but I had to sell them off to scrap dealers. That business was ruined. Then I got hurt and then after that . . . ’.

680 S: *tab matlab*(.) *problem ho gaya:?=*
then means problem happen go-pst

681 J: *ha: problem phir ga:riya:* (-) {S: *ha:*} [*maka:n bana: diya*
yes problem then car-pl yes building make give

‘Yes. Problem. Then the cars . . . I built the house.’

→682 D: [*bacce us ta:im to* (.) {S: (-)}
children that time dm

→683 *bacco ko parha:na tha >cote the*↑ *bohot cote the*↑< {S:*ha::*}
children dat educate had small pst very small was

→684 *baccelogo ko PARHA:YA likaha:ya phir*(.) *me-meri beti*↑.
children-pl acc educate write-caus then I-gen daughter

'The children had to be educated: they were young very young at that time. We educated the children. My daughter . . .'.

685 *>jo bic wali hæ na:*↑< {S:*ha:ji*} *usne*↑*:: a:t- >a::thwi me*
rel.pro middle noz cop dm yes-DM she(erg) Eight in

686 *parhti thi wo blaind ko tyushen:: deti thi*< {S:*acca:*}
study past she/nom blind dat. tuition give past okay

'(My daughter) – the middle one – was in the eighth standard when she used to give tuitions to the blind.'

687 *or:: usne twe:lft ke ba::d phir usne steno kia*↑, {S:*hm:*} *steno bhi*
and she(erg) twelfth of after then she steno did steno also

688 *karti thi sa:th me tyushen parhati thi >serswati viha:r< ja::karke*
did past with loc tuition teach pst Saraswati Vihar go-do-cpm

'Then, after her twelfth, she did a course in stenography while also giving tuitions at Saraswati Vihar.'

689 S: *acc*↑*ha:* °*ba::pre*°
okay my god

→690 J: *'M.henat kari usne* {S: *ha:*} °*us lerki ne*° {S: *acca:*}
hard work did she(erg) yes that girl erg okay

'That girl has worked hard.'

→691 D: *=phir uske ba::d usne job kari* {S:*ha:*} *phir uski p- sha:di*
then that after she(erg) job did then s/he gen marriage

692 *bho:t jeldi ho gayi thi* > ° *wo jeb twe:nti yers ki thi*↑
very early happen go-pst she when twenty years of pst

693 *uski sha:di ho gayi*< ° =
her marriage happen go pst

'Then, after that, she did (a) job and then she was married very early when she was twenty years old.'

((3 lines deleted: S confirms if it is the eldest daughter or the middle one that they are talking about.))

697 D: *ha: bic wa:li phir usne ba:d me si bi a:i me servis ki* (.)
yes middle noz then she/he(erg) later in C B I in service did

698 {S: *ha:*} *phir uskA: bacca hua* (-) (-)
yes then s/he-gen child happened

'Yes – the middle . . . one. Then later on she worked at CBI and then she had a baby.'

→699 D: *wo bohot mehnati* (*hæ*) *bohot mehnati hæ:*
very hardworking pres very hardworking pres

'She is very hard working.'

((S's turn deleted in which she says that this seems as if she has done something with her life.))

701 J: =>*DUKH sukh to a:dmi ka: ata: hi hæ zindegi me*↑*wo koi* (.)
sorrow happiness dm man gen come emph pres life loc that some

→702 *a:dmi ka: hæ<a::j mere pa::s maka::n: hæ ye he wo hæ<*
man gen pres today I-gen near building pres this pres that pres

703 *>kal ka: to <u>pata:</u> hi nahi insa:n ka:< kya: hona: kya: hæ*
tomorrow gen dm know emph neg human gen what happen what pres

'Sorrow and happiness keep coming to man in life. Some man may say, "Today I have buildings . . . this and that but people do not know what might happen tomorrow".'

J starts his TCU in line 656 above with a preface, *nei: wo shtrent to esa: hæ* ('No, about strength it is like this') – it sets the stage for his abstract in the same line, *din bure bhi: a:ye* ('Days that were bad had also come'). Significantly, he does not use D's name or an honorific pronominal like *inhone* (she/he) in line 657 – he uses the common noun *wa:if* ('wife') while explaining that D had done door-to-door sale–purchase. He uses *ye* ('this') in line 357 followed by twin pauses '(.)' in lines 357 and 358, which helps him initiate 'self-repairs' to reorient his sentence. Following a question as to when this happened, D and J through lines 660–71 exhibit features of 'duetting' (Coates 2005). Recall from our discussion earlier that the key features of *collaborative talk* are that it involves (1) two narrators making contributions to the story which join together seamlessly (latched utterances marked with '=' which indicate that turns follow each other seamlessly); (2) frequent repetition; (3) frequent rephrasing of each other's ideas using different words; (4) shared construction of utterances; and (5) frequent backchannel support to signal acceptance of the other's speech (Coates 2005: 91–92). D and J use a number of *latched utterances* (note the lines marked by '='), *overlapping speech* (marked by '['), *repetitions* and *rephrasing*, and even *consult each other* (lines 665–71) as to the year when D had done door-to-door sale and purchase to support the family in bad times (lines 667–68). J's use of *echo words* are also highly idiosyncratic; instead of the usual /w/ sound that occur at the beginning of echo words in Hindi, he uses echo words highly idiosyncratically with a reduplicated sound of the first consonantal sound of the preceding word: for example, *ga:riyo guriyo* (lines 673, 674), *kabariyo kuboriyo* (line 677), or his own formulation like *cot put* (line 678).

Following the 'duetting' in which they 'perform' their coupledom J takes the floor, and in lines 673–81, he narrates about how after his transport business had failed, he had to sell off his commercial vehicles to scrap dealers and then got badly injured.[2] Significantly, there is no detailing as to how J got injured and the pause (0.2) in line 679 of his narrative clause *probably indicates a discomfort at the remembrance of the difficult time.* S's turn in line 680 serves as a potential evaluation for J's narrative on hard times and shows that as a listener/interviewer, she felt a need to sympathize with the narrator for a positive face. Just as J begins to resume his narrative with another temporal clause in line 681 D takes the floor from him with a possible *progressional onset* and starts her own narrative about the children – how they were very young at that time and were yet to be educated. It must be noted that D's use of overlapping speech in line 682 below to take the floor from J, who also had started to speak about making the house in line 681, is not at a TRP given that J has resumed his narrative. It is an interruption, but it is also an independent narrative that serves as an added evaluation of J's narrative on hard times. Following Labov, we call this 'waves of evaluation' that penetrate and are distributed throughout the narrative structure without being confined to one clause (Labov 1972: 369).

D's turn about the upbringing of their three daughters in her long TCU of seven lines between 682 and 688 is in itself a narrative, but, as noted above, it adds an evaluative dimension to J's preceding narrative on hard times. Following S's turn in line 689, J takes the floor in line 690 and this time it is he who gives the evaluation of his wife's narrative; she is talking about their hardworking daughter. This evaluation not only shows J's attempt at 'duetting' (joint storytelling) with his partner but, at another level, can be seen as J's attempt to reiterate the importance of his wife's narrative thereby avoiding the 'So what?' situation which can cause the failure of a narrative. Crucially, his evaluation comes after an expressive backchannel by the author in line 689 (*ba::pre*).[3] This joint telling of a story is definitely a feature of collaborative talk as noted in Coates (2005) and others but the two important dimensions that are added here in terms of co-narration are that: (1) partners may share aspects of the narrative form – here, one partner provides the evaluation of the other's narrative (for example, J evaluates D's narrative with his turn in line 690); (2) the 'waves of evaluation' may happen through ensconced narratives – D's narrative about their children's upbringing with reference specially to the middle daughter serves to aggrandize the evaluative component of J's narrative. D continues with two temporal sequences using *phir* ('then') in lines 691–92 where she talks about her daughter's job and subsequent wedding. It is crucial to note at this point that D uses the first person singular genitive pronominal *meri* in line 684 while identifying which daughter she is talking about – she does not use *hama:ri* ('our'), almost as if in recognition of the fact that the upbringing of her three daughters was *her* (the mother's) responsibility. Another interpretation of this stretch is that because her husband had been disabled following his accident, the burden was on her to educate her daughters: *bacce logo ko parha:ya: likha:ya*: ('I educated the children'). Her burden is also shared by her daughters – the middle daughter started giving tuitions when she was very young (in class 8). In all, D uses the temporal word *phir* ('then') at least five times between lines 687 and 698 to hold the narrative floor, and in line 699 she rephrases her husband's evaluative line (line 690) about their hardworking daughter with her own evaluation following the narrative clauses with *phir* ('then') in lines 691–98. Finally, following a turn by S when she appreciates their efforts, it is J who utters a TCU which serves as the coda for his wife's narrative on their daughter's upbringing as well as his own narrative earlier on tough times when his wife did door-to-door sale and purchase.

Lines 701–03 are J's generalization on 'life' and acts as what Jefferson (1978) calls 'exit talk'. It is very important to note that even in his exit talk J mentions the importance of having house/property even though he talks about these in relation to the uncertainty that life brings (see note 1 regarding the uncertainties this couple faced owing to J's compromised health on account of his accidents). D continues these with reiterative lines that they have truly worked hard and seen money in their lives.[4] D's embedded evaluative narratives regarding the education of her daughters and how hard they, particularly the middle one, worked follow J's narration about the tough times the family faced functions as a form of 'duetting'. The features of co-narration, viz. latched utterances, repetition, overlapping speech, joint construction of sentences, consultation (Coates 2005), are all exemplified through lines 660–71 above. The joint narration in this case also happens via sharing of features of narrative form – J in line 690 evaluates D's narrative who repeats the former's evaluation in her TCU in line 699. Finally, J winds up their co-narratives with his coda on the unpredictability of times (lines 701–03).

However, apart from this *performative* aspect of coupledom, the narrative extract performs other important functions; though the initial narrative of J emphasizes D's role in the hard times they faced, the latter gives a more *positive* face to the narration. She emphasizes how the children, especially the middle daughter, made the most of the circumstances through her hard work and emerged as a successful person who not only studied and did jobs, but also retained 'core Indian values' by giving tuitions to 'the blind' (implying that she was helping those in need when she was just a young girl in class 8; lines 685–86), getting married at a young age and having a baby. As we saw earlier in our discussion on narrative form (see the second section of chapter 3 titled 'The Narrative: Form, Function and Plots'), the 'narrative form is inevitably shaped by the social context in which it occurs and . . . narrativity as a discursive mode is at the core of our social and institutional world' (Thornborrow and Coates 2005: 7). In that chapter, we also discussed Blum-Kulka's (2005) distinction between 'tale', 'teller' and 'telling', wherein the tale delimits the story itself (the narrative sequence of events), the teller is the narrator, and the telling specifies the context within which the story is told. In the extract cited above, D's 'tale' is about their daughter and delimits how she had worked very hard, was very studious and industrious; the tellers in this case are the proud parents who acknowledge the fact that their daughter has worked hard in life (*mehnat kari hai*), and the telling specifies not only the context of the narration wherein the married couple 'performs' their heterosexuality through joint narration but also positions them as successful parents. Following Winslade (2003) and Monk (2005), their 'position calling' (especially of D since she uses the first person singular pronoun in line 684) is that of proud and successful parents who have inculcated traditional values in their children. Here D's delineation of their good life is consistent with the conscientious upbringing of the daughter who gave tuitions to the blind, and D and J's joint narrative functions not only to establish their social identity as husband–wife who exhibit their togetherness through co-narration but also reflects the cultural values of Indian middle-class parents. In this sense, this narrative also becomes what McAdams calls a 'cultural text' (McAdams 2005: 127) and fulfils the functions of the narrative as (1) social identity, (2) performance in discourse and (3)cultural identity (Thornborrow and Coates 2005: 7). In this context we can also cite Bonn and Tafarodi who noted that 'the tendency for South Asians to define a good life in spiritual, moral and beneficient terms . . . is consistent with scholarly characterizations of Indian culture as essentially spiritual and tolerant of diversity (Palkivala 2002; Vyas 1992)' (Bonn and Tafarodi 2014: 744).

In the last few extracts of this chapter let us examine more narrative structures which establish social norms in tune with the 'cultural imaginary' as theorized by Mackenzie ([2000] 2005). If, as Bruner (1990, 1991) contends, the narrative holds a key position in a social and cultural world, how gendered roles are played out and hegemonic patriarchy performed in narrative structure will showcase another functional aspect of the narrative. The extract of U below shows how these concepts of the performance of gender come into play, and how hegemonic patriarchy finds expression within the contours of the storyline as defined by the culture within which it is spoken; in the Indian sociocultural scenario, it is surmised that it is the woman who heeds the handed down advice of her mother to be a dutiful and faithful wife who is deemed 'good'. The life events in U's narrative (Life Story 7) can be interpreted as 'My mother's life. My (subsequent and consequent) life.' What precedes U's positioning of herself as the good wife is however another stretch of conversation in which her husband R is stating what is good in his wife. The final extract of this chapter is another narrative extract by M – whose narratives were featured in the last chapter and who was also present when the author interviewed his sister U and his brother-in-law R. M's earlier narratives in chapter 4 helped us understand how the issue of life plans and the 'good life' structure life plans and figure in the narratives of couples in conversation in the process defining their selfhood, while his narrative cited in this chapter helps us understand received notions of gendered identity.

The final three extracts in this chapter by these three relatives (R, his wife U and her brother M) on two separate occasions help to turn our attention to the idea of goodness itself: how *received* ideas of goodness from the cultural imaginary (re-)define notions of selfhood and identity. If, following Taylor, 'We have a sense of who we are through our sense of where we stand to the good', goodness and selfhood are inextricably related (Taylor 1989: 105). In quite a few stretches of narratives within conversation, the idea of happiness is linked to stereotypically *gendered* notions of goodness – for instance, U's narrative cited below in Extract G shows how received notions of goodness function not only as yardsticks of identity but also become the basis for happy life. For U in this narrative, her good life was ensured because she appropriated her mother's ideals of a compliant and loyal wife. Her narrative exhibited ways in which *cultural notions of gender identity* come to have a bearing on, and influence, individual identity. The implication of the half/full *chapati* metaphor is that no matter what the circumstances are, a 'good wife' in U's sociocultural milieu is defined by her ability to cope with her husband, be compliant and feel happy with him. Startlingly, her sister-in-law N's evaluative lines to her husband M (U's brother) cited in Extract H below reflect and invoke the same kind of sociocultural dictates of the uncomplaining good wife who ensures a good and happy life. Again startlingly, there is also a subtle emphasis on *fidelity* in both U's narrative (Life Story 7) – when she reports her mother as advising her daughter that she must not look towards another man or covet for better things in life which can be provided by another man – and in N's lines in her husband's narrative (Life Story 8).

We begin with looking at the preceding context of conversation: as mentioned above, what is pertinent is that U's narrative cited in Extract G follows a stretch of conversation where her husband R speaks of goodness (Extract F below). Asked to speak of an occasion when his wife provided him support, R does not respond with any particular incident, unlike J (in Life Story 5 cited in Extract E) who said that D did door-to-door selling in tough times to support him. However, R expresses in extremely general terms that U supported him *by doing whatever he asked her to do* (lines 622–26 in Extract F below). He even attributes his success in life to this supporting nature of U. On her part, when asked of a good quality in her husband, U responds by saying that she had a good life with him and that was good about him (line 634). R crucially then goes on to say in his subsequent turn (lines 636–39) that he considers the human being who listens to him to be good – in other words, obedience is crucial for recognition as being 'good'. In this case, the idea of the 'good' wife is dependent upon compliance with the husband's wishes which in turn hinges upon stereotypical and cultural images of the husband as the master of the household.

Life Story 6:[5] *'With Me, For Me . . .'*

Transcript Details:	[RSB A5 0803]
Participants:	U, her husband R and her brother M; U and R's six children and the author
Language of Interaction:	Hindi
Narrative Context:	Conversation has been on for more than thirty minutes in the presence of U's husband, their children and S. R is asked to speak of an occasion when he found strength or inspiration in his wife
Narrative Highlights:	Generalizations regarding gendered roles (generic life statements); goodness as related to the man's (husband/father) self-respect

Extract F

621 R: =>*nahi..esa: to vakya hua:*↑ *hæ<esi ba::t nahi. par: ye hæ ki*↑
neg like dm event happen pres like talk neg but this pres that

→622 *JO mæne kaha: usne ye kiya:*↓ {S:*acca:*} *jaha: mæne kaha: ki*
what I-erg say s/he-erg this do-pst okay where I-erg say that

623 *yaha: khada: hona: hæ khade the* {S:*acca:*} *ba::ki*
here stand happen pres stand pst okay rest

'Episodes like this have happened. It's not like this. Rest, whatever I said, she did it. Wherever I asked her to stand, she stood. Rest. . . .'

624 *YE nahi ki mana:: kara ho mere ka:m ke liye* {S:*ha:*} *bara:bar sa:th*
this neg that refuse do happen i-gen work gen for yes equal company

625 *diya: hæ isi ke ad::ar par a:j ham stert khade hæ*
give pres this-emph gen basis loc today e-h-nom straight stand pres

626 *acce se*
good with

'It's not as if she refused to do any work of mine. She has given me equal company. It is because of her that I am standing her today.'

((Two lines deleted; S asks what U thinks is R's best quality; asks her to think.))

630 U: *socna: ke kya: bata:ye jo acca: ka:m karte hæ wo acci ba:t hæ*
think-inf cpm what say1 rel pro good work do pres that good talk pres

'What is there to think here? The good things that he does are good, that is good'.

((Three lines deleted/ S says that people usually have qualities that others like and U says that R has many qualities.))

→634 U: *sabse acca: to zindagi acci kat gayi ye acca: hæ*
all from good dm life good pass go-pst this good pres

'The best thing is that life has passed by well.'

((Two lines deleted/ S asks R same question regarding U.))

→636 R: *insa::n mera: ke↑hna: ma::n le to me use*
human I-gen say-inf accept take then I-nom s/he-acc

→637 *acca: samajhta:: hu* {S:*acca:*} *mera: kehna: ma::n le↑bhei mæ jese*
good understand pres1 okay I-gen say-inf accept take I-nom like

638 *kehta: hu wo ma::ne* {S:*hm*} *mæ USI KO ACCA: samajhta: hu*
say-masc pres that accept hm I-nom that emph acc good understand pres

639 *jo nahi ma::nta: hæ to phir apni marzi se karo*↑ {S: *acca:*}
rel pro neg accept pres then then self wish with do2 okay

'What is good is that – I think the person who listens to me is good . . . whatever I say if she/he agrees, I consider that person to be good. If she/he doesn't agree, then do as per your wish.'

As noted earlier, U on being prodded by the author on what are her husband's good qualities, says in line 630 that the good deeds that he does are good and in line 634 comes to a 'generic life statement' that life has been spent well. R in his TCUs starting at line 621 and then in line 635 talks about the solid back-up support that his wife proffers; also he pertinently uses the generic word *insa:n* (human being) in line 636 to refer to his wife's good quality. The strategy to move from *a specific to a generic* statement on an obedient person being a good one is two-pronged: it *obfuscates* the identity of the wife as a life partner and *superimposes* the human being identity. R, the head of the household, thinks that the human being who is obedient to *him* is a good individual (lines 636–38). It is expected that cultural notions of the good wife and good children are also expected to be internalized by all six children (four daughters and two sons) of R and U who were present at the time of the interview. Such conversational contexts thus provide *cultural models* for others to follow. Bonn and Tafarodi note:

> It is a core tenet of cultural psychology that *how one understands, interprets, and relates to the surrounding world is guided largely by cultural models* (Markus and Kitayama 2003; Quinn 2003; Shore 1996). The social scripts (Miller *et al.* 1996, 1997) and biographical templates (Habermas and Bluck 2000) that are recognized from early childhood onward provide ready-made patterns through which individuals learn to organize their own internal narratives and evaluate their experiences. Stories reproduced within social contexts provide frameworks within which activities and experience can be causally and thematically connected to each other: They allow for the meaningful contextualization of isolated experiences (Berntsen and Bohn 2009; Snibbe and Markus 2005). (Bonn and Tafarodi 2014: 742; emphasis added)

This prompts us to conclude, along with Mackenzie (2005) and others cited in Bonn and Tafarodi (2014) above, that the *cultural imaginary* (our personal repertoire of images and representations that shape our core values, desires, emotions, beliefs and self-conception) does indeed affect our selfhood. But does it circumscribe our autonomy of who we are or who we can be even within our narratives? U's narrative below gives the semblance of an answer.

Life Story 7: *'Like Mother, Like Daughter . . .'*

Transcript Details:	[BRB10002]
Participants:	Same as Extract F (U, her husband R and her brother M; U and R's six children and this author)
Language of Interaction:	Hindi
Narrative Context:	Conversation has continued beyond Extract F; U starts talking about her mother who had recently expired. She narrates how she is endeavouring to follow in the latter's footsteps of being a faithful and dutiful wife
Narrative Highlights:	Cultural moorings of gendered identity; culture threatening narrative and culture-conforming individual; narrative pseudo-event as breach in canonical script; goodness and good life

Extract G

→685 U: *mammi ki- uspe HAM cal rahe hæ↑::: (.) mammi ne*
mother of on I-hon-nom go prog pres mother erg

686 *bola tha ki >"beta:↑<*{S:*hm:*} *JO kuc he 'pati ke hi*
said past that TA what all is husband of emph

687 *gher me hæ"* (0.3) *kehte hæna: ki doli*[8] *me sajke a:te hæ*
house loc pres said pres.dm that in decorate come pres

688 *or erthi*[9] *pe ja:te hæ* {S:*hm::*} *to wei hama:ri kaha::ni hæ*↑
and on Go pres then that our story pres

'I am going (on the path) as my mother asked. Mother had said that "My daughter, for you, everything is at your husband's house." As they say, a woman comes in her *doli* and leaves on her *erthi*. So that's my story too. . . . '

→689 *>ki dusre ke elava-<(.) sirf ek a:dmi ke elava: (.) kisi dusre ke*
that other of leaving only one man of leaving any other-of

→690 *lie nei (.) ki bhei >dusra acca: kha raha hæ, acca: keh raha*
for neg that dm other good eat prog pres good say prog

691 *hæ↑< uspe koi* (-) {S:*hm:* }
pres on any hm

'. . . that other than any other man, other than only one man . . . should not be for someone else. Not that someone else eats good or talks good. Nothing (for such person).'

→692 *↑JO::: tereko pati de↑ USI↑ me khus rehna:* {S:*acca:*}
whatever you-dat husband give that in happy stay-fut okay

693 *>A:DHI roti de ya: ca-catni se kha:< USI↑ me khus reh*
half roti give or chutney with eat that loc happy stay-fut-imp

694 *ye↑ nei- hæ ki >wo acca: kia to uske sath bha:g ja:*
this not pres that he good did then he gen with run go-fut

695 *wo acca kahe to uske sath cali ja<* {S: *ha:*}
he good say then he gen with walk go-fut yes

→696 *↑YE mat kar* (.) {S: *ha:*} *MERI jindegi bes: MÆNE jese*
this don't do-imp-fut yes my life just I-erg how

697 *ka::ti hæ na:↑* {S:*hm:*} *wese hi tu reh* {S:*acca:*}
live pres dm like emph you-nh stay-fut-imp okay

'Whatever your husband provides, be happy with that. Whether he gives half a *chapati* or you get a full *chapati* with chutney, stay happy with that. Not that someone else is doing good or saying good things so you should go off with that person. Don't do that. Just as I have lived my life, you should live yours.'

→698 U: *to wa↑↓hi hamne ye apna:ya tha↑ ki pal↑↓le me ba:ndh li*
then that I-hon-erg this accepted past that loc tied take

699 *ma: ki ba:t↑* {S:*ha*} *ki jo kuc hæ: pati ke sa:th*
mother of talk yes that what little pres husband of with

700 *me khus rehna:* (.) *ca:he a:dhi roti mile* - {S:*hm:*} (.)
in happy stay whether half roti get

→701 *paresha:ni uthaii:: To HAM DONO NE SATH MILKAR*{S:*ha*}
trouble take up then we two erg together meet-cpm

'So that's what I accepted: tied it to my *palla* that whatever little husband provides, stay happy with that whether it is half a *chapati* or with chutney. Troubles were taken up and faced by both of us together.'

→702 *uska sa:mna kara:* (.) *na ye bhage paresha:ni se na me DUR*
that face did nor he-hon ran trouble from nor i-nom far

703 *hati ki bhai >ye paresha:ni me tumhe chodke bhag jaye*
move that dm this trouble in you-acc leave run go-fut

704 *cal tu paresha:n hæ to choR ke ja rahi hu<* (-) *paresha:n hæ*
go you-nh trouble pres then leave after go prog pres Troubled pres

→705 *to DONO ne:::* (.) *paresha:ni ka:: sa:mna kara:*
then both erg trouble of face did

→706 *isliye ye bhi acce* [*hæ or* (-)
this-for this also good-h-agr pres and

'Not that he ran off from his troubles or I moved away from them. Nor did I run off in the face of trouble. Both of us together faced them. That is why he is good and . . .'.

707 S: *[a::p bhi acce ho hehehe*
you-h also good cop

'You are also good?! Hehehe.'

((Three lines deleted – unclear.))

→711 U: *hehehe BURE to bohot wakt a:ye the* (.) *HA::RE nahi ham*
bad dm much time come pst lose neg we

→712 *<u>himmat nahi ha::Ri</u>* (.) *ki KAB TAK bhagwa::n hame bure wakt*
courage neg lose that when till god we-acc bad time

→713 *dikha::yega↑: 'kabhi to acche din ayenge* {S:*ha:*} *isliye ham*
show-masc some dm good days come-fut yes that-why we

714 *acce hæ ye* (.) *ham (CUKI) ham <u>dono</u> ne milke sa::mna kara:*
good pres this ham because we both erg together face do

'Bad days, there were quite a few; we did not lose. We did not lose courage. Till when would God show us bad days? Sometime or the other good days would come. That is why we are good. Both of us faced difficulties together. . . .'

715 *dono me se KOI BHI pi::che nahi hata:* {S: *acca:*} ((…)) *ye piche*
both loc from some also back neg move okay she/he back

→716 *hat ja::yenge m((…)) piche hat ja::u isliye↑ <zindegi acci kati>*
move go-fut I-nom back move go-1 this-for life good pass=pst

→717 *>or KHUSI se kati ye nahi pata: laga:: ki hama:ri bis*
and happy with pass this neg know feel that we-gen twenty

718 *ikkis sa:l <u>kidhar</u> ko cale gaye<, ye pata: nahi laga:*
twenty one years where acc go go-pst this know neg feel

'Neither of us stepped back . . . (if) he moves back I will move back. That is why life passes by well. And it passed by happily. We never knew where and how twenty–twenty-one years of our lives went.'

Just prior to U's first cited TCU in Extract G (line 685), she was talking about her parents – she mentions that her father had died when her younger brother M (our featured storyteller of chapter 4) was very young. She then starts talking about her mother: U begins her narration with an abstract of her story in line 685: how she is going along the 'path' that her mother had prescribed (unable to find the right word – possibly for 'diktat' – she uses *uspe* 'on that'). The orientation is already introduced by her turn in line 685 so it is clear to her story recipients that the story will be about her mother and *she uses quotative voice through lines 686–87 to literally become her mother's (cultural) voice*. U launches on her narrative by telling about how her mother had taught her that a woman's whole life ought to be with her husband once she is married off, and uses clichéd expressions of a woman coming to her husband's home after marriage in a palanquin and leaving only on her death.[11] In fact, she overtly uses the story mode in lines 687–88 to claim it as her life story (*to wei hama:ri kaha:ni he:* 'So that is my story.'). Quite like the earlier extract of D and J, this latter evaluative line of U starts off a 'wave of evaluation'. Her lines 689–90 are semantically ambiguous: *ek a:dmi ke ela:va kisi dusre ke liye nei* can mean 'other than one man, she should not *be* for someone else' ,which prompts her to follow it up with a clarificatory repair in the second part of line 690 – *dusra: acca: kha: raha: he ya: dusra: acca: kehraha hæ* ('[If] someone *else* is wearing good [clothes] or saying good [things]' she should not covet it. Her TCU here talks about a '*pseudo-event*' (elopement with another man) and initiates the so-called breach in the canonical script (Bruner 2001) which makes a narrative interesting and 'tellable' (Polanyi 1985).

The intensity with which U narrates about her late mother's belief finds expression as social norms (in faithfulness to the husband under all circumstances) and this intensity is captured by her use of *loud speech* and *emphatics* (for example, lines 692, 693, etc.). The latter also linguistically locates the appropriation of culturally rooted ideas of the good wife.[12] Juxtaposed with this intensity is incongruity as well as the unrealized possibility of D's running off with someone with better prospects; it successfully establishes U as a culture-conforming individual while her narrative itself becomes culture-threatening. What follows in line 692 is a reiteration of the stereotypical role of the husband as the provider and the wife as the dependant: *JO::: tere ko pati de USI me khus rehna:* ('Stay happy with whatever your husband provides you'). The social norms are enumerated through the strategic use of various comparators[13] (Labov 1972: 380–87): U uses negatives/futures/imperative form in lines 690, 692, 693, 694, 695, 696 and 697, not only for the narrative voice of her mother but also to emphasize her own conforming to such social norms – her most emphatic of these voices of her mother is in line 696 when she says '*YE mat kar*' (don't do this).[14] Her shift to her own voice in line 698 with pitch variations (↑↓) signals her return to her own mental world and the conversational present. She thus successfully positions herself as a loyal wife and good daughter within her self-proclaimed life story. Her moral positioning fulfils the condition of a good narrative.

Corresponding to the moral obligation to stand by her husband in good and bad times is the *chapati* metaphor – the *a:dhi roti* (half *chapati*) serves as the metaphor for bad times while *roti* with chutney is symbolic of good times (lines 692–93). It is noteworthy that while U uses first person *MÆ* (Hindi 'I') in line 697 to quote her mother (*MERI zindagi . . . MÆNE*), she mostly uses the first person honorific form for herself – line 685 and again in line 698 above. This can be said to indicate that U has an exalted sense of self in adopting what her mother had taught her. It does her proud and elevates her status as a daughter and wife that whatever her mother taught she could implement in her life with her husband. The stereotypical gender roles of the husband as provider (lines 692–93) and the suppliant wife who must stay happy under all circumstances in her husband's home is earmarked in lines 686–87, and also repeated as her story's 'evaluation' in lines 698–700. U uses figurative language that she tied her mother's words to her '*palla*' – the loose flowing end of a saree – indicating the cultural injunction of being obedient to her mother and husband. Her mother's words become part of her everyday consciousness through being tied to her. U goes on to link these notions of goodness with togetherness in her narrative's resolution. U's story here encodes the recognition of as well as the solution to the moral issues at hand and establishes her 'moral self'; in appropriating her mother's moral maxims as defined by 'Indian culture', her narrative makes morality a traditional thing that is passed on from mother to daughter.

The fact that this conversation happens in the presence of the couple's six children – including four daughters – is an indication that they are performing this aspect of hegemonic patriarchy for their children to emulate. It is expected that the children will appropriate such ideals of compliant Indian wives who stay happy in their husbands' homes and are content with whatever the latter provide them with. It proves that 'narratives are highly portable discursive units' (Brigss, ed. 1996: 29), which not only reveal aspects of individual identity (U's sense of exaltedness in using *ham*) but give hints of social identity by being already steeped in a particular culture (in this case, the patriarchal Indian family). Contrasting South Asian culture with Chinese culture, Bonn and Tafarodi (2014) note that while Chinese culture emphasizes a practical Confucian philosophy extolling the virtues of hard work and education, the importance of independent obligations and the cultivation of relationships,

> South Asian culture, on the other hand, is bound to a more transcendental worldview, derived from Hindu, Muslim, and other more ascetic traditions.

> It emphasizes the importance of virtue, good work,selfless service,purity, and a balance between worldly and sacred concerns (Jahanbegloo 2008; Mongia 2005). Much of this can be understood in relation to the concept of *karma* – the belief that one's actions matter for spiritual progression; that good and bad intentions and deeds are rewarded or punished, whether in this lifetime or the next. This spirituality is evident in the worldview of many South Asians (Babb 1983). (Bonn and Tafarodi 2014: 744)

Deeply seeped in her cultural moorings of the 'suppliant Indian wife' who comes to her husband's place in the bridal palanquin and leaves only on her death bed, U's narrative is evocative of these cultural and constitutive elements of selfhood that are passed on inter-generationally. This analysis of U's narrative not only throws up subjective meanings but also functions as an interpretation of the social realities constitutive of them and vice versa. It facilitates a deconstructive process where 'the interest is not only in what the author himself or herself may have meant by a particular utterance but what the text itself means' (Freeman 1993a: 34). In Ricouerian terms, the importance of U's narration lies not so much in the relevance of it (she is talking about her mother) but the importance of it via having established a linguistic dimension of her 'self' that is culturally sustained. She connects the events of her mother's teachings with the story of her life in the process investing it with a meaning it may not have had incipiently. In this sense, it also comprises what Ricouer (1984) calls the configurational (non-chronological) aspect of storytelling; U significantly uses sentences with the discourse marker *to* ('so') in lines 688, 698 and 705 – *to wei hama:ri kaha:ni hæ* ('So that is my story'), *to wahi hamne ye apna:ya: tha*: ('So that is what I accepted') and *to dono ne milkar paresha:ni ka: sa:mna: kia* ('Both of us faced troubles together') to underscore this configurational dimension of her storytelling. Ricoeur also notes that in joining the configurational dimension together with the episodic dimension that confers the succession (this happened and then that happened), the narration juxtaposes time and memory to configure a linguistic identity not apparent at the beginning of the narrator's telling (ibid.): this is seen in line 706 where U unexpectedly says that *isiliye ye bhi acce hæ* ('That's why he is also good'). Her use of *bhi* ('also') prompts S to teasingly say she (U) also is good, following which U brings up her exit talk in 706–11 to elaborate on the goodness and happiness of both husband and wife by saying how they both stood up to bad times courageously. U post-poses the subject positions in line 711 to highlight the 'goodness' factor, *HA::RE nahi ham* (We did not lose despite the bad times that came).[15]

U's TCUs in the above lines can be seen to draw a link between her past and present – her narrative shows a backward movement of time while a forward movement of development is encoded in her lines 712–13 where she uses a comparator (a question) to ask till when God would show them bad times, that good times *would* follow, that there was *karma* after all,[16] and that they did not realize where twenty years of their married life had gone. The narrative here functions as a conduit to express the fact that good times *had* followed. In Freeman's terms, 'the backward movement of narrative . . . turns out to be dialectically intertwined with the forward movement of development' (Freeman 2004: 77) and it facilitates a 'rewriting of the self'. U's whole narrative in Extract G above can also be interpreted as a re-reading of her relationship with her husband R in the light of her following her mother's advice; given what her mother had said, she established her identity as a dutiful daughter and wife, and this facilitated their leading a good, happy life. *Gendered identity is as much in evidence here as coupledom*; by speaking of the good times together that were facilitated by their facing bad times, her identity as the dutiful wife is established and her symbolic role as co-partner in her husband's life is asserted. Towards this end U uses variations of *ham dono ne milkar* ('Both of us together') in her TCUs, especially in lines 701, 705, 712 and 714 above. Even in the earlier transcript (Extract E) where D and J are engaged in a narration of the daughter's industriousness, we surmised that they are also constructing their identities as successful parents in the process of eulogizing their daughter's success while simultaneously 'performing' their heterosexuality through 'duetting'. This cardinal role of duetting also hints at the prime role of the 'other' and establishing one's narrative identity is seen to be concurrent with establishing the identity of the other, thus making identities *dialogical, culture-conforming and context-dependent.*

In this final extract of this section from U's younger brother M, we shall examine one more instance whereby the cultural imaginary comes into play in the forging of gendered identities. M's first TCU here in line 330[17] is from their interview (conducted earlier than that of U and R) and follows a stretch of conversation where he and N are telling how they never fight and in fact laugh at other couples in their neighbourhood who fight. M's turn here is preceded by a narrative of N about their neighbours. The two narrative sequences where M first talks about how they do not fight and then both M and N talk about each other's good qualities are marked Extract H and Extract H(i), respectively.

Life Story 8: *'The Good Wife Who Cooks for the Good Man Who Earns'*

Transcript Details:	[MNK A2 0407]
Participants:	Same as Extracts B, C and D (M, his wife N and their three children the eldest of whom was studying in Class 2 and the current author).
Language of Interaction:	Hindi
Narrative Context:	'NM' interview on for more than ten minutes. The kids sing songs and the author interacts with the children about whether they like their mother more or father more. S then asks if the couple fights and N promptly says no. Following N's narrative (lines 306–23, not cited here) about neighbours who fight, M remarks that they have set up a 'world record' of not fighting. This prompts S to make a remark showing incredulity to M's contention, following which he starts his TCU below. N proffers new information by saying that others in their neighbourhood tease them about the kind of married couple they are since they do not fight. The author then teased them asking how it was possible that they had not fought even once in eleven years, at which M launches into his TCU reported in line 330 below.
Narrative Highlights:	Looped narratives by M marking narrative pseudo-events; distancing from non-ideal narrative identity by moving from first-person to second-person account; stereotypical gendered notions of goodness; culture-threatening narrative and culture-conforming individual; narrative pseudo-event as breach in canonical script; goodness and good life as related to happiness

Extract H

330 M: ↑*pa:c sa:l mæ apni didi ke ghar reh ke a:ya:*
five years I-nom self elder-sister gen home stay cpm came-masc

331 *>guruji< ek din bhi mæne kabhi* (.) *na to *inne* ((*constricted form of
TA one day also I-erg ever nor dm s/he-erg *inho:ne*))

332 *didi ko ye kaha: ki mujhe wo-ye nehi la:ke dia*
elder sister dat this said that I-gen that this neg bring-cpm gave

'I stayed with my sister for five years, not even a day did she complain to sister that "he has not brought this for me . . .".'

333 {S:*ha::*} *na mæne ye kaha: ki bhei mujhe roti bana:ke*
yes nor I-erg this said that brother I-dat roti make-cpm

→334 *nehi di* {S:*accha*} *cakkar*(.) *sabse badi setti*N *hama:ri* <*YE HÆ*
neg gave okay issue of-all big setting we-gen this pres

335 *sa↑r, ki ham log na:, a:pas me, ek dusre ki galti ko*
sir that we people dm within loc one other gen mistake gen

336 *(kamfart) karte hæ*> {S:*acca:*} >*matlab*< *ab mæ hu↑* {S:*ha:*}
? do-prog pres okay means now I-nom cop yes

'Nor have I ever said that she did not make *roti* (lit. did not cook food) for me. Our biggest setting is that both of us ('comfort') each other's mistakes. . . . Means now take me (for instance) . . .'.

((M probably uses '*kamfart*' here to mean something like 'complement'))

→337 *dyuti hæ meri ca:r baje tak* {S: *ha:*} >*or mæ kahi*
duty pres I-gen four o'clock till yes and I-nom somewhere

338 *bhi (ha:tne) nikal- nikal jau ra:t ko a:u sa:re gyara: bara:*
too roam out out go night acc come1 half eleven twelve

339 *baje*<, {S:*ha:*} *to isme biwi bacco ki kya: galti hæ↑?*
o'clock yes then this-loc wife children gen what fault pres

'My duty is till 4–4.30 pm and if I go out after that and come back at 11–12 o'clock at night, then what is the fault of my wife and children . . . ?'

→340 {S: *ha:*} >*jo ghar me mil jaye kha:ne ko wo kha↑o or*
yes what home loc get go-fut eat-inf acc that eat2 and

→341 *so ja:o*< {S: *ha:*} *bhei galti to tumha:ri hæ tum*
sleep go yes brother fault dm you-gen pres you

342 **bha:nd*[18] *ke a: rahe ho idhar udhar* {S:*ha:*}
cpm come prog pres here there yes

'Whatever you get to eat just eat it up, drink some water and go to sleep. After all the fault is yours that you were roaming here and there . . .'.

343 *bai ca:ns, agar ka:m karke a: rahe ho tum↑,* >*dyuti karke*
by chance if work do-cpm come be-impf cop2 you duty do-cpm

344 *a: rahe ho*<, *to tum dyuti se PHON karo* {S:*ha:*}
come prog cop2 then you duty from phone do2-nh yes

345 *ki bhei mæ dyuti pe hu* {S:*ha:*} >*mere liye kha:na: cahiye*
that brother I-nom duty loc cop1 yes I-gen for food need

→346 *ye cahiye wo ca:hiye<* {S:*ha:*} *wo to thi:k hæ*
this need that need-pres yes that dm right pres

'By chance, if you are to come back from work, you are coming from duty, then you call from duty – that "I am on duty: I need my food, I need this, and I need that." That is alright.'

→347 {S:*accha*} *ab tu↑m* (.) *masti ma:r rahe ho kah↑in*
okay now you fun hit prog cop somewhere

348 *ghu:m rahe ho kah↑in, phir ghar me a:ke larh rahe ho*
roam prog cop2 somewhere then home loc come-cpm fight prog cop

'Now you are having fun somewhere, roaming around somewhere and then coming home and fighting . . .'.

349 *ki ji* "*@kha:na: kyu nehi hæ@*" {S:*ha:*} *'esa: thode hi*
that dm food why neg pres yes like little emph

350 *hota: hæ* {S: *ha:*} *>jo mil gaya: wo kha: lo,*
happen pres yes what get go-pst that eat take2

→351 *pa:ni piyo so jao<*
water drink2 sleep go2 nh

'. . . that "Why don't I have my food?" It is not like that – whatever you get, just eat it, drink water and go to sleep.'

((One line deleted.))

353 M: *=is kar ke larai nahi hoti hæ °guruji°* {S:*accha:*} *agar*
this do cpm fight neg happen pres TA okay if

354 *meri galti hæ mæne apni galti ko ma:n liya:* {S:*hm:*} *↓inko*
I-gen fault pres I-erg self fault acc agree take s/he-hon-acc

355 *kuc nei kehna:* {S:*hm:*} *agar* (.) *inki galti hæ, inhone*
something neg say-inf if s/he-hon-gen fault pres s/he-hon-erg

356 *apni galti ko ma:n liya: kuc nahi kehna:* {S:*accha:*}
self fault acc agree take something neg say-erg okay

'That is why we do not fight. If it is my fault, I admit my mistake, she does not have to say anything, if it is her fault she admits her mistake I do not say (anything).'

((Twenty lines of M's TCU are deleted here – see Extract 2 in Appendix for these lines where M narrates how he and his mother and brothers 'do not fight'. The ideal family is constructed and reiterated by him both for his joint family as well as his nuclear family. S then asks M what he thinks is his wife's best quality to which he answers with his TCU in Extract H[i] below.))

Extract H(i)

Transcript Details: [MNK [A20628]]

→384 M: =*MATLAB sabse acca ye HE::, ki agar meri koi dyuti*
means of all good this pres that if my someone duty

385 *sube ca:r sare ca:r baje ki lagade na*↑ {S: *ha::*}
morning four half-past four o'clock of give dm yes

386 *ya: ra:t ke sa:re ba:ra: ek ki laga:*↑*de* {S: *ha:*} *'tab bhi*
or night dat half-past twelve one dat give yes then also

387 *mujhe khana milega*↓ {S:*acc(h)a* (.) *aur wo bhi ekdum first class*
i (dat) food get okay and that too full

388 *bana: hua >turant bana hua<=*
made past immediately made perf

'Means the best thing is that if someone gives me duty for half past four in the morning or for eleven thirty or twelve at night, then also I shall get my food. And that too made (in) first class (manner), made there and then.'

((S's turn deleted))

→390 M: *itna sabkuc*(.) *>to bohot acca: lagta hæ:<* {S: *accha*}
so much everything then very good feel pres okay

391 *>ki* ↑*bhai< a:dmi jab* <u>*KAMA*</u>*:NE ja: raha:* ↑*hæ::* {S: *ha::*}
that brother man when earn inf go prog pres yes

392 *aur usko ulta pulta kha:ne ko mile to man to*
and he-nh-dat topsy-turvy eat-inf dat get-inf than mind dm

393 *>wahi se hi ghar se hi< khara:b ho ja[ta: hæ:*
there-emph from emph home from emph bad happen go pres

'So much so, then it really feels nice. That when the man is going out to earn and he gets to eat junk, then one feels bad right from home only . . .'.

394 S: *[paresha:ni*
trouble

'(One gets) troubled.'

→395 M: *aur AGAR ghar se hi wo acca: kha:ke ja:: raha hæ:*↑*:*
and if home from-emph he good eat-cpm go prog pres

→396 *aur acca: dekh raha hæ: ghar ki setting .hhh*
and good see prog pres house dat setting

→397 *>a::ge to phir hæ: hi< apna*(.) °*acca hi*°
future then after pres emph self good emph

'And, if from home itself he goes out after eating well, and sees that his home's setting is good, then ahead it is only good.'

398 *ki bhei a:dmi jab ghar se hi acche mu::d me niklega*
that brother man when home from-emph good mood loc go -out

→399 *to ka::m bhi acca karega:*
then work also good do fut

'That when the man goes from his home itself in a good mood, then he will also work well . . .'.

((N is then asked what she thinks are her husband's good quality in line 400; when S teases that she will make them fight, she responds with her TCU below.))

410 N: *nehi to hama:re se kuc hota hi nahi hæ °bas:°:*
no then our by something happen emph neg pres enough

411 *lara::i jhagra to hamne sikha hi nahi ↑hæ,* {S: *ha::*}
fights fights dm We-erg learn emph neg pres yes

412 *na: ma: ba:p ne sikhaya ki tum ja:ke lara:i jhagra karna:*
nor mother father erg teach that you go-pm fight fight do-inf

413 *ya is chi:j ke liye lar↑na:* (.) *>°ye kuc nehi hæ:°<*
or this thing of for fight-inf this something neg pres

'No, something like this does not happen with us. That's it. Fights are not possible by us. Nor have (my) parents taught that you go fight. Or fight for this thing – nothing of this sort.'

414 *apni jo marji se la:: de- >de denge< la:ke kha:ne ke*
self that wish with bring give give give fut bring eat-inf of

415 *liye wo kha len↑ge itna: jaru:r sikhaya ma: ba:p*
for that eat take This much definitely teach mother father

416 *ne hama:re [me*
erg our in

'As per his wish, whatever he brings to eat, I eat. This much (my) parents have definitely taught (me).'

417 S: *[accha=*
okay

→418 N: *=ye nahi hæ ke tum ja:ke pati* (.) *jæse* (.) *lara:i ho*
this neg pres that you go-cpm husband like fight happen

419 *ja:ti hæ:, to uske piche lara:i ho gayi*
go pres then that-of after fight happen go-2-fem

420 *ki* *apne* *ghar* *cali* *gayi* {S:*hm*} *hamne* *a::j* *tak*
that self home went-fem go-2- fem I-hon-erg today till

421 *esa:* *kabhi* *nahi* *hone* *dia:* {S: *accha:*}
like ever neg happen give okay

'It is not that you go and like, fight with your husband or fight about that thing. (Something like) she left for her home. I have never let that happen even once till today.'

422 N: (.) >*kabhi* *bhi*< (.) *gyara:* *sa:l* *ho* *gaye*↑, {S: *ha::*}
ever emph eleven years happen past yes

423 *a:j* *tak* *hama:re* *ma:* *ba:p* *ko* *ye* *nahi* *pata:,* (.) *ki*
today till I-hon-gen mother father dat this neg know that

424 *kya* *hota:* *hæ:* *waha:* *pe* {S:*acca:*} *KESE* *rehte* *hæ:* *ye*
what happens pres there loc okay how stay pres they

'Never. It has been eleven years, till today my parents do not know what happens there – how they live.'

→425 N: *sab* *yehi* *dekhte* *hæ* *ki* *ha:* *khus* *hæ* >*ham* *HÆ* *hi*
all this-emph see-inf pres that yes happy pres we pres emph

426 *khus*< {S: *ha::*} *apne* *ghar* *reh* *rahe* *hæ* *ham* *sabse*
happy yes self home stay prog pres we of all

427 *barhiya:* *reh* *rahe* *hæ:*
very good stay prog pres

'All people see is that "Yes – they are happy." We are happy. We live at our own home, we are living in the best possible way.'

In M's long TCU through lines 330 to 380 (in Extract H above and Extract 2 in Appendix), *he extols the virtues of the non-confrontational wife* all in the form of pseudo-narratives – his initial appreciation is actually for the fact that his wife never once complained even when M did not provide her with things she required (line 332) during all the five years that they initially stayed at his elder sister (U)'s place in Jahangirpuri. He 'returns' the favour by never complaining about the food she cooked (line 333). This in itself *creates and reifies the stereotypes of the male as provider and the woman as dependent care-giver who stands by the former through all circumstances.*[20] He *modulates his voice*, lapses into *slow speech* and also uses *emphatics* along with overt term of expression from the author when he elaborates his 'biggest setting' (line 334–36) of how they achieve their non-fighting or non-confrontationalist attitude: '*kamfart*' each other (in line 336) – by which he probably means something like complement. His pseudo-narrative launches with the prefatory line '*ab mæ hu*' (Now take me) – and we are now ready for the story that M *knows* he is the hero of. He uses a comparator for an elaborate question posed to the listener in lines 337–39 – 'My duty is till 4–4.30 pm and if I go out after that and come back at 11–12 o' clock at night, then what is the fault of my wife and children . . . ?' Significantly, however, the narrative persona that M has taken on in his narrative – that of the errant husband prone to night binges who neglects his wife and children – is not to his liking and now he has to manage that with the context of the conversation. M's first person account of the example he is citing, about the errant husband who in coming late after duty should not blame the wife or kids, suddenly changes into a second person account in line 341 – '*galti to* ***tumha:ri*** *hæ* ***tum*** *bha:nd ke a: rahe ho idhar-udhar* (The fault is yours – you have been roaming here and there)'. His verbalized form of the expletive *bha:nd* (pimp) shows his utter disregard for such irresponsible behaviour which merits no special treatment – (in that case) one (deservedly) should eat whatever one gets. This conversion from a first person account to a second person account is probably his way of distancing himself from such unwanted behaviour as well as the narrative identity created in the situation of interlocution.

It is important to note in this connection Mackenzie's ([2000] 2005) notions of the 'internal audience' and the 'internal observer' which she likens to the relations between the *person's point of view* and her *self-conception*, respectively. For Mackenzie, the internal audience is 'caught up within the imaginative project and emotionally identifies with it' while the internal observer 'stands outside the imaginative project; may react to it emotionally in a range of different ways; and reflects on and evaluates the desires, emotions and beliefs represented or manifested in the imagining' (Mackenzie 2005: 285). The internal audience simulates different emotions in a person, while the internal observer responds to these emotions with reactive emotions. In M's narrative, his construction of the problem of the errant husband starts in line 336 when he depicts a '*hypothetical self*' with the preface *ab mæ hu* (Now take me, for instance). As he proceeds with his narrative of this *mæ*, he as the 'internal audience' is caught up with the description of this self's characteristics (he roams around till late at night while his wife and children are at home; lines 337–39). However, to the internal observer that 'stands outside' the reflective project (going on in his narrative and in the conversational present), it becomes apparent that this is *not* the ideal self that he is/wants to be. As a response to this, M uses (what is being called here) the '*distancing principle*' and starts his conversion to the second person account. He first switches to second person verbs of lines 340 and 341 (*khao/jao* – 'eat/go') and then to the second person pronominal *tumha:ri* on which he shifts the blame (*bhai galti to tumaha:ri hæ* – 'The fault is yours'). *M's point of view here has constructed a self that is not idealistic – an irresponsible husband and father who roams around after duty hours and neglects his family; consequently, he uses the distancing principle in his language to work his way out of his narrative* (lines 353–56). These strategies indicate the way in such cultural notions of good selves have a bearing on gendered identity. There is a corresponding example in N's speech a few turns later when such distancing/appropriation of idealized selves are at work. Following M's turn in lines 330–80 cited in Extract H above, he extends his TCU to talk about his mother and family (relevant lines cited as Extract 2 in Appendices), and when asked what he considers to be his spouse's best quality, M responds with his TCU lines 384 onwards. The same question is also posed to N who at first does not say anything but following the interviewer's remark that since N had nothing good to say about her husband it would make them fight (not cited), N responds with her TCU with lines 411–22. She says that she has not learnt to fight and nor has she been taught to fight by her parents. In other words, she has had an ideal upbringing.

In M's TCU (lines 384–95 in Extract H[i] above), he uses the comparator *acca* as many as seven times to emphasize what he considers good qualities in his spouse: ensuring timely meals for her husband so that he can go out and work well. The onus then rests simply and solely on the woman to provide the man with good food and take care of his 'family setting' so that he is in a positive frame of mind. N, on the other hand, sub-/unconsciously deflects from the question posed to her to say what she thinks are his good qualities to shift the focus on her good upbringing; she has been taught by her parents not to fight. It is after this that, significantly, she too uses the distancing principle, like M does in his narrative above for distancing her constructed self from a non-ideal self. If, for M, this non-ideal self is the irresponsible husband who roams around even after duty hours to the utter neglect of home and family (lines 336–51), for N, it is the temperamental wife who fights with her husband and goes off to her maternal home (lines 418–21). M distances it with *galti to tumha:ri hæ* ('The fault is yours' [line 341]) and N does it with *ye nahi hai ki tum ja:ke pati jæse larai ho ja:ti hæ,* 'It's not that you go and like fight with your husband' [line 418].) Also, again like her husband who has spoken about his good family in his earlier lines (Extract 2 in Appendix), she too emphasizes her ideal family background whose teachings she has appropriated, so much so that in almost eleven years they do not even now know how she lives (lines 422–24).[21] In her subsequent lines she notes how people – others[22] – see that they are happy (*sab yehi dekhte hæ . . .* – line 425) and it is attributed to her ideal upbringing. N's moral position is augmented by the emphatic *ham HÆ hi khus* ('We <u>are</u> happy' [lines 425–26]) and she goes on to say that since they stay in their own home, they feel good. *In return for being provided for by her husband, she is happy with him.*[23] These gendered notions of goodness and happiness seem to imply a cultural injunction to become good selves. Just as M positions himself as the responsible father/husband which in turn circumscribes him (he distances himself from the non-ideal narrative self his story throws up unexpectedly by moving from a first person to a second person account), his explicit gendered notions of his wife's symbolic role delimit her selfhood – she must provide him with fresh and hot food whatever the time of his duty.

To sum up this exploration of the gendered self and gendered ethics, we can say that Life Stories 5 and 6 exemplified duetting within narrative by the self–other in which episodic stories were often seen to be narrated by husbands while configurational dimensions were provided by wives; moreover, cultural notions of goodness and good selves dictate the kinds of stories we narrate about ourselves and while our narratives can be culture-threatening to retain their tellability, the narrative selves that they conjure up are often culture-conforming.

> . . . *conceptions of the good implicitly work themselves into individual identities by providing points of motivation, comparison, and evaluation within personal narratives. Individuals internalize a sense of what is good or worthwhile from their surroundings.* This anchors their internal evaluations and provides context for how they construct stories about their lives and how they come to understand themselves. Whether their related experiences are positive or negative, *individuals can be expected to speak more about topics that are culturally emphasized than those that are not.* (Bonn and Tafarodi 2014: 742; emphases added)

Finally, even if a non-ideal self does prop up unexpectedly in the narrative, the narrator can use a certain *distancing principle* to dissociate from the narrative identity being presented and move to a more positive articulation of self. As such, even our most intimate projections of selfhood within conversation are in relation to and with others, contextually accomplished *and* culturally conforming.

Notes

[1] D and J belonged to a mid-socio-economic group (defined in Barua [2012a] as earning up to Rs 50,000 per month). At the time of the interview, D and J owned twin flats (divided into four parts) on two floors in a residential colony of Delhi, and had given out three parts of the flats on rent while staying in one part themselves. J, male, then aged 66, had migrated to Delhi from Pakistan (in 1951 or so) as a child with his parents after India's Independence, and D was born (in 1948) and brought up in Delhi. The rents were their source of livelihood especially after J got partially disabled following an accident in which he badly injured his leg (J had a permanent limp on his right foot). They led retired lives since J gave up his business following an acid attack on him due to some political reasons (J had been a volunteer of a political party). D had been self-employed earlier (as salesperson/tuition teacher) but gave up working following the marriages of their three daughters. While J spoke both Hindi and Punjabi, D claimed to speak only in Hindi (although she was seen to converse with her husband in Punjabi at times).

[2] In the context of the overall interview of D and J that was undertaken for the author's PhD (Barua 2012a), J's narrative here is actually a repeated narrative; he had already spoken on the transport business, his getting injured and his making the house in extended narratives much earlier during their interview (lines 244–53, 544–601). He narrates about the transport business, cars and acquiring the flat again in at least two more subsequent narratives in the interview – lines 709–11 and lines 1081–113. His repeated narratives on these issues also indicate the *salience* these aspects have for J, especially with regard to roles and positioning, in the constitution of his identity (Burke 2003, cited earlier).

[3] *Ba:pre* is a vocative non-standard colloquial expression. Literally *ba:p* means 'father' but the expression can be culturally translated into something like 'Oh God!' or 'Oh dear!'. That D and then J continue to speak and add to the narrative even after this expressive backchannel by their listener (current author) shows that the 'organizational, and organic, control over the complex . . . "body" of a narrative is indeed exercised by the small, and on the face of it irrelevant, interventions and "repairs" produced by participants during the process of story-telling' (Nair 2003: 253).

[4] The rest of these lines feature significantly in the next chapter on the ancillary narrative.

[5] At the time of the interview U and her husband R were in their forties and living in two-room sets in *bastis* (low-income neighbourhoods) in West Delhi. They belong to the low socio-economic group, had been married for over twenty years and had six children, all of whom were present when the interview was conducted. R had migrated to Delhi from Uttar Pradesh in 1976 in search of a better job and his wife, U, had come to Delhi following their marriage in 1986. The author knew them

through M who worked at her hostel as a member of the cleaning staff. His elder brother-in-law R was employed as a sweeper in the University of Delhi, while R's wife U was working as cleaning staff at a private computer institute. They speak Hindi and Gamaru (see note 1, chapter 4).

[6] Although U and R's lives are far from over, U here speaks as if life has been completed – this is necessitated contextually since they have to, in retrospect, invest meaning to their lives. Narratives revolving around life stories are seen to often contain these 'generic life statements' (let us call these GLS for now) that help narrators and individuals come to grips with the vagaries of life and thereby render the uncertain into certainties of the conversational present. These narrative certainties are of course fragile, contextually bound and conversationally dependent on self–other dynamics. It would be a very 'bad' listener who would contest a narrator's GLS.

[7] See Extract 1 in Appendices where R relates his children's obedience to his self-esteem. That particular extract was in response to what the biggest priorities were for U and R as a couple, to which he says that their children should learn to take responsibility and obey him.

[8] Traditional Indian bridal palanquin in which the bride is sent off to her in-laws'/husband's home after marriage.

[9] Funeral pyre of a Hindu.

[10] '*Palla*' is the loose end of the saree in Hindi.

[11] Bonn and Tafarodi (2014: 742) note: 'Individuals' internal narratives, the stories they tell themselves about who they are, emerge from a lifelong process by which personal experiences are reconciled with the stories that prevail within the social milieu (McAdams 2001; Quinn 2003)'.

[12] Labov (1972: 378–79) notes that intensifiers like expressive phonology, gestures, quantifiers, repetition and ritual act as internal evaluative device which selects a narrative events in order to strengthen or intensify it.

[13] Comparators include 'negatives, futures, modals, quasimodals, questions, imperatives, *or*-clauses, superlatives and comparatives more or less in increasing order of syntactic complexity. . . . A comparator moves away from the line of narrative events to consider unrealized possibilities' (ibid.: 387; cited earlier). It is a clause internal evaluative device.

[14] This is a cultural injunction in U's narrative voice of her mother to not run off with another man. The inherent moral position is reminiscent of Sellars' (1968) 'We intentions' (cited earlier) – U's narrative here seems to say that 'We are not that sort of women that run away with other men.'

[15] U's narrative here that moves to overt notions of goodness and where they stand in relation to it becomes a condition of their very existence. In this sense 'orientation to the good is not some optional extra, something we can engage in or abstain from at will, but a condition of our being selves with an identity' (Taylor 1989: 68; cited earlier on page 30).

[16] To deduce these connotations of the narrator's life story, one would require what Nair (2003: 265) calls *implicultural* ability: for Nair, unlike Labov, stories may be particularly 'fragile' when they are blatantly offered as stories about extraordinary rather than everyday events, and ordinary story material has to be made reportable

if it is not to be criticized as boring ('why are you telling me this?') (ibid: 274). It adds to the point cited above about U's citing the discourse marker *to* ('so') – it helps to give credibility to the ordinary tale that she is narrating.

[17] As has been mentioned earlier, transcript narrators who have multiple narratives cited in this work have retained the original transcript number lines to give a sense to the reader as to when the narrative occurred during the situation of interlocution. In the case of M's Life Story 2 (Extract B) of chapter 4, he launched into his narrative right in his first TCU in line 3. Here, in Life Story 8, the lines begin from 330 and hence it is clear that this narrative occurs much later than Extract B.

[18] **bha:nd* is a swear word that means agent of a prostitute; it has been verbalized here by M to mean someone who roams around

[19] N and M had just completed their ten years of married life – here she speaks of the ongoing eleventh year of marriage as an already completed term.

[20] This is reminiscent of U's narrative cited earlier whether the half a *chapati*/fuli *chapati* with chutney metaphor implies a wife who stands by her husband through thick and thin – it shows the cultural affinity and salience of the people whose life stories abide by cultural gendered notions of what constitutes a good husband or wife. 'Ignorant of the possibility of freedom, *women live as inferiors because they deem it given in their situation*' (de Beauvoir 1997; cited earlier on page 45).

[21] Her sister-in-law U (in Life Story 7) uses the same tactic of saying intra-narrative that they were not conscious of how twenty years had passed by. That both women are in separate interview situations on different days and yet use the same strategies to invoke a good self and good wife speaks of the cultural models that root their narratives (Bonn and Tafarodi 2014; cited earlier).

[22] Recall her husband M's narrative (Life Story 4) reported in chapter 4, in which he too mentions how others' recognition of him as a man with a regular job means a lot and adds to his self-esteem.

[23] 'Childlike in the vulnerability of their dependence and consequent fear of abandonment, they claim to wish only to please, but in return for their goodness they expect to be loved and cared for' (Gilligan 1982: 67; cited earlier on page 63).

6

Why I *Paused* . . . and Then Told *Another* Story

The Ancillary Narrative

Any enquiry into how the self reveals itself in language would be incomplete if we do not acknowledge the possibility that there may be aspects of the self *not* revealed in language. A narrative is a shared cognitive space – the narrator and the listener are both engaged in an imaginative world where characters and situations are interpreted towards a certain *end*. Playing on the semantic ambiguity of the word, 'end' suggests both an end to a story as well as the aim of the narrative. Thus, reaching the former end – the end of the story – accomplishes the *how* of the narrative, while reaching the latter end – the aim of the story – accomplishes the *why* of the narrative. In the case of life stories, this shared cognitive space is a contested one – the narrator invites the listener to share her story world but does not want any contestation so that her narrative identity is safe in the moment of interlocution. But humans are complicated beings and have an acute sense of the 'personal'. Hence, even in the shared mental space which the narrator of a life story shares with his audience, there can be contextual assertions of identity and safeguarding of the most private aspects of one's life – those that the storyteller does *not* want the listener to gaze into – and hence these aspects would need protection from any invasion of mental space in the story world.

> Dennett tells us that narrative activity is our chief mode of self-creation. I argue further that *narrative is probably an important instrument of self-protection as well.* It provides, by convention as well as by implication, a format for defining an individual's social territory, and thereby, that individual's unique identity within a community. (Nair 2003: 18; emphasis added)

How exactly can a person protect her *self* while portraying *herself* in her own life story? Is there even a way for the individual to safeguard the most private aspects of his life and protect them from the storytelling urge that pervade humans? Human beings are social – they want recognition *from* the other and altruism dictates that they reach out *for* the other. So how would they protect the self from being deconstructed *by* the other in the narrative space? Which aspects of their lives would people not want to narrate about? It is safe to assume that there are few aspects that remain shrouded with the veil of privacy – these could range from (1) aspects that are potentially face-threatening, i.e. ones that may make a person lose self-worth; to (2) aspects of sexual life that necessarily fall with the private life of an individual; to (3) traumatic episodes that may invoke painful memories.

In Life Story 1 in chapter 3, we saw N struggling to *not* reveal details of a damaging rumour that her gossip-mongering friends purportedly spread about her when she shared a stroll with a male classmate. In that case, N sequesters information within her narrative that could potentially threaten her positive face and narrative identity. We saw how, towards the end of the narrative she redeems her moral ground by positioning her peers, the others, as 'that type' (vicious gossipers) whom there is no use confronting. In Life Story 2 also, we saw M screen out details of what the troubles were that he faced in his village even though he 'headlines' it by saying that the trouble pertained to 'what they would eat and what they would earn', implying a poverty-stricken living. In that narrative, M redeems his narrative identity through the salience of his job which has ensured that he could provide for his children. Below, we look at another narrative in which details of information regarding a traumatic memory are sequestered. Speaker I here was asked by the author as to what she considered to be her spouse's best quality. And even though, in the first instance, the query pertained to when speaker I found strength or inspiration from her spouse (then partner), the life story she narrates has a traumatic experience – the accident and subsequent death of her younger brother. As a narrator, she efficiently sequesters details of the accident and 'edits' the memory, possibly, so that the most painful portions are not relived at the moment of interaction.

Life Story 9:[1] *'Where I Was When He Died . . .'*

Transcript Details:	[BMP B40005]
Participants:	I, her husband B and the author (S).
Language of Interaction:	Hindi and English
Narrative Context:	'IB' interview on for over 60 minutes. Speaker I was asked about her spouse's best quality, or any occasion when she found some kind of strength or inspiration – something that made them go on despite the odds. She starts her turn with a pause in line 5 that is indicative of anxiety; B gets up for a break then and she starts her narration. 'He'/ 'him' in lines 7–9 is B here, while he/him and he/ his in lines 11–19 refer to I's brother who had died in an accident. On being asked specifically about where the accident occurred, I goes on to narrate where she was at the time of the accident while totally sequestering other details of the accident and hence the painful memory.
Narrative Highlights:	Showcases how I sequesters details of brother's accident that are emotionally traumatic while conversing about the time she found strength in her husband (then partner).

Extract I

1 S: *>matlab aapko laga ho bas↓ 'iske sivae aur koi nahi bacha sakta'<=*
meaning you feel happen that's it he-gen other and anyone neg save can
'Means you felt "no one other than him can save . . .".'

→2 I: *hahaha <ye to hamesha hi hota hæ (hehe)*
this dm always emph happen pres
'That always happens ((laughs)).'

→3 S: *hehe nei some* (.) *you kn↑↓ow* (.) *some↑. <u>some</u> kind of.><u>agar</u> aisa huwa hai<* (.) *ki* (.)
no if like this happen pres that
'No! You know, some . . . some kind of . . . if it has happened that . . .'.

→4 *you know* (.) *you felt like giving it all up* ((*and you found strength*))

→5 I: (0.4) *i thin↑k 'se↓e.* ((B gets up for a break))°*so so far the*

→6 *most difficult time*° *for <u>ME</u> as a person was my brother's:::*

7 °*death*°. {*S: hm::*} *and:: the WAY he was with <u>m</u>↑↓<u>e</u>< and my family↑>*

8 *<and ev↑↓en after that↑>*(0.5) *i::: i felt a <u>lot</u> of strength, GOT lot of*
9 *streng↓th* {S:*hm::*} *from him* (.)
10 S: *to unka: kaha:* (.) *æksident hua: tha:*↑?
dm s/he-h-gen where accident happen

'So where had he met with the accident?'

→11 I: *>it it happened in japiur↓<. >me:: jaipur meth i↑: or i*(.)*i had shifted to*
I-nom Jaipur loc pst and

'I was at Jaipur and . . .'.

13 *delhi↓<*{S:*accha::*} *and he was living with me::↑ in <u>jaipur</u>.* {S: *hm:*} *so ><u>HE</u> had*
okay

14 *his exams in decem↑↓ber<*{S: *accha:*}*wahA: pe parha raha: tha: >rajasthan*
okay there loc study prog-masc pst Rajasthan

15 *yuniversity me<. so he said that:: 'i'll finish my exams and then i will come*
university loc

'He was studying there in Rajasthan University . . .'.

16 (.)*to you'*{S: *hm::*}(0.3) *so my mother went to hi↑m, to live with hi↑m, till*
17 *he* (.)*writes his exam.* (.) *IN that- during that period also* (.) *only he* (.)°*met*
→18 *with an accident*°. {S:*accha↓:*} *so I HAD shifted to de↑↓lhi, >it was hardly*
19 *<u>THREE</u> months<, <three- four months>*{S: *hm::*}:°*i came in in august and it*
→20 *happened in december*°(.) *so:: that's ho↓w* ((*it happened*)). *then bikram:::, i think*
→21 *HE got the news, he came to me and took me to jaipur. E::>and ALL THE*
22 *WHI↑↓LE and even <u>after</u> that we felt so LOST↓ and:: >°so i think↑ that was the*
23 *time↑ when i felt that* (.) *my <u>strength</u>*°(.) *WILL come, always come from him,*
24 *if it comes at this difficult time.*

(0.8)((B comes back here))

I's first Turn Construction Unit (TCU) in response to the author's question is laughter – since, crucially, the question itself had an imaginary situation built into it, that of a 'saviour'. I then laughingly says that it was inevitably the case and it always happens. S's next turn in line 3 is also crucial – it elaborates on the question turn forcefully, almost insistently, that *if* any such a situation had happened and she felt like giving it all up and found strength in her partner/husband 'B'. This TCU by S, in retrospect, seems to be a face-saving one since I's laughter to her initial query seems a potentially dismissive one. Hence the forceful appeal to respond to the question occurs in S's turns in lines 3–4. The strategy is successful as, after a pause, I launches into her TCU in lines 5–9, where she admits that the most difficult time she faced as an individual was her brother's death. Her choice of language is also interesting – the conversation was going on in Hindi and both S and I's initial turns are in Hindi, but I's entire TCUs and narratives between lines 5 and 28 are in English.[2]

Tellingly, her voice becomes softer (indicated by '° °') when she mentions her brother's death, and she says that she had found a lot of strength in her husband (then partner) 'because of the way he was' with her and her family – in implicit terms, this alludes to B as a source of strength for her. Since S knew that I had lost her brother in an accident, she asks for specifics about the incident, as to where it had happened (line 10), and I launches into her narrative regarding the incident in her TCU in lines 11–22. The abstract of the story is that 'it happened in Jaipur' and then the narrator shifts the focus away from a traumatic memory by refraining from narrating the exact details but instead narrates about the placement of other people: where she was at that time; where her mother was, and what her brother was doing at that time (he was living in Jaipur with her and planning to join her in Delhi after his exams). While the story moves in the 'narrative present' (I uses clauses with present tense 'till he writes his exam' in line 17), she shifts to past tense. There were a lot of *pauses* and *pitch variations* in her narrative that indicate a guarded *emotional response* since invoking the memory of the accident would have been traumatic. This time I is talking about her brother's fatal accident and instead of saying how the accident occurred, she narrates about what her brother was doing and where she was when the incident happened. And even though she mentions in line 20 that 'that's how it happened', her narrative has never really given exact details of *how* the accident happened. In other words, the traumatic memories are subverted by being *not* narrated. She mentions that her husband Bikram[3] had got the news and he went to take her to Jaipur. Again, details are glossed over and only the affective component is retained ('we felt so lost' in line 22). The loud voice with which she utters the phrase 'all the while' brings her back to the conversational present and she performs the exit talk of her narrative as well as performs a preferred adjacency pair to S's question asked way back in line 1 regarding finding strength in the partner. The intra-narrative changes in pitch, and timed and untimed pauses that signal I's emotional trauma and the shift of focus – from when and how the accident occurred to where the other characters of the narrative (family members) were present – accomplish her sequestration of experience. There is a long silence after this (after line 24), signifying both the narrator and the listener still being into the story domain and the silence is broken only when B – who had gone out for a break – returns to the room.

In this last Extract J below, we shall examine one more remarkable example of sequestration of experience – one that is being called, following Barua (2012a and b), *the ancillary narrative*. The use of narrative structures as a sequestration of experience comes out extremely forcefully in the case of J: following a series of accidents, J had been partially disabled and an acid attack on him due to politically motivated reasons had left him with permanent scars on his person (see note 1 of chapter 5). During the course of the interview the issue is specifically raised by the current author only on one occasion in line 255, when J is asked if he had had an accident (till the time of the interview, S had assumed that the scars were possibly burn marks, and only during the interview in D's TCU cited below did she come to know that it was from a purposive acid attack and that J was not a burn victim but an acid attack victim). Significantly, J's wife D answers for him and says it was not an accident but 'acid had fallen' on him. Her use of the agentless passive construction in line 256 is pertinent – it could still be interpreted as an accidental falling of acid on J. In response to S's question in line 258 J uses overlapping speech and quickly specifies that it was in 'party politics' that the acid had fallen. There is a long silence (in line 261) following S's reaction to J's turn – no one takes the floor and since it clearly showed a defensive state of mind, S refrained from asking any more questions and switched to a new question in line 262 about what languages they spoke at home.

[JDS: A2 0230]

→256 D: *nei æsid:: (.) æsid gir: gaya: tha:=*
no acid acid fall go- pst

'No – acid had fallen on him.'

257 J: *=æsid*
acid

258 S: *ÆSID gira: [tha:?*
acid fall pst

'Acid had fallen?'

→259 J: *[↓ha: >ye pa:rti politiks me<*
yes this party politics loc

'Yes. In this party politics . . .'.

260 S: <*acca:* *acca:*>
okay okay

→261 (0.8)

Unexpectedly, however, D herself brings up the issue of the acid attack in one of her turns much later in the interview. The interview had been going on for over thirty minutes and D and J were talking about the tough times they had faced following S's question about finding strength in each other in lines 651–55. The couple exhibited features of duetting in their subsequent narratives (this stretch of conversation was cited as Extract E in chapter 5). J had narrated about the time when D had done door-to-door sales and his transport business, following which D had narrated about their daughters, and J summarized the ongoing narrative on life and good and bad times in his coda in lines 702–03. The lines that are cited below are actually in continuation of J's coda (in Extract E) where D's progressional onset in line 704 gives a configurational dimension to their joint narratives about good and bad times. J performs duetting when he repeats/rephrases her speech in lines 705 and 707, and goes into another narrative to repeat the story about his cars, etc.

LIFE STORY 10: *'I worked hard . . . [acid thrown on him] . . . I worked hard'*

Transcript Details:	[JDS B1 0351]
Participants:	Same as Extract E (D, J and the author,S)
Language of Interaction:	Hindi
Narrative Context:	The couple were asked about an occasion when they found come kind of strength or inspiration. Following the extensive narrative sequence and duetting as exemplified in Extract E, they talk about all kinds of time and D suddenly brings up the acid attack topic in her TCU in line 714 which is a particularly traumatic memory for J.
Narrative Highlights:	Exemplifies the ancillary narrative that sequesters traumatic memories/experience of the narrator even in the conversational moment that it becomes unexpectedly evoked.

Extract J

→704 D: *'me::nat bhi kari [hæ jindegi me pesa:: bhi dekha: hæ*
hard work also do pres life loc money also see pres

'(We) have worked hard also and seen money also in life . . . '

705 J: *[me:nat kari hæ*
hard work do pres

'(We) have worked hard.'

→706 D: *koi kam[i bhi nei dekhi* {S: *acca*}
some paucity also neg see-pst okay

'(We) have seen paucity of anything in life.'

707 J: *[kami <u>PESE</u> ki nahi hui* {S: *acca:*} *zindagi me*
paucity money gen neg happen okay life loc

708 *bas wo jo >thoda: bohot hota: hi rehta: hæ< sa:l do: sa:l*
just that rel pro little much happen emph stay pres year two year

709 *kisi cakkar me* (.) {S: *hm:*} *wese ga:riya: <u>THI</u> KHADI THI*
some circle loc otherwise cars pst-fem stand pst-fem

'There was no paucity of money as such. In life these little things do keep happening every one or two years. Otherwise, the cars were there, they were standing . . .'. ((Probably meaning the cars could have been used)).

710 *phir sha:diya: kari↑,* {S: *hm*} *phir wo gariya: <u>bech</u> di↓*
then wedding-pl do-pst then those cars sell give

711 *kabariyo ko bech di* {S:*hm:*}[(-)(-) *da::l di* (-) *da:l di*
scrap-dealer dat sell give put give put give

'Then did (arranged) the weddings, then sold off the cars to scrap-dealers; put (?) . . .'.

→712 D: *[wo to dekhi hæ*
that dm see pres

→713 *sab kuc dekha: hæ, <u>har tarah</u> <u>ka:</u> <u>taim</u> dekha: hæ* {J:*ha:* }{S: *ha:*}
all some see pres every type gen time see pres yes yes

'That we have seen; saw everything . . . times of all kinds . . . '

→714 *he:↑? æsid pad gaya: inpar* ((---))[4]
Q into acid fall go-pst he-hon-loc

715 ((Initiates a self-repair and again specifies the year and month of the acid attack/deleted here))

→716 *æsid para hæ: inke upar* {S: *acca*} *to ab kitne::*
acid fall pres s/he-gen top okay dm now how

717 *sa::l ho gaye*
year happen go-pst

'Isn't it? Acid fell on him in (year); it was in (year) that acid had fallen on him. So it's been so many years now . . .'.

718 S: ((year deleted)) *me ha:: [acca: to-* (-) (-)
loc yes okay dm

'In 19 . . .? Okay. So . . .'.

→719 J: *[>HAM TO KARTE RAHE<* *ye* (.) *ye* (.)
I-hon-nom dm do-h prog this this

720 *wo* (.) *tra:::nsport ka: karte rahe* {S: *hm*}=
that transport gen do-h prog

'I kept on working; did that transport work.'

721 D: *=inki [pro:blam*
s/he-h-gen problem

'His problem . . .'.

→722 J: *[PÆLE SHURU SHURU me to mæ:* (.) *jab mætrik ki*↑,
first beginning beginning loc dm I-nom when matric do-pst

723 *>uske ba:d phir mæne::: thekeda:ri ki<* {S: *acca:*}
that-gen after then I-erg contract do-pst okay

'In the beginning right after my matric exams, I did contract work . . .'.

724 *>wo kisi: ke pa*↑↓*:s karta: tha: ka:m* {S:*hm*} *wo hama:ra: tha*↑*::*
that some gen near do-masc pst work that we-gen pst-masc

725 (.)*A::bhai: saha::b the <si pi dabliu di> me ka::m karta: tha:*
brother sir cop c p w d loc work do-masc pst-masc

726 *usne theka: lia: hua: tha:* {S:*hm*} *wo sarvent*(.) *gomant*
s/he-nh-erg contract take happen pst-masc s/he servant government

'I had worked with someone. . . . He was a brother who worked in CPWD. He was a government servant . . .'.

726 *sarvent tha: o::r wai:f ke na:m pe theka: le- le*
servant cop and wife gen name loc contract take take

728 *rakkha: tha:* {S: *acca:*} *jo* (-) (-) *si bana rakhi: thi:* {S: *acca:*}
keep pst okay rel-pro like make keep pst okay

→729 *us>usne naya: ka:m shuru kara:: tha: MÆ GAYA: THA:<*
s/he-nh-erg new work beginning do pst I-erg go pst-masc

'. . . and he had taken up construction work under his wife's name. He had made something like a (?). He had newly started work – I had gone there . . .'.

730 {S: *hm:*} (.) >*mæne ek sa:l ka:m kara: tha:*< *ra:::t* (.)
I-erg one year work do pst-masc night

→731 <*gharwa:le soye hote the*↑ *cala: ja:ta: tha:*↓ *gharwa:le*
home-noz asleep happen pst go-masc go-masc pst-masc home-noz

→732 *so ja:te the*↑ *'tab a:ta: tha:*↓> {S:°*acca*°} *mehnat badi*
sleep go pst then come pst-masc okay hard work much

'I worked there for one year. . . . My family used to be asleep (at night/early morning) when I used to go. And they used to be asleep when I would return. I worked very hard . . .'

733 *kari* {S:*acca(ha)*::} *phir usko usko PE*↑↓::*LE kehdiya: tha:*
do-pst okay then s/he-nh-acc s/he-nh-acc first say give pst

734 >"*bhei hame ka::m sikhna: hæ:*"< {S: *hm*} *ha*↓*: phir uske*
brother I-h-acc work learn-inf pres yes then that

735 *ba:d me*(.) *mæne panja::b me theka: liya:* {S: *acca:*} (-) (-)
after loc I-erg punjab loc contarct take-pst okay

→736 *o:l in o:l tha: wa:ha:* {S:hm:} *sa:ra: usme karta: dherta:* [(*mætha:*)
all in all cop there all that-loc doer I-nom pst

'Then I had told him right at the beginning that I want to learn work and then after that I had taken up contract in Punjab. I was the all-in-all there. I was the in-command.'

J's TCUs in lines 705 and 707 are rephrasings and repetitions of D's TCUs, following which he continues to take the floor and launches into his narrative through lines 709–11. By *phir sha:diya: kari:* in line 710, J means that he got his three daughters married. His repeated narrative about his cars[6] sets off a contest for the floor by D in line 712. She however again gives a *configurational* dimension to his narrative by saying they had seen all kinds of times, and thereafter unexpectedly brings up the acid attack topic in line 714. Her TCU in this line was probably meant to emphasize 'all kinds of times' that they had seen together for so many years, but it turned out to be a potentially damaging turn because of the re-introduction of the acid attack topic in the current conversation. D does a self-repair in line 715 and reiterates that it has been many years since the incident. To subvert D's potential turn-taking as well as to divert the narrative from its potentially damaging aspect, J launches his TCU in loud speech overlapping in line 719 parallel with S's turn in line 718 to emphasize that he kept on working at his transport business. When D tries to continue her turn by referring to his 'problem' in line 721, he again uses *loud speech to usurp the floor and launches into an ancillary narrative about his early career* starting from right after his Class 10 board exams – it is a long TCU that he takes to narrate about his work (lines 722–35), and with this ancillary narrative on his career and work he sequesters his traumatic memory associated with the acid attack.

J's narrative above is not only an attempt to sequester the painful memories of the acid attack that had been brought up suddenly in the conversation, but *also a subtle reiteration of his own masculine identity*. Significantly, he starts his TCU with the honorific *ham to karte rahe* in line 719; the loud speech ensures him the floor and he starts his narrative by stating that he had started work right after his Class 10 (lines 722–23). In his elaborate orientation (lines 724–29), he goes on to speak about how he had gone to a brother (who had newly started work in the construction line in the name of his wife). Much like I in the preceeding extract, J here strategically uses the orientation of his narrative (1) to continue with the narrative floor, and (2) to make sure that the earlier topic of the acid attack is completely deflected. Notably, his orientation actually *follows* a narrative clause (line 723). Labov (1972: 364–65), in speaking of the structural placement of the narrative orientation, remarks that elaborate orientations can work as strategic devices – for example, in portraits of the main character(s) being narrated about. It appears that elaborate orientations within the ancillary narrative function to hold the narrative floor and subvert a potentially traumatic memory. Looked at only from a Conversation Analysis perspective, J's TCU in line 719 can be seen as an attempt to usurp the floor and establish conversational dominance. However, as we have just seen, from a narrative perspective such turns actually launch an ancillary narration to deflect a damaging topic. This analysis clearly demonstrates the advantages of examining a narrative simultaneously from the CA and the narrative perspectives. Nair (2003) notes that narrators typically *compress* their narrative in order that their turn is not challenged:

> The fragility of stories is, paradoxically, an 'interactional' or cooperative feature in conversations because the logic of conversation decrees that it is *recipients* who must play a crucial role in determining which aspects of a story a teller 'may not have . . . right'. Tellers therefore use a number of strategies to protect their narratives. One such method, Sacks suggests, is to *compress* their length and detail so that recipients have fewer opportunities to challenge them. (Nair 2003: 263)

On the contrary, however, as we saw above, it is because one of J's listeners – his wife, who was also his narrative duetting partner – *threatens* his narrative identity with the bringing up of a traumatic memory, that J launches into extensive ancillary narrative and, rather than compressing, he *elaborates* on his life story starting with completion of the Matric exams when he started his work life. The onset of the complicating action and resolution of his narrative are signalled by the loud assertive statement, *MÆ GAYA: THA* ('I had gone') in line 729, and his *position calling* within this ancillary narration is also made clear – *he is the hard-working provider for his family*. He shifts to slow speech to focus on that aspect in lines 730–31 – he would go to work when his family was asleep at night, and by the time he returned after a hard day's work, his family would be in bed. He reaches the explicit evaluation of his narrative in lines 732–33 when he says, *mehnat badi kari* ('I worked very hard'), and he reports telling his brother/employer that he was keen on learning work. Through another temporal clause he says that he subsequently had taken up work independently in Punjab and his narrative resolution claims that he was the 'all-in-all' there – the sole person in command. This narrative on career, and specially the emphasis on hard work and the last line where he categorically states that he was the 'all-in-all', can be seen as an assertion of J's masculine identity. Any doubt cast on his capacity to provide for his family and his (real/symbolic) role as the breadwinner is then 'unjustified' – he kept on doing his transport business (line 719) just as he had worked hard in the initial days of his life when he had provided for his family. In this sense, not only is this narrative a sequestration of the traumatic experience of the acid attack but an assertion that the incident did not leave him de-masculinized.

With regard to storytelling that reports extraordinary events, Nair (2003) argues:

> Over-emphasis on the extraordinary by story-tellers often has the paradoxical consequence that recipients are bored. Since stories typically put the 'selves' of teller and listener into conversational contact, they offer a series of glimpses into the organization of inner landscapes. Mental territories are opened out and we get to compare how weirdly similar our minds are – how extraordinarily ordinary. (Nair 2003: 278)

Here, a self has faced an extraordinarily difficult situation (an acid attack) – and there was the opportunity of narrating an unbelievable tale of heroism, optimism and courage. However, instead of narrating about the particularities of the event – when and where it happened, how did he feel, how much of a painful experience it was, how did his family cope – he traces the entire trajectory of his being from his very first landmark experience (his

Matric exams) to how he managed his first decent job. For a person who had faced such extraordinary circumstances to try and narrate about *other* things speaks volumes of the power of narrative to both reveal and protect the self. As a screening-off device for potentially harmful topics, the ancillary narrative proved to be a potent discursive strategy and a good *defensive linguistic technique* by which a narrator avoids talking about an event in the past that can potentially trigger painful memories. It has been suggested by the author (in Barua 2012b) that narrative structures can encode and establish the positioning of the narrator vis-à-vis the sociocultural dynamics of her/his world, but ancillary narratives can themselves be differently oriented. For example, the ancillary narratives of husband–wife dyads may be *potentially different* from those centered around peer-group culture in terms of self–other positioning – the former *may be more self-protective* and latter *more self-preserving*. In the case of J (in Life Story 10), the sequestering was more inwards and self-directed (there were aspects of the narrator's past and experiences that were sought to be withheld from the person himself), whereas in the context of the young Assamese university student narrating about the peer group (in Life Story 1), the narrative sequestered information was more outwards and other-directed (the information withheld would have revealed what the *other* thought about the narrator). It remains to be seen what other aspects of selfhood and otherness the ancillary narrative may reveal; for the moment it suffices to say that when a person *says* more in a narrative, it does not necessarily *reveal* more about his/her self.

Notes

[1] Extract I is from an interview of I and B conducted for the author's PhD (Barua 2012a). At the time of the interview, the high-income couple (defined in the study as earning more than Rs 90,000 per month) IB stayed in South Delhi in a rented apartment. B had been staying in Delhi intermittently since 1990 for his education and then his stints at various jobs; I came to Delhi just prior to their marriage in 2005. At the time of the interview, I was not working full time and was doing part-time work from home in order to take care of their infant son. B was working on international projects earlier and at the time of the interview was working with an NGO. B later gave up his job and opened his own firm while I did a Master's degree from a foreign university and took up full-time work. I and B spoke Hindi between themselves at home, while with extended relatives I spoke Maithili and B spoke Karampuri.

[2] This choice of language could be on account of the fact that this high-end couple who had been informed at the beginning of their interaction with the author – then a researcher – that they could converse in either Hindi or English, chose to answer

most of their questions in English. Was it on account of an underlying belief that interlocution with a PhD student should be in English, or the fact that English, being their second language, was more 'emotionally distant' and hence I switched to English here? It is a matter of surmise here but for multilingual speakers, choice of L1 or L2 are also significant markers of their salient identity at the moment of speaking.

[3] Name changed to preserve anonymity.

[4] D cites year of occurrence, which is deleted here to protect identity.

[5] A government department dealing with public construction in India.

[6] J has already talked about his transport business and cars that he had to sell off to scrap-dealers in lines 244–49, 557–59, 673–79 of the interview earlier, which indicates the salience this transport business had for him in his life.

7

Moral of the Story? 'Good Selves in Good Narratives'

We began this exploration into life stories with the intention of precisely locating the phenomenon of linguistic identity within the structure of the narrative. We started our enquiry by looking at how and why human beings started telling stories and how minds starting from childhood are storied worlds. Through explorations of the question of morality and goodness we arrived at our primary contention that *it is in the stories we tell about our lives that our selfhood gets expressed* – in talking about the 'good life' we aspire for, our narratives position us as 'good' selves. This necessitated a brief detour into the concept of selfhood amongst the philosophical positions that we found tenable for the postulation of an ethico-moral self within the narrative. We also looked at gendered notions of self and ethics, and then took a framework for studying the narrative structure. So what have these life stories taught us about narratives? As a discursive strategy that locates the ideals of goodness within notions of reflexive good life circumscribed by a cultural matrix, we can agree with Bonn and Tafarodi (2014) that in the personal narrative,

> . . . the sense of personal coherence and sameness that allows a mature person to plan for the future and commit to given courses of action and relationships (i.e., identity; see Erikson 1950, 1968) is highly dependent upon role-based expectations defined within the context of cultural narratives. The story lines along which individuals organize their lives, the scripts that they see and hear played out in their surroundings everyday, become the templates by which they learn to structure and evaluate their own personal narratives (Bauer *et al.* 2008;

> Hammack 2008; White 2006). Individuals' internal narratives, the stories they tell themselves about who they are, emerge from a lifelong process by which personal experiences are reconciled with the stories that prevail within the social milieu (McAdams 2001; Quinn 2003). (Bonn and Tafarodi 2014: 742)

University student N's narrative in Life Story 1 sees her circumscribed within the peer culture who gossip and spread needless malicious rumours. Her narrative is thus interspersed with linguistic symbols of hesitations and hedges – she ultimately capitalizes on a turn by an other (her interviewer/listener) to resurrect her narrative identity. A cleaning staff member engaged in a hostel, M's Life Stories 2, 3 and 4 help him rise above his station in life through the salience of his job; the metaphor of biscuits as a life of plenty defines his position of a provider who did a better job than his own parents at parenting since he was able to provide at least half a meal to his children in the evening if they had had a full one by day. M's life partner N (different from the speaker N of Life Story 1 above who was a university student) turns a duetting partner as she provides configurational dimensions to M's stories and they perform their coupledom. This later becomes even more pronounced in the case of D and J in Life Story 5, who have been married for many more decades than N and M, and do exquisite duetting in their narratives. Gendered identity surfaces in R and U's narratives in Life Stories 6 and 7 whereby cultural notions of goodness and patriarchy lurk beneath the narratives as deep assertions of identity. It gets reiterated and typified in like narratives by M and N in Life Story 8. Finally, aspects of self that seek to remain hidden or protected are sequestered through the ancillary narrative in Life Stories 9 and 10 of I and J. These teach us that 'storytelling' can tellingly be about what we do not wish the other to know about us.

But to end this story about the story now, have we derived any moral from our endeavour?

> Stories obey a *linguistic law of 'necessary incompleteness'* . . . this is so because all discourse genres, of which narrative is arguably just the most prototypical example, are embedded in the cognitive context of conversation. Language may primarily be a tool of thought, but discourse genres – jokes, riddles, lectures, novels, poems, rap, tall tales, etc. – cannot but be at least 'two-party'. They are specifically designed to turn talk into text – that is, to call up perlocutionary inferences. (Nair 2003: 261; emphasis added)

The incompleteness that you, the reader or I, the author may be feeling owes a lot to the essence of storytelling. This necessary incompleteness, though, is not the fate of the narrative alone but of that human connection. So, just as I started this book by addressing you, I draw out the moral of *this* story by addressing *you*.

From a self's/speaker's perspective, the revelation possibly occurs thus: I want to share an episode of my life with you. Through this sharing, I tacitly want to establish that I am a good self and I want you, as my listener, to acknowledge that I am this good self as projected in my narrative identity itself. You co-construct this good self when your turns do not challenge me. Where they do challenge me, I must protect my own sense of self and gendered personhood by deflecting away – it can be a simple strategy such as *the distancing principle*, or it can be an ancillary narrative. I also might want you to know my culture, my people, my problems, but ultimately, I want to establish a good self who is inhabited by culture, so much so that I cannot extricate my selfhood from my culture to stand there stripped of identity so to speak. In the fragility of my conversation with you, I narrate and thereby take a *linguistic selfie* (Barua 2016b: 309) – so that when you take the reiterable character of narratives to re-narrate my story, you also remember to use this perspective with which this selfie was taken.

From the other's/listener's perspective, the revelation possibly occurs thus: I want to listen to you as I wish to know you better and, more importantly, I have the altruistic desire to make you, the narrator and myself, the listener, relevant. I backchannel and use other markers to acknowledge that I am indeed in the conversational moment and yet have entered your story world. If I find any inconsistencies, I may knowingly or unknowingly challenge you, but overall, my turns help to chisel out your story because I too have narrated it. I share cultural knowledge with you of what constitutes a story, and if your story was worth anything to me, I contribute with various aspects of the narrative form thereby co-constructing both your narrative and you. As co-conversationalists, we have equal rights to hold the floor, but as a story-listener, I suspend my rights momentarily to allow you the luxury of a monologue for at least the complicating action and resolution of your narrative. When you take that linguistic selfie, it has me in the backdrop and thereby your subjectivity is not yours alone. In orienting to your 'good' self, I too emerge as a good 'other'.

As to what we will discuss when we do meet in person, well, *that* is another story.

Appendix

Additional Extracts

Extract 1: Goodness as related to the father's self-esteem

[RSB A5 0115]

(('UR' interview has been on for nearly forty minutes; R here replies to a query as what is their topmost priority in life; he says the children are his biggest responsibility and they should be eligible for the sake of his name)).

→527 R:	[*mera:*	*to yahi*	*hæ*								
	I-gen	dm this	pres								
528	*ki*	*JO*	*BACCA:*	*AGAR*	*APNA:*	*SA::RI*	*ZIMMEDA::RI*	*APNA:* (.)			
	that	rel	prochild	if	self	all	responsibilities	self			
529	*bacce*	*la::yak*	*hæ*	*to sab*	*kuc*	{S: *acca:*}	*sab kuc*	*hæ*	*ya::ni*↑		
	children	eligible	pres	then all	thing	okay	all thing	pres	means		
→530	*bacce*	*mere*	*ya::ni* ↑ (.)	*meri*	*ba::t*	*na:*	*khara::b*	*kare*	*jese*	*mæne*	
	children	I-gen	mean	I-gen	talk	neg	bad	do	like	i-erg	

'For me it is this that child of mine … s/he is full responsibility. If my children are eligible means … that is everything. My children should not spoil what I say. . . .'

→531	*nahi*	*ki:*	*hæ*	{S: *ha:*}	*meri*	*ijjat*	*ko*	*dhabba:*	*nehi*	*hæ*	{S: *ha:*}	
	neg	that	pres	yes	I-gen	respect	acc	taint	neg	pres	yes	
→532	*sab*	*se*	*badi*	*YE CHIJ*	*HÆ*	{S: *ha:*}	*agar*	*meri*	*ijjat*	*thik*	*hæ*	
	all	from	big	this thing	pres	yes	if	I-gen	respect	right	pres	

→533 *to sab kuc hæ nahi:to kuc bhi nahi* {S:*acca:*} *'bacce ke mere to*
dm all thing pres neg dm some also neg okay children gen I-gen dm

534 *yahi hæ ki apna:: mæ to nahi parha: likha:* {S: *hm*}
this pres that self I-erg dm neg read write

535 *ba:ki bacco ka: mæ ca::hta: hu mere se acca: parhe likhe*↑
rest children gen I-nom wish-masc pres I-gen from good read write

'My respect should not get tainted . . . that is the biggest thing. If my respect is right then it is everything, otherwise there is nothing. About the children it is that . . . I am not educated. Rest, I want my children to be better educated than me.'

536 S: *sahi ba:[:t hæ*
right talk pres

'That is right.'

537 R: [*acchi sosaiti*↑ *me BETHE* {S: *hm*} *acchi ba*↑ *::te sikhe*↑ {S:*hm*}
good society loc sit-pl-3 good talk learn

538 *mæne to nahi kuc kia: mæne jo bhi kuc hæ: meri jindegi*
I-erg dm neg some do-pst I-erg rel pro also come pres I-gen life

539 *to a::dhi kat gayi* {S: *hm*} (.) *a::dhi o:r jese marji kat ja::yegi*
dm half pass go-pst half and like wish pass go-fut

540 {S: *hm*} (-) (-) (-) *ba:ki mæ baccõ se yahi kahunga:*
rest I-nom children with this say-fut-masc

'They should sit in good society, learn good things. . . . Whatever it is, my life is half-gone and rest will go as I wish it. . . . Rest, what I would tell my children.'

541 *ki jo hæ a:pna: jo hæ acci ba::te sikho acche sosaiti me*
that pres self rel pres good talk learn2 good socity loc

542 *betho*{S: *hm*} *or acci::: ya::ni ka::m karlo jaldi (ta::ke tumha::ri)*
sit2 and good means work do2 quickly so that you-gen

543 *koi bad na::mi na: ho*
some bad name neg happen

'Learn good things, sit in good society and do good things quickly so that (you) do not get a bad name.'

((S's line deleted))

→545 R: *sabse bari ijjat hæ*↑ {S:*hm*} *agar ijjat hæ to sab kuc hæ*
all from big respect pres if respect pres then all thing pres

546 *nahi to kuc bhi nahi*
neg dm some also neg

'Respect is the biggest thing . . . if there is respect there is everything. If not there is nothing.'

Extract 2: M's narrative on ideal family who does not fight

[MNK A2 0520]

(('NM' has been on for about fifteen minutes. N and M are saying how they do not fight. The extract cited here is following N's narrative about how they laugh at neighbours who do fight, and M's narrative about how he stayed for five years at his sister's place where he and M never quarrelled. He attributes this 'setting' to lessons learnt from his home. It is pertinent that though M is speaking about an ideal family whose members do not fight and have a non-confrontational attitude, he reports his mother and elder brother as using abusive speech when they are angry – line 362.))

357 *or ye SETTIN hamne dekhi he apne ghar se* {S: *accha:*}
and this setting we-erg see pres self home from okay

358 *ham ca:r bha:i hæ*↓ {S:*hmm*} *MA:*↑(.) *or bada: bha:i*↓{S: *hm::*}
we four brothers cop mother and big brother

359 *agar kuc kehne lag ja:ye na: hame*↑: {S:*hm:*} *bai ca:ns*
if something say-inf join go-fut dm we-acc by chance

'And this setting we have seen from our home. We are four brothers. If mother or elder brother start saying something to us – by chance . . .'.

360 *wo gussa: kabhi kar ja:te hæ or ga:li dene*
they anger sometimes do go-impf pres and scolding give-inf

361 *lagte hæ bha:i* (.) *or ma: bhi* (.) *ga:li dene*
join-impf-2 pres brother and mother also scolding give-inf

→362 *lagti hæ* >"@*kutte kamine ye nei karte wo nei*
join-impf-2-fem pres dog scoundrel this neg do that neg

363 *karte, esa hæ wesa hæ*@"<, *to ham ti:no bha:i khisak*
do-impf this pres that pres then we three-incl brothers slip

364 *lete hæ*=
take-impf-1 pres

'. . . they get angry sometimes and start scolding us – both mother and elder brother: "You dogs/scoundrels/rascals – you do not do this, you do not do that", then we three brothers just slip out.'

((S's turn/laughter deleted))

366 M: *matlab,* *<unka:* *sa:mna* *nei* *kar[te>*
means their-hon front neg do-perf

'Means we do not confront them'.

367 S: [*nei* *karte* *ha::*
neg do-perf-2 pres

'Do not do – yes.'

368 M: *or(.)* <u>*pandhra:*</u> *minute* *ba:d* *ya:* *ghante* *ba:d* *unke* *sa:mne*
and fifteen minutes later or hour later their-hon front

→369 *ham* *jayenge* *ek* *ek* *karke,* {S:*accha::*} ↑*phir* *phæmili* *ikkathi*
we go-fut-1 one one do-cpm okay again family together

'And after fifteen minutes or one hour we go in front of them one by one – the family is together again.'

((S's line deleted))

371 M: *us* *gussa:* *ka* *agar* *ham* *sa:mna:* *karenge,* *>unko* *to* *gussa*
that anger gen if we-nom front do-fut-2 they-acc dm anger

372 *a↑::* *hi* *raha:* *hæ,* {S:°*hm*°} *hame*↑ *bhi* *gussa:* *ayega:*
come emph prog pres we-acc also anger come-fut

373 *or* *ham* *bhi* *kuc* *bol denge,* *wo* *to* *hame* *gussa:* *kar* *hi*
and we-nom also something say give-1 that dm we-acc anger do emph

374 *rahe* *hæ,* *agar* *hamne* *thoda:* *sa:* *bhi* *kuc* *bol* *dia*
prog pres if we-erg little cl also something say giv-pst

375 *phir* *jhagra:* *or* *bhi* *barh* *jayega:* <{S: *accha:*} *is* *kar ke*
then fight more also grow go-fut okay this do cpm

'If we confront that anger, they are already angry and we also will get angry and say something. They are already angry with us and if we say even a little thing, then the fight will only increase. So . . .'.

376 *hamne* *piche* *se* *hi* *apni* (.) *phæmili* *se* *hi* *settiN*
we-erg back from emph self family from emph setting

377 *ye* *bohot* *acci* *si:kh* *li* *hæ* {S: *acc(h)a:*} *bh(h)ai*
this very good learn take pres brother

'. . . then the fight will just get extended. So we have learnt this setting back from our family only that . . .'.

378 *apni* *galti* *ka:* *ehsa:s* *karo* {S: *ha:*} *bhai* *ye* *galti* *meri*
self fault gen realization do yes brother this fault I-gen

379 *hæ* *yaha:* {S: *ha:*} *ye* *galti* *unki* *hæ* {S: *hmm*}
is here yes this fault s/he-hon-gen is yes

380 *to* *a:pas* *me* *jhagra:* *hone* *ka:* *sawa:l* *hi* *nei* *utthta::*
then within loc fight happen gen question emph neg arise

'. . . realize your own fault – this fault is mine and this fault is yours. Then there is no question of fights amongst yourselves.'

Bibliography

Abrams, D. and M.A. Hogg (1990), *Social Identity Theory: Constructive and Critical Advances*, London: Havester-Wheatsheaf.

Acker, J. (1991), 'Hierarchies, Jobs, Bodies: A Theory of Gendered Organizations', in J. Lorber and S.A. Farrell, eds, *The Social Construction of Gender*, Thousand Oaks, CA: Sage Publications.

Alcoff, L.M. and E.F. Kittay, eds (2007), *The Blackwell Guide to Feminist Philosophy*, United Kingdom: Blackwell Publishing.

Amos, V. and P. Parmar (1984), 'Challenging Imperial Feminism', *Feminist Review*, vol. 17, pp. 3–20.

Anderson, E. (1999), 'What is the Point of Equality?', *Ethics*, vol. 109, no. 2, pp. 287–337.

Anderson, W.T., ed. (1996), *The Fontana Postmodernism Reader*, London: Fontana Press.

Aries, E.J. (1982), 'Verbal and Non-Verbal Behaviour in Single-Sex and Mixed-Sex Groups: Are Traditional Sex Roles Changing?', *Psychological Reports*, vol. 51, pp. 127–34.

Armbruster, H. and U.H. Meinhof (2005), 'Storying East-German Pasts: Memory Discourses and Narratives of Readjustment on the German/Polish and Former German/German Border', in J. Thornborrow and J. Coates, eds, *The Sociolinguistics of Narrative*, vol. 6, Amsterdam and Philadelphia: John Benjamins Publishing Company, pp. 41–65.

Atkins, K., ed. (2005), *Self and Subjectivity*, United Kingdom: Blackwell Publishing.

Babb, L.A. (1983), 'Destiny and Responsibility: Karma in Popular Hinduism', in C.F. Keyes and E.V. Daniel, eds, *Karma: An Anthropological Inquiry*, Berkeley: University of California Press, pp. 163–81.

Banton, M. (1965), *Roles*, London: Tavistock.

Barua, S. (2005), 'Conversational Dominance and Gender Construction among Primary School Children: A Case Study', MPhil dissertation, University of Delhi, Delhi.

—— (2012a), 'Revelation of Self in Language: A Conversation Analysis of Hindi-Speaking Couples', PhD thesis, University of Delhi, Delhi.

—— (2012b), '"Tell-tale Stories": Cross-cultural Perspectives on the Role of the Ancillary Narrative', paper presented at the 34th All India Conference of Linguists (AICL), NEHU, Shillong, November.

—— (2014), 'Women and the Injunction to Care: A Case Study of Reminiscences', *Journal of Higher Education and Research Society*, vol. 2, no. 1, pp. 10–20.

—— (2016a), 'Othering in Self-ascription: A Case for the Linguistic Selfie', in V. Dhanaraju, ed., *Voice of the Other: Understanding Marginal Identities*, New Delhi: GenNext Publication, pp. 298–310.

—— (2016b), 'Marginalizing the Marginalized: The Feminine Narrative Voice and/as Exclusionist Language', in D.P. Nath, ed., *Women's Narratives from North East India: Lives in the Margins*, Guwahati: Purbanchal Prakash, pp. 48–64.

—— (2016c), 'The Meaning of *Ma:ne*: A Conversational Filler, a Structural Necessity and a Cognitive Endowment', in M. Barbora and G.K. Borah, eds, *Aspects of Modern Assamese*, Guwahati: Bhabani Books, 2016, pp. 192–213.

—— (2017), 'Locating Exclusion in Male Peer Talk', *Journal of Exclusion Studies*, vol. 7, no. 1, 2017, pp. 76–89.

—— (2018/2020), 'Symbolic Acts, Implied Character: Constructing the Peer Identity', in Om Prakash and Rajesh Kumar, eds, *Linguistic Foundations of Identity: Readings in Language, Literature and Contemporary Culture*, New Delhi: Aakar Books, pp. 48–62 (2018 edition); London: Routledge (2020 edition); DOI: https://doi.org/10.4324/9781003106807.

Bauer, J.J., D.P. McAdams and J.L. Pals (2008), 'Narrative Identity and Eudaimonic Well-being', *Journal of Happiness Studies*, vol. 9, pp. 81–104.

Bell, V. (1999), 'On Speech, Race and Melancholia: An Interview with Judith Butler', *Theory, Culture and Society*, vol. 16, no. 2, pp. 163–74.

Benhabib, S. (1986), 'The Generalized and the Concrete Other: The Kohlberg-Gilligan Controversy and Moral Theory', *Praxis International*, vol. 5, no. 4, pp. 402–24; reprinted in E.F. Kittay and D.T. Meyers, eds, *Women and Moral Theory*, New Jersey: Rowman and Littlefield, 1987, pp. 154–77.

—— (1992), *Situating the Self: Gender, Community and Postmodernism in Contemporary Ethics*, Oxford: Polity Press.

Berntsen, D. and A. Bohn (2009), 'Cultural Life Scripts and Individual Life Stories', in P. Boyer and J. Wertsch, eds, *Memory in Mind and Culture*, Cambridge: Cambridge University Press, pp. 62–82.

Blum-Kulka, S. (2005), 'Modes of Meaning in Young Children's Conversational Storytelling', in J. Thornborrow and J. Coates, eds, *The Sociolinguistics of Narrative*, vol. 6, Amsterdam and Philadelphia: John Benjamins Publishing Company, pp. 149–70.

Bonn, G. and R.W. Tafarodi (2014), 'Chinese and South Asian Conceptions of the Good Life and Personal Narratives', *Journal of Happiness Studies*, vol. 14, pp. 741–55.

Boyd, B. (2009), *On the Origin of Stories: Evolution, Cognition, Fiction*, Cambridge, MA: Harvard University Press.

Brigss, C., ed. (1996), *Disorderly Discourse: Narrative, Conflict and Inequality*, Oxford: Oxford University Press.

Bruner, J. (1987), 'Life as Narrative', *Social Research*, vol. 54, no. 1, pp. 11–32.

—— (1990), *Acts of Meaning*, Cambridge, MA: Harvard University Press.

—— (1991), 'The Narrative Construction of Reality', *Critical Inquiry*, vol. 18, pp. 1–21.

—— (2001), 'Self-Making and World-Making', in J. Brockmeier and D. Carcaugh, eds, *Narrative and Identity: Studies in Autobiography, Self and Culture*, Amsterdam: John Benjamins, pp. 25–28.

Burke, P.J. (2003), 'Introduction', in P.J. Burke, T.J. Owens, R.T. Serpe and P.A. Thoits, eds, *Advances in Identity Theory and Research*, New York: Kluwer Academic/Plenum Publishers.

Burman, E. (1994), *Deconstructing Developmental Psychology*, London: Routledge.

Butler, J. (1993), *Bodies that Matter: On the Discursive Limits of Sex*, London: Routledge.

—— ([1990] 1999), *Gender Trouble: Feminism and the Subversion of Identity*, New York: Routledge.

—— (2000), 'Critically Queer', in A. Tripp, ed., *Gender*, New York: Palgrave, pp. 154–67.

Button, G. (1990), 'Going Up a Blind Alley: Conflating Conversation Analysis and Computational Modelling', in P. Luff, N. Gilbert and D. Frohlich, eds, *Computers and Conversation*, London: Academic Press, pp. 67–90.

Calhoun, C., ed. (1994), *Social Theory and the Politics of Identity*, Cambridge, MA: Blackwell Publishing.

Cameron, D. (1995), 'Rethinking Language and Gender Studies: Some Issues for the 1990s', in S. Mills, ed., *Language and Gender: Interdisciplinary Perspectives*, London: Longman, pp. 31–44.

—— (1997), 'Performing Gender Identity: Young Men's Talk and Construction of Heterosexual Masculinity', in S. Johnson and U. Meinhof, eds, *Language and Masculinity*, Oxford: Blackwell, pp. 47–64.

Cameron, D. and D. Kulick (2003), *Language and Sexuality*, Cambridge: Cambridge University Press.

Card, C., ed. (1991), *Feminist Ethics*, Kansas: University of Kansas Press.

Carr, H. (1988), 'In Other Words: Native American Women's Autobiography', in B. Brodzki and S. Schenck, eds, *Life/Lines: Theorizing Women's Autobiography*, Ithaca: Cornell University Press.

Chodorow, N. (1974), 'Family Structure and Feminine Personality', in M.Z. Rosaldo and L. Lamphere, eds, *Woman, Culture and Society*, Stanford: Stanford University Press.

—— (1978), *The Reproduction of Mothering*, Berkeley: University of California Press.

Cixous, H. ([1983] 1992), 'The Laugh of Medusa', in E. Abel and E.K. Abel, eds, *The Signs Reader: Women, Gender and Scholarship*, Chicago: Chicago University Press.

Cixous, H. and C. Clement ([1975] 1986), *The Newly Born Woman*, Minneapolis: University of Minnesota Press.

Clark, H.H. (1996), *Using Language*, Cambridge: Cambridge University Press.

Coates, J. (1996), *Women Talk*, Oxford: Blackwell.

—— (1997a), 'One-at-a-Time: The Organization of Men's Talk', in S. Johnson and U.F. Meinhof, eds, *Language and Masculinity*, Oxford: Blackwell, pp. 107–29.

—— (1997b), 'The Construction of a Collaborative Floor in Women's Friendly Talk', in T. Givon, ed., *Conversation: Cognitive, Communicative and Social Perspectives*, Amsterdam: John Benjamins, pp. 55–89.

—— (2005), 'Masculinity, Collaborative Narration and the Heterosexual Couple', in J. Thornborrow and J. Coates, eds, *The Sociolinguistics of Narrative*, vol. 6, Amsterdam and Philadelphia: John Benjamins Publishing Company, pp. 89–107.

Cook-Gumperz. J. and M. Szymanski (2001), 'Classroom "Families": Cooperating or Competing – Girls' and Boys' International styles in a Bilingual Classroom', *Research on Language and Social Interaction*, vol. 34, no. 1, pp. 107–30.

Cote, J.E. (1986), 'Traditionalism and Feminism: A Typology of Strategies Used by University Women to Manage Career-Family Conflicts', *Social Behaviour and Personality*, vol. 35, no. 5, pp. 133–43.

Coupland, N., P. Garrett and A. Williams (2005), 'Narrative Demands, Cultural Performance and Evaluation: Teenage Boys' Stories for Their Peer Groups', in J. Thornborrow and J. Coates, eds, *The Sociolinguistics of Narrative*, vol. 6., Amsterdam and Philadelphia: John Benjamins Publishing Company, pp. 67–87.

Cranny-Francis, A., W. Waring, P. Stravropoulos and J. Kirby (2003), *Gender Studies: Term and Debates*, New York: Palgrave Macmillan.

Crenshaw, K. (1992), 'Whose Story Is It Anyway? Feminist and Antiracist Appropriations of Anita Hill', in T. Morrison, ed., *Race-in Justice, En-gendering Power*, New York: Pantheon Books.

Crismore, A. and W.J. Vande Kopple (1990), 'Rhetorical Contexts and Hedges', *Rhetoric Society Quarterly*, vol. 20, no. 1, pp. 49–59.

Daiute, C. and C. Lightfoot (2004), 'Editors' Introduction: Theory and Craft in Narrative Inquiry', in C. Daiute and C. Lightfoot, eds, *Narrative Analysis: Studying the Development of Individuals in Society*, California: Sage Publications, pp. vii–xviii.

de Beauvoir, S. (1997), *The Second Sex*, edited and translated by H.M. Parshley, London: Vintage; first published in French as *Le Deuxième Sexe*, Paris: Editions Gallimard, 1949.

Derrida, J. ([1967] 1973), *Speech and Phenomena*, translated by D. Allison, Evanston, Illinois: Northwestern University Press.

—— ([1967] 1976), *Of Grammatology*, translated by G. Spivak, Baltimore: The John Hopkins University Press.

—— ([1967] 1978), *Writing and Difference*, translated by A. Bass, London: Routledge.

—— ([1977] 1988), *Limited Inc*, translated and edited by by S.Weber, J. Mehlam, and G. Graff, Evanston Illinois: Northwestern University Press.

—— (1998), *Monolingualism of the Other or The Prosthesis of Origin*, translated by P. Mensah, Stanford: Stanford University Press.

Dressler, R.A. and R.J. Kreuz (2000), 'Transcribing Oral Discourse: A Survey and a Model System', *Discourse Processes*, vol. 29, no. 1, pp. 25–36.

Dunbar, R. (1997), *Grooming, Gossip, and the Evolution of Language*, London: Faber and Faber.

Eakins, B.W. and R.G. Eakins (1978), *Sex Differences in Human Communication*, Boston: Houghton Mufflin.

Eckert, P. and S. McConnell Ginet (2003), *Language and Gender*, Cambridge: Cambridge University Press.

Erikson, E.H. (1950), *Childhood and Society*, New York: Norton.

—— (1960), 'The Problem of Ego Identity', in S.M. Stein, A.J. Vidich and D.M. White, eds, *Identity and Anxiety: Survival of the Person in Mass Society*, New York: The Free Press.

—— (1968), *Identity: Youth and Crisis*, New York: Norton.

Falk, S. (1980), 'The Conversational Duet', in *Proceedings of the 6th Annual Meeting of the Berkeley Linguistic Society*, vol. 6, pp. 507–17.

Fausto-Sterling, A. (2000), 'How to Build a Man', in A. Tripp, ed., *Gender*, New York: Palgrave, pp. 109–14.

Fishman, P. (1978), 'Interaction: The Work Women Do', *Social Problems*, vol. 25, pp. 397–406; reprinted in B. Thorne, C. Kramarae and N. Henley, eds, *Language, Gender and Society*, Rowley, MA: Newbury House, 1983, pp. 89–101.

Foucault, M. (1972), *The Archaeology of Knowledge and the Discourse on Language*, translated by A.M. Sheridan Smith, New York: Pantheon Books.

—— ([1988] 1990), 'An Aesthetics of Expereince', interview by A. Fontana, in L.D. Kritzman, *Michel Foucault: Politics, Philosophy and Culture: Interviews and Other Writings, 1977–1984*, New York and London: Routledge, pp. 47–53.

—— (1994), *The Order of Things*, New York: Vintage Books.

Frankfurt, H. (1971), 'Freedom of the Will and the Concept of the Person', *Journal of Philosophy*, vol. 68, pp. 5–20.

Freeman, M. (1991), 'Rewriting the Self: Development as Moral Practice', in M.B. Tappan and M.J. Packer, eds, *Narrative Approaches to Moral Development: New Directions for Child Development,* vol. 54, pp. 83–101.

—— (1993a), *Finding the Muse: A Sociopsychological Inquiry into the Conditions of Artistic Creativity*, Cambridge: Cambridge University Press.

—— (1993b), *Rewriting the Self: History, Memory, Narrative*, London: Routledge.

—— (2004), 'Data Are Everywhere: Narrative Criticism in the Literature of Experience', in C. Daiute and C. Lightfoot, eds, *Narrative Analysis: Studying the Development of Individuals in Society*, California: Sage Publications, pp. 63–81.

Freud, S. ([1905] 1961), 'Three Essays on the Theory of Sexuality', in J. Strachey, trans. and ed., *The Standard Edition of the Complete Works of Sigmund Freud*, vol. 8, London: The Hogart Press.

—— (1908), 'Civilized Sexual Morality and Modern Nervous Illness', in *The Standard Edition of the Complete Works of Sigmund Freud*, vol. 9, London: The Hogart Press.

—— (1925), 'Some Psychical Consequences of the Anatomical Distinction Between the Sexes', in *The Standard Edition of the Complete Works of Sigmund Freud*, vol. 19, London: The Hogart Press.

—— (1930), 'Civilization and Its Discontents', in *The Standard Edition of the Complete Works of Sigmund Freud*, vol. 21, London: The Hogart Press.

Friedman, M. (1997), 'Autonomy and Social Relations: Rethinking the Feminist Critique', in D.T. Meyers, ed., *Feminists Rethink the Self*, Boulder: Westside Press, pp. 40–61.

—— (2000), 'Feminism in Ethics: Conceptions of Autonomy', in S. Fricker and J. Hornsby, eds, *The Cambridge Companion to Feminism in Philosophy*, Cambridge: Cambridge University Press.

Friedman, M. and A. Bolte (2007), 'Ethics and Feminism', in L.M. Alcoff and E.F. Kittay, eds, *The Blackwell Guide to Feminist Philosophy*, UK: Blackwell Publishing, pp. 81–101.

Gay, M. (1992), 'Talking with Adolescents', *British Journal Hospital Medicine*, vol. 47, no. 3, pp. 207–18.

Gazzaniga, M. (2000), *The Mind's Past*, Berkeley: University of California Press.

—— (2008a), 'Forty Five Years of Split Brain Research and Still Going Strong', *Nature Reviews Neuroscience*, vol. 6, pp. 633–59.

Gazzaniga, M. (2008b), *Human*, New York: Harper Collins.

Giddens, A. (1991), *Modernity and Self-Identity: Self and Society in the Late Modern Age*, UK: Polity Press and Basil Blackwell.

Gilligan, C. (1982), *In a Different Voice: Psychological Theory and Women's Development*, Cambridge, MA: Harvard University Press.

Gilligan, C. and M.F. Bellenky (1980), 'A Naturalistic Study of Abortion Decisions', in R. Selman and R. Yando, eds, *Clinical Developmental Psychology: New Directions for Child Development*, no. 7, Sam Francisco: Jossey-Bass.

Glynn, S. (2002), 'The Freedom of the Deconstructed Postmodern Subject', *Continental Philosophy Review*, vol. 35, The Netherlands: Kluwer Academic Publishers, pp. 61–76.

Goffman, E. (1955), 'On Face-Work: An Analysis of Ritual Elements in Social Interaction', *Psychiatry: Journal of the Study of Interpersonal Processes*, vol. 18, no. 3, August, pp. 213–31.

—— (1956), *The Presentation of Self in Everyday Life*, Edinburgh: University of Edinburgh.

—— (1971), *Relations in Public*, London: Allen Lane.

—— (1981), *Forms of Talk*, Oxford: Basil Blackwell.

Goodwin, M.H. (2002), 'Exclusion in Girls' Peer Groups: Ethnographic Analysis of Language Practices on the Playground', *Human Development*, vol. 45, pp. 392–415.

Gottschall, J. (2013), *The Story Telling Animal: How Stories Make Us Human*, New York: Mariner Books.

Grice, H.P. (1991), *Logic and Conversation* in *Pragmatics: A Reader*, edited by Steven Davis, Oxford: Oxford University Press.

Gumperz, J.J. (1982), *Language and Social Identity*, Cambridge: Cambridge University Press.

Haan, N. (1975), 'Hypothetical and Actual Moral Reasoning in a Situation of Civil Disobedience', *Journal of Personality and Social Psychology*, vol. 32, pp. 255–70.

Habermas, T. and S. Bluck (2000), 'Getting a Life: The Development of the Life Story in Adolescence', *Psychological Bulletin*, vol. 126, pp. 748–69.

Hall, K. and M. Bucholtz, eds (1995), *Gender Articulated: Language and the Socially Constructed Self*, New York and London: Routledge.

Hammack, P.L. (2008), 'Narrative and the Cultural Psychology of Identity', *Personality and Social Psychological Review*, vol. 12, pp. 222–47.

Haraway, D. (1991), 'A Cyborg Manifesto: Science, Technology and Socialist Feminism in the Late Twentieth Century', in *Simians, Cyborgs and Women: The Reinvention of Nature*, New York: Routledge, pp. 149–81.

Harding, S. (1987), 'The Curious Coincidence of Feminine and African Moralities: Challenges for Feminist Theory', in E.F. Kittay and D.T. Meyers, eds, *Women and Moral Theory*, New Jersey: Rowman and Littlefield, pp. 296–315.

Hegel, G.W.F. (1977), *Phenomenology of the Spirit*, translated by A.V. Miller, Oxford: Clarendon Press; first published in German as *Phanomenologie des Geistes*, 1952.

—— (1991a), *The Encyclopedia Logic: Part 1 of the Encyclopaedia of Philosophical Sciences*, translated by T.F. Geraets, W.A. Suchting and H.S. Harris, Indianapolis: Hackett Publishing; first published in German as *Enzyklopädie der philosophischen Wissenschaftenim Grundrisse*, 1812–1816.

—— (1991b), *Elements of the Philosophy of Right*, translated by H.B. Nisbet and edited by A.W. Wood, Cambridge: Cambridge University Press; first published in German as *Grundlinien der Philosophie des Rechts*, 1820.

—— (2005), 'Phenomenology of Spirit, "Self-Consciousness: Lordship and Bondage"', in K. Atkins, ed., *Self and Subjectivity*, UK: Blackwell Publishing.

Heidegger, M. (1962), *Being and Time*, translated by J. Macquarrie and E. Robinson, Oxford: Blackwell.

Held, V. (2006), *The Ethics of Care: Personal, Political and Global*, New York: Oxford University Press.

Hesse, M. (1980), *Revolutions and Reconstructions in the Philosophy of Science*, Bloomington: Indiana University Press.

Hollway, W. (1995), 'Feminist Discourses and Women's Heterosexual Desire', in S. Wilkinson and C. Kitzinger, eds, *Feminism and Discourse: Psychological Perspectives*, London: Sage.

Holstein, C. (1976), 'Development of Moral Judgment: A Longitudinal Study of Males and Females', *Child Development*, vol. 47, pp. 51–61.

Horner, M. (1968), 'Sex Differences in Achievement Motivation and Performance in Competitive and Noncompetitive Situations', PhD dissertation, University of Michigan, Michigan.

Horner, M.S. (1972), 'Toward an Understanding of Achievement Related Conflicts in Women', *Journal of Social Issues*, vol. 28, pp. 157–75.

Hutchby, I. and R. Wooffitt (1998), *Conversation Analysis: Principles, Practices and Applications*, Cambridge: Polity Press.

Irigaray, L. (1981), 'This Sex Which is Not One', in E. Marks and I. de Courtivron, eds, *New French Feminisms*, London: Harverster.

—— (1997), *The Sex Which Is Not One*, translated by C. Potter with C. Burke, Ithaca: Cornwell University Press; first published in French as *Ce Sexe Qui n'en est pas un*, Editions de Minuit, 1977.

Itakura, H. (2001), 'Conversational Dominance and Gender: A Study of Japanese Speakers in First and Second Language Contexts', *Pragmatics & Beyond*, New Series, vol. 89, Amsterdam and Philadelphia: John Benjamins Publishing Company.

Jahanbegloo, R. (2008), *The Spirit of India*, New Delhi: Penguin India.

James, W. (1890), *Principles of Psychology*, New York: Holt Rinehart and Winston.

Jefferson, G. (1978), 'Sequential Aspects of Storytelling in Converstaion' in J. Schenkein, ed., *Studies in the Organization of Conversational Interaction*, New York: Academic Press.

—— (1983), 'Notes on Some Orderliness of Overlap Onset', *Tilburg Papers in Language and Literature*, vol. 28, Department of Linguistics, Tilburg University.

—— (1986), 'Notes on Latency in Overlap Onset', *Human Studies*, vol. 9, pp. 153–83.

—— (1989), 'Preliminary Notes on a Possible Metric Which Provides for a "Standard Maximum Silence" of Approximately One Second in Conversation', in D. Roger and P. Bulls, eds, *Conversation: An Interdisciplinary Perspective*, Clevedon and Philadelphia: Multilingual Matters, pp. 166–96.

Jesperson, O. (1922), *Language: Its Nature, Development and Origin*, London: Allen and Unwin.

Jones, D. (1987), 'Family Pattern, Critical Method, Narrative Model', *Journal of Narrative Technique*, vol. 17, no. 1, pp. 12–24.

Kaufmann, W. (1968), *Basic Writings of Nietzsche*, New York: Modern Library.

Kittay, E.F. and D.T. Meyers, eds (1987), *Women and Moral Theory*, New Jersey: Rowman and Littlefield.

Kitzinger, C. (2002), 'Doing Feminist Conversation Analysis', in P. McIlvenny, ed., *Talking Gender and Sexuality*, Philadelphia and Amsterdam: John Benjamins Publishing Company, pp. 49–77.

Kivisto, P., ed. (2021), *The Cambridge Handbook of Social Theory, Vol. II: Contemporary Theories and Issues*, Cambridge: Cambridge University Press.

Kohlberg, L. (1958), 'The Development of Modes of Thinking and Choices in Years 10 to 16', PhD dissertation, University of Chicago, Chicago.

—— (1976), 'Moral Stages and Moralization: The Cognitive-Developmental Approach', in T. Lickona, ed., *Moral Development and Behaviour: Theory, Research and Social Issues*, New York: Holt, Rinehart and Winston.

—— (1981), *Essays in Moral Development*, Vol. 1: *The Philosophy of Moral Development: Moral Stages and the Idea of Justice*, San Fransisco: Harper and Row.

—— (1982), 'A Reply to Owen Flanagan and Some Comments on the Puka-Goodpaster Exchange', *Ethics* , vol. 92, pp. 312–37.

—— (1984), *Essays in Moral Development*, Vol. 2: *The Psychology of Moral Development*, San Fransisco: Harper and Row.

Konner, M. (2010), *The Evolution of Childhood*, Cambridge, MA: Harvard University Press.

Kristeva, J. (1980), *Desire in Language: A Semitic Approach to Literature and Art*, Oxford: Blackwell.

Kritzman, L.D., ed. (1988), *Michel Foucault: Politics, Philosophy and Culture – Interviews and Other Writings 1977–1984*, translated by A. Sheridan, London: Routledge.

Kuhn, T. (1962), *The Structure of Scientific Revolutions*, Chicago: University of Chicago Press.

Kvale, S. (1996), 'Themes of Postmodernity', in W.T. Anderson, ed., *The Fontana Postmodernism Reader*, London: Fontana Press.

Labov, W. (1966), *The Social Stratification of English in New York City*, Washington D.C.: Center for Applied Linguistics.

—— (1972), 'The Transformation of Experience in Narrative Syntax', in *Language in the Inner City: Studies in Black English Vernacular*, Philadelphia: University of Pennsylvania Press, pp. 354–96.

Labov, W. and J. Waletzy (1967), 'Narrative Analysis: Oral Versions of Personal Experience', in J. Helm, ed., *Essays in the Verbal and Visual Arts*, Seattle, Washington: University of Washington Press, pp. 12–44.

Lakoff, R. (1973), 'Language and Women's Place', *Language and Society*, vol. 2, pp. 45–79.

—— (1975), *Language and Women's Place*, New York: Harper Colophon.

—— (1990), *Talking Power*, New York: Basic Books.

Le Page, R.B. and A. Tabouret-Keller (1985), *Acts of Identity: Creole-based Approaches to Language and Ethnicity*, Cambridge: Cambridge University Press.

Leet-Pellegrini, H.M. (1980), 'Conversational Dominance as a Function of Gender and Expertise', in H. Giles, W.P. Robinson and P.M. Smith, eds, *Language: Social Psychological Perspectives*, Oxford: Pergamon Press, pp. 97–104.

Lever, J.R. (1976), 'Sex Differences in the Games Children Play', *Social Problems*, vol. 23, pp. 478–87.

Liddle, J. and S.M. Rai (1993), 'Between Feminism and Orientalism', in M. Kennedy, C. Lubelska and V. Walsh, eds, *Making Connections: Women's Studies, Women's Movements and Women's Lives*, London: Taylor and Francis.

Locke, J. (1948), *An Essay Concerning Human Understanding II*, edited by R. Wilburn, London: Dent and Sons.

Lovibond, S. (2000), 'Feminism in Ancient Philosophy: The Feminist Stake in Greek Rationalism', in S. Fricker and J. Hornsby, eds, *The Cambridge Companion to Feminism in Philosophy*, Cambridge: Cambridge University Press.

Lyotard, J.F. (1984), *The Postmodern Condition: A Report on Knowledge*, translated by G. Bennington and B. Massumi, Minneapolis: University of Minnesota.

Mackenzie, C. ([2000] 2005), 'Imagining Oneself Otherwise', in C. Mackenzie and N. Stoljar, eds, *Relational Autonomy: Feminist Perspectives on Agency, Autonomy and the Social Self*, Oxford: Oxford University Press; also in K. Atkins, ed., *Self and Subjectivity*, UK: Blackwell Publishing, 2005.

Maltz, D.N. and R.A. Borker (1982), 'A Cultural Approach to Male–Female Miscommunication', in J.J. Gumperz, ed., *Communication, Language and Social Identity*, Cambridge: Cambridge University Press, pp. 196–216.

Mandelbaum, J. (1987), 'Couples Sharing Stories', *Communication Quarterly*, vol. 35, no. 2, pp. 144–70.

Markus, H. and S. Kitayama (2003), 'Culture, Self, and the Reality of the Social', *Psychological Inquiry*, vol. 14, pp. 277–83.

May, R. (1980), *Sex and Fantasy*, New York: W.W. Norton.

McAdams, D.P. (2001), 'The Psychology of Life Stories', *Review of General Psychology*, vol. 5, pp. 100–22.

—— (2005), 'A Psychologist Without a Country, or Living Two Lives in the Same Story', in G. Yancy and S. Hadley, eds, *Narrative Identities: Psychologists Engaged in Self-Construction*, London and Philadelphia: Jessica Kingsley Publishers, pp. 96–113.

McClelland, D.C. (1975), *Power: The Inner Experience*, New York: Irvington.

Mead, G.H. (1934), *Mind, Self and Society*, Chicago: University of Chicago Press.

Miller, J.B. (1976), *Towards a New Psychology of Women*, Boston: Beacon Press.

Miller, P.J., H. Fung and J. Mintz (1996), 'Self-construction through Narrative Practices: A Chinese and American Comparison of Early Socialization', *Ethos*, vol. 24, pp. 237–80.

Miller, P.J., A. Wiley, H. Fung and C.H. Liang (1997), 'Personal Storytelling as a Medium of Socialization in Chinese and American Families', *Child Development*, vol. 68, pp. 557–68.

Milroy, L. (1980), *Language and Social Networks*, Oxford: Basil Blackwell.

Mohanty, C. (1988), 'Under Western Eyes: Feminist Scholarship and Colonial Discourse', *Feminist Review*, vol. 30, pp. 61–88.

Mongia, S. (2005), *Brand India*, Delhi: B.R. Publishing.

Muldoon, M. (2002), *On Ricoeur*, Belmont: Wadsworth/ Thomson Learning.

Murphy, J.M. and C. Gilligan (1980), 'Moral Development in Late Adolescence and Adulthood: A Critique and Reconstruction of Kohleberg's Theory', *Human Development*, vol. 23, pp. 77–104.

Nair, R. (2003), *Narrative Gravity: Conversation, Cognition, Culture*, USA and Canada: Routledge.

Nakamura, K. (2001), 'Gender and Language in Japanese Preschool Children', *Research on Language and Social Interaction*, vol. 34, no. 1, pp. 15–43.

Nietzsche, F. (1956), *The Birth of Tragedy and The Genealogy of Morals*, F. Golffing, Garden City, NY: Doubleday Anchor.

—— (1968), *The Will to Power, W. Kaufimann and R. Hollingdale*, translated and edited by W. Kaufimann, New York: Vintage, Random House.

—— (2005), 'The Genealogy of Morals', in K. Atkins, ed., *Self and Subjectivity*, UK: Blackwell Publishing.

Noddings, N. (1984), *Caring: A Feminine Approach to Ethics*, Berkeley: University of California Press.

O'Hara, M. and W.T. Anderson (1996), 'Psychotherapy's Own Identity Crisis', in W.T. Anderson, ed., *The Fontana Postmodernism Reader*, London: Fontana Press.

Oakeshott, M. (1975), *Of Human Conduct*, Oxford: Oxford University Press.

Oatley, K. (2008), 'The Mind's Flight Simulator', *Psychologist*, vol. 21, pp. 1030–32.

Paley, V. (2004), *A Child's Work: The Importance of Fantasy Play*, Chicago: University of Chicago Press.

Palkivala, N. (2002), *We, the People*, New Delhi: UBS Publishers and Distributors.

Pascarella, E.T. and P.T. Terenzini (2005), *How College Affects Students, Vol. 2: A Third Decade Of Research*, San Francisco: Jossey-Bass.

Piaget, J. ([1932] 1965), *The Moral Judgment of the Child*, New York: The Free Press.

Polanyi, L. (1982), 'Literary Complexity in Everyday Storytelling', in D. Tannen, ed., *Spoken and Written Language: Exploring Orality and Literacy*, Norwood, NJ: Ablex, pp. 155–70.

—— (1985), 'Conversational Storytelling', in T.A. van Dijk, ed., *Handbook of Discourse Analysis, Volume 3: Discourse and Dialogue*, London: Academic Press, pp. 183–201.

Ramachandran, V.S. (2011), *The Tell-Tale Brain: A Neuroscientist's Quest for What Makes Us Human*, Haryana: Random House India.

Richards, M.P.M. (1974), *The Integration of a Child onto a Social World*, Cambridge: Cambridge University Press.

Ricoeur, P. (1981a), *Hermeneutics and the Human Sciences*, Cambridge: Cambridge University Press.

—— (1981b), 'Narrative Time', in W.J.T. Mitchell, ed., *On Narrative*, Chicago: University of Chicago, pp. 165–86.

Ricoeur, P. (1984), *Time and Narrative*, vol. 1, translated by K. McLaughin and P. Pellauer, Chicago: University of Chicago Press.

—— (1985), *Time and Narrative*, vol. 2, translated by K. McLaughin and P. Pellauer, Chicago: University of Chicago Press.

—— (1988), *Time and Narrative*, vol. 3, translated by K. McLaughin and P. Pellauer, Chicago: University of Chicago Press.

—— (1991), *A Ricoeur Reader: Reflection and Imagination*, edited by M.J. Valdes, Toronto: University of Toronto Press.

—— (1992), *Oneself as Another*, translated by K. Blamey, Chicago: University of Chicago Press; first published in French as *Soi-même comme un autre*, Seuil, Paris, 1990.

Ritzer, G. (2011), *Sociological Theory*, US: McGraw Hill Companies.

Ritzer, G. and B. Smart, eds (2001), *Handbook of Social Theory*, London: Sage Publications.

Robson, D. (2021), 'Our Fiction Addiction: Why Humans Need Stories', available at https://www.bbc.com/culture/article/20180503-our-fiction-addiction-why-humans-need-stories, accessed 15 September 2021.

Rorty, A.O., ed. (1976), *The Identities of Persons*, California: University of California Press.

Rorty, R. (1989), *Contingency, Irony and Solidarity*, Cambridge: Cambridge University Press.

Sacks, H. (1972), 'On the Analyzability of Stories by Children', in J. Gumperz and D. Hymes, eds, *Directions in Sociolinguistics*, New York: Holt, Rinehart and Winston, pp. 325–45.

—— (1995), 'Lectures on Conversation', vols 1 and 2, edied by G . Jefferson, Oxford: Blackwell.

Sacks, H., E.A. Schegloff and G. Jefferson (1974), 'A Simplest Systematic for the Organization of Turn-Taking for Conversation', *Language*, vol. 50, pp. 696–735.

Sampson, E.E. (1993), *Celebrating the Other: A Dialogic Account of Human Nature*, London: Harverster-Wheatsheaf.

Sarbin, T.R. (2005), 'The Poetics of My Identities', in G. Yancy and S. Hadley, eds, *Narrative Identities: Psychologists Engaged in Self-Construction*, London and Philadelphia: Jessica Kingsley Publishers, pp. 13–35.

Sassen, G. (1980), 'Success Anxiety in Women: A Constructivist Interpretation of Its Sources and its Significance', *Harvard Educational Review*, vol. 50. pp. 159–67.

Schegloff, E.A. (1968), 'Sequencing in Conversational Openings', *American Anthropologists*, 70, pp. 1075–99.

—— (1982), 'Discourse as an Interactional Achievement: Some Uses of "uh huh" and Other Things That Come Between Sentences', in D. Tannen, ed., *Analyzing Discourse Text and Talk*, Washington, D.C.: Georgetown University Press, pp. 71–93.

—— (2007), *Sequence Organization in Interaction: A Primer in Conversation Analysis*, Volume I, New York: Cambridge University Press.

Schegloff, E.A. and H. Sacks (1973), 'Opening up Closings', *Semiotica*, vol. 8, pp. 289–307.

Sellars, W. (1968), *Science and Metaphysics*, London: Routledge and Kegan Paul.

Shore, B. (1996), *Culture in Mind: Cognition, Culture, and the Problem of Meaning*, New York: Oxford University Press.

Shotter, J. (1974), 'The Development of Personal Powers', in M.P.M. Richards, ed., *The Integration of a Child onto a Social World*, Cambridge: Cambridge University Press.

Smith P. (1979), 'Sex Markers in Speech', in K.R. Scherer and H. Giles, eds, *Social Markers in Speech*, Cambridge: Cambridge University Press, pp. 10–46.

Smith, A.M. (1995), 'The Regulation of Sexual Identity through Erasure: The Case of Jennifer Saunders', in K. Jay, ed., *Lesbian Erotics*, New York: New York University Press.

Snibbe, A.C. and H.M. Markus (2005), 'You Can't Always Get What You Want: Educational Attainment, Agency, and Choice', *Journal of Personality and Social Psychology*, vol. 88, pp. 703–20.

Snow, D.A. and Oliver, P.E. (1995), 'Social Movements and Collective Behaviour: Social Psychological Dimensions and Considerations', in K. Cook, G.A. Fine, and J.S. House, eds, *Sociological Perspectives on Social Psychology*, Boston: Allyn and Bacon, pp. 571–700.

Solomon, R. and D. Sherman, eds (2003), *The Blackwell Guide to Continental Philosophy*, UK: Blackwell Publishing.

Speer, S.A. and J. Potter (2002), 'From Performatives to Practices: Judith Butler, Discursive Psychology and the Management of Heterosexist Talk', in P. McIlvenny, ed., *Talking Gender and Sexuality*, Philadelphia and Amsterdam: John Benjamins Publishing Company.

Stets, J.E. (1995), 'Role Identities and Person Identities: Gender Identity, Master Identity and Controlling One's Partner', *Sociological Perspectives*, vol. 38, no. 2, pp. 129–50.

Stets, J.E. and P.J. Burke (2000), 'Identity Theory and Social Identity Theory', *Social Psychology Quarterly*, vol. 63, pp. 224–37.

Strawson, P. (1977), *Individuals: An Essay in Descriptive Metaphysics*, London: Metheun.

Streitmatter, J. (1993), 'Gender Differences in Identity Development: An Examination of Longitudinal Data', *Adolescence*, vol. 41, no. 4, pp. 55–66.

Stryker, S. (1968), 'Identity Salience and Role Performance', *Journal of Marriage and the Family*, vol. 4, pp. 558–64.

Stryker, S. and R.T. Serpe (1982), 'Commitment, Identity Salience and Role Behavior: Theory and Research Example', in W. Ickes and E.S. Knowles, eds, *Personality, Roles and Behaviour*, New York: Springer-Verlag.

Sugiyama, M.S. (2005), 'Reverse Engineering Narrative: Evidence of Special Design', in J. Gottschall and D.S. Wilson, eds, *The Literary Animal*, Evanston, Illinois: Northwestern University Press.

Tafarodi, R.W., G. Bonn, H. Liang, J. Takai, S. Moriizumi, V. Belhekar and A. Padhye (2012), 'What Makes For a Good Life? A Four-Nation Study', *Journal of Happiness Studies*, vol. 13, pp. 783–800.

Tannen, D. (1990), *You Just Don't Understand: Women and Men in Conversation*, New York: Ballantine Books.

Taylor, C. (1989), *Sources of the Self*, Cambridge: Press Syndicate of the University of Cambridge.

Taylor, C. (1976), 'Responsibility for Self', in A.O. Rorty, ed., *The Identities of Persons*, California: University of California Press.

Thornborrow, J., and J. Coates (2005), 'The Sociolinguistics of Narrative: Identity, Performance, Culture', in J. Thornborrow and J. Coates, eds, *The Sociolinguistics of Narrative*, Vol. 6, Amsterdam and Philadelphia: John Benjamins Publishing Company, pp. 1–16.

Traugott, E.C. and M.L. Pratt (1980), *Linguistics for Students for Literature*, New York: Harcourt Brace Jovanovich.

Trevarthen, C. (1975), 'Early Attempts at Speech', in R. Lewin, ed., *Child Alive*, London: Temple-Smith.

—— (1979), 'Communication and Cooperation in Early Infancy', in M. Bullowa, ed., *Before Speech: The Beginning of Interpersonal; Communication*, Cambridge: Cambridge University Press.

Trudgill, P. (1974), *The Social Differentiation of English in Norwich*, Cambridge: Cambridge University Press.

—— (1983), *On Dialect*, Oxford: Basil Blackwell.

Vidich, A.R. and S.M. Lyman (1994), 'Qualitative Methods: Their History in Sociology and Anthropology', in N.K. Denzin and Y.S. Lincoln, eds, *Handbook of Qualitative Research*, London: Sage Publications.

Vyas, R.N. (1992), *Nature of Indian Culture*, New Delhi: Concept Publishing.

Wardhaugh, R. (2010), *An Introduction to Sociolinguistics*, sixth edition, Great Britain: Wiley-Blackwell.

Warrington, M. and M. Younger (2011), 'Life is a Tightrope: Reflections on Peer Group Inclusion and Exclusion Amongst Adolescent Girls and Boys', *Gender and Education*, vol. 23, no. 2, pp. 153–68.

Weinreich, H. (1978), 'Sex Role Socialization', in J. Chetwyand and O. Hartnett, eds, *The Sex-Role System*, London: Routledge and Kegan Paul.

West, C. (1995), 'Women's Competence in Conversation', *Discourse and Society*, vol. 6, no. 1, pp. 107–31.

West, C. and A. Garcia (1988), 'Conversation Shift Work: A Study of Tropical Transitions Between Women and Men', *Social Problems*, vol. 35, no. 5, pp. 551–75.

West, C. and D.H. Zimmerman (1983), 'Small Insults: A Study of Interruptions in Conversations Between Unacquainted Persons', in B. Thorne, C. Kramarae and N. Henley, eds, *Language, Gender and Society*, Rowley, MA: Newbury House, pp. 102–17.

White, S.C. (2006), 'The Cultural Construction of Wellbeing: Seeking Healing in Bangladesh', ESRC WeD, Working Paper 15, Bath, UK: Wellbeing in Developing Countries ESRC Research Group (WeD).

Whiting, B.B. and C. Edwards (1988), *Children of Different Worlds*, Cambridge, MA: Harvard University Press.

Wilson, D.S. (2003), *Darwin's Cathedral*, Chicago: University of Chicago Press.

Winslade, J. (2003), 'Discursive Positioning and Theory and Practice: A Case for Narrative Mediation', PhD dissertation, University of Waikato, Hamilton, New Zealand.

Wittig, M. (1983), 'The Point of View: Universal or Particular?', *Feminist Issues*, vol. 3, no. 2, Fall.

Zimmerman, D.H. and C. West (1975), 'Sex Roles, Interruptions and Silences in Conversation', in B. Thorne and N. Henley, eds, *Language and Sex: Difference and Dominance*, Rowley, MA: Newbury House, pp. 105–29.

Index